MANAGEMENT AND THE BRAIN

AN INTEGRATIVE APPROACH TO ORGANIZATIONAL BEHAVIOR

compiled and edited by
R. Carlton Bessinger and Waino W. Suojanen

1983

Business Publishing Division
COLLEGE OF BUSINESS ADMINISTRATION
GEORGIA STATE UNIVERSITY
Atlanta, Georgia 30303

Library of Congress Cataloging in Publication Data

Main entry under title: Management and the brain.

Includes bibliographical references.
1. Organizational behavior. I. Bessinger, R.
Carlton. II. Suojanen, Waino W.

HD58. 7.M36 1983 658.3'001'9 82-24161
ISBN 0-88406-161-2

Business Publishing Division
College of Business Administration
Georgia State University
University Plaza
Atlanta, Georgia 30303
Telephone: 404/658-4253

First Printing 1983

Georgia State University is a unit of the University System of Georgia
and is an equal educational opportunity institution and an equal
opportunity/affirmative action employer.

Printed in the United States of America

Cover design by Richard Shannon

For Dan, Danyne, Rachel, Noah, and Sarah.

Contents

PART III
Addictive Personal and Management Behavior

PART IV
Creativity, Education, and Management for the Future

vii

Preface

Management and the Brain is a collection of previously published and unpublished articles, lectures, and papers, covering the period 1970-1982. Some of these as printed here may differ in minor ways from the published originals because of the nature of the editorial process. Several articles appearing in the later chapters have been edited to eliminate duplication. Other material has been retained and repeated if the editors felt it was essential to the reader's understanding. Also, while most of the chapters have been edited to include updated information, others have retained their original language but are provided with addenda that reflect the predictive content of the original work.

This volume may be read in two ways. One way is to pick an area of interest and read chapters selectively. The other way is to read the book straight through from beginning to end. In this manner the reader can build a better understanding of organizational behavior and management from the perspective of the integrative theory. Whatever the approach, it is the editors' hope that the reader will gain new insight into the subjects of the individual, management, and organizational behavior.

This book is intended to help managers and students understand how the brain works and its relationship to management. Organizational behavior is viewed from the standpoint of what we have learned from the biobehavioral (biohavioral) sciences in the last couple of decades, using information drawn from the fields of biology, ethology, sociobiology, neurophysiology, biochemistry, and psychobiology. These sciences and the findings of recent brain research enable us to look at human behavior in a way that is different from the standard approaches of psychology, sociology, and anthropology. This new approach allows us to better understand why people act in certain ways and what behavior is appropriate in various situations. This improved understanding of individual behavior in turn provides a better understanding of organizational behavior. The areas of stress, addiction, creativity, and education are examined.

Throughout the book, numerous references to the brain use the acronyms A QUIVER and SCANS. A QUIVER refers to the left new brain and stands for *A*nalytical, *QU*antitative, *I*ntellectual, *VE*rbal, *R*ational. The acronym A QUIVER is used to depict the different functions performed by the left side of the new brain. These functions are related to the manager in the organization, who traditionally has been a monolingual male. This distinction is necessary because recent research indicates females and bilinguists have verbal abilities spread out over the two new brains as opposed to being localized in the left new brain. SCANS is an acronym referring to the different functions of the right new brain and stands for *S*ynthesizing, *C*reative, *A*rtistic, *N*ormative, *S*patial.

Additionally, references are made to the *mind(s) of man* and to *man as animal* and *man as man*. The word *man* in this context is used generically to refer to a human being, person, or mankind, whether male or female. The pronouns *he* or *his* are also used in a generic sense, as appropriate, to avoid cumbersome problems of syntax.

Finally, compiling and editing a book would not be possible without the guidance and assistance of certain people. We would like to thank everyone at the Business Publishing Division, College of Business Administration, Georgia State University. Special thanks go to R. Cary Bynum, Director of the Business Publishing Division for his initial enthusiasm about the project and to Peggy Stanley, the editing supervisor, whose patient and perceptive skills led to a more readable and understandable book.

List of Contributors

R. CARLTON BESSINGER received his M.B.A from Georgia State University, Atlanta, Georgia. He formerly taught Accounting and Finance at Clemson University and was a manager and management development trainer for the State of Georgia. Mr. Bessinger is now researching/writing in collaboration with Dr. Waino Suojanen on the effects of biology, the brain, and addictive behavior on individual and managerial behavior.

WAINO W. SUOJANEN received his B.S. from the University of Vermont, his M.B.A. from the Harvard Graduate School of Business Administration, and his Ph.D. from the University of California, Berkeley. Dr. Suojanen is Professor, Department of Management, and Professor, School of Urban Life, at Georgia State University, Atlanta, Georgia. Dr. Suojanen's research in recent years has focused on the development of the integrative theory, which combines brain evolution and functioning with neurochemistry to explain human behavior. He has written and lectured extensively on the management of addiction and is involved in applying self-help concepts to change personal as well as professional behavior. His more than one hundred publications include three books. In 1966, his book *The Dynamics of Manage-*

ment won the McKinsey Foundation Award. Dr. Suojanen is listed in *Who's Who in America* and *American Men and Women of Science.*

ASTERIOS G. KEFALAS, Professor of Management, University of Georgia, Athens, Georgia.

DONALD R. HUDSON, Associate Professor of Management, University of Miami, Coral Gables, Florida.

RICHARD C. GROEPPER, National EAP Coordinator, Crawford and Company, Atlanta, Georgia.

GARY B. ROBERTS, Assistant Professor of Management, University of Tennessee, Knoxville, Tennessee.

WAYNE W. SUOJANEN, Attorney, Pepper, Hamilton and Scheetz, Philadelphia, Pennsylvania.

Introduction

The media bear witness to the fact that American industry today is faced with a disaster of major proportions. Consumers evidence dissatisfaction with product quality, while worker dissatisfaction with management runs strong and deep. Something is drastically wrong—we appear to have been managing our way into economic decline since the end of World War II.

Popular concepts of management appear to have little value in the current assumptions about human behavior and are being overturned on every hand by the research findings of the biological sciences.

Increasingly, neurophysiological evidence suggests that man has both an old, visceral brain that mediates animal behavior and a new brain that controls the individual's behavior as man. The new brain is divided into two parts—a left new brain and a right new brain. The left new brain of the human being mediates behaviors that are analytical, quantitative, intellectual, verbal, and rational; the right new brain controls those behaviors that are synthetic, creative, artistic, normative, and spatial.

Another way of viewing the three brains is by their orientation toward different situations. The left new brain focuses on routine-oriented situations, the right new brain focuses on knowledge-oriented behavior, while the old brain focuses on crisis-oriented circumstances.

When we refer to the left new brain and the right new brain, we mean that part of the brain that other writers have called left half brain and right half brain or left hemisphere and right hemisphere. We use the terms *left new brain* and *right new brain* because we view the brain as actually being three brains in one—an old, or visceral, brain and a new brain divided into the left and right.

Management theory since World War II has focused almost totally on left-new-brain, routine-oriented behavior. An obsessive concern for efficiency and profit in the short run have become not only means but ends in themselves. Now that the United States is beginning to press the limits of growth, long-term considerations must be substituted for this fixation on short-term efficiency and profit.

In the immediate future, reindustrialization or industrial revitalization will call for visceral brain, crisis-oriented behavior to solve such problems as inflation, the energy crisis, the deterioration of the work ethic, and increases in crime and terrorism. Knowledge-oriented behavior mediated by the right new brain will come into its own, as the United States moves from an industrial service society to an informational society and once again focuses its attention on such issues as investment, research and development, and entrepreneurship--areas that have been seriously neglected in recent years.

The integrative theory, as it has been developed by Waino W. Suojanen in recent decades, looks to biology, ethology, sociobiology, neurophysiology, and other sciences for guidance in understanding human behavior. The assumptions of the integrative theory are based on research data from the biological sciences. By contrast, current management theory draws all its assumptions from psychology, sociology, and anthropology. We now know that many of the assumptions of the social and behavioral sciences are incorrect.

We also know enough about how biology influences behavior and how the brain functions to suggest that the selections in this volume can provide part of the foundation needed for a restructuring of management theory to meet the challenges of a crisis/knowledge-oriented, continually changing world. This restructuring of management theory and its application to management practices will establish the United States once again as the leader/teacher of the world economies.

Part I

The Role of Ethology in Organization

1

Evolution, Ethology, and Organization

Waino W. Suojanen

The phenomenon of the development of life and the accompany-ing emergence of organization can be usefully approached from an evolutionary point of view. The failure of functional theory to provide means by which man's interrelations and habits may be studied is a matter of record. We hope to demonstrate that the evolutionary approach offers a rational and internally consistent approach that explains how organizations came to be and how they have evolved to save the ever-increasing demands of man. This "Evolutionary Experiment" is based on increasing amounts of scientific evidence that suggest that the origins of the universe and the origins of behavior were simultaneous and should be discussed together rather than separately.

The initiation, evolution, and continuance of life on earth is uniquely and inseparably related to the physical and chemical environment. Given this unique environment, prebiological forms (proto-organisms) originate. These forms develop into biological organisms and continue up the evolutionary scale until the vertebrates, the primates, and, ultimately, man, emerge. Contrary to older beliefs (still tenaciously held by some), the progression

Reprinted with permission from the *Southern Journal of Business*, vol. 5, no. 4, October 1970. The author is deeply indebted to Steven Brooke, Institute of Molecular Evolution, University of Miami, Coral Gables, Florida, for helping to bring to fruition many of the ideas developed in this chapter.

from the abiological to the prebiological to the biological is a gradual one with no defined or exact limits to any step in the progression; it is simply not possible to state exactly where the prebiological ends and the biological begins.

This approach is based on the assumption that evolution is the central process that links together the biochemical, psychological, and organizational continua in our world. In other words, order begins with the various kinds and concentrations of elements in the chemical world. Given the appropriate physical conditions, proteinoid microspheres—a possible precursor of life forms—emerge, and over the course of time become more complex and more highly organized and integrated. The process of evolution continues and higher forms of life develop, with man ultimately appearing at the top of the phylogenetic scale. From this point of view, evolution may be viewed as an internally systematic, self-ordering, and nonrandom process.

In terms of heredity, man may be viewed as an animal with much behavior determined by genetic endowment. In common with other animals, man has developed from the very simple to the very complex, as the following classification indicates:

1. Simple reflex
2. Complex reflex—instinct
3. Conditioned reflex
4. Instrumental conditioning
5. Operant conditioning
6. Simple problem solving
7. Complex problem solving
8. Concept formation
9. Linguistic behavior

Without question experimental psychologists, for example, will continue to study the more simple behavior of white mice and rats for many years to come and will continue to extrapolate assumptions about human behavior based on data derived from such studies. However, these studies normally involve isolating an animal in space and time and extensive efforts are generally devoted to discovering what the animal can be made to do rather than to what it does in the natural field situation. Consequently, comparative studies tend to consist of comparison of a few species of animals and the evaluation of their abilities to perform a limited number of artificial tasks.

As a matter of methodology, several schools of psychology dealing with animal behavior have not only neglected field study but also the physiological, genetic, and biochemical bases of the responses being studied. Because of this, a large amount of data has been collected with few heuristic schemes resulting. Attempts to categorize or classify animals psychologically have not proven fruitful. Rejecting this approach, we have presented in outline form a classification of behavioral elements. The principle behind this classification emphasizes the degree of freedom of the individual or the organization from the environment. The importance of this will become obvious in the following discussion.

In order to develop this classification, we accept the findings of ethology that indicate that if we strip away the patina or veneer of culture, then much of human behavior is simply animal behavior. In terms of the Evolutionary Experiment, man as an animal can never escape a genetic endowment based on approximately 4,600,000,000 years of life on Earth. Neither can he escape the approximately 100,000,000 years of development which were required to produce man as we know him today.

The ethological approach differs quite radically from the American behavioral approach as typified by such scholars as B. F. Skinner and J. B. Watson. Whereas the behavioral approach stresses causation, the ethological scheme places primary importance on evolution, function, and survival. Rather than the artificial situation of the laboratory, the ethologist first studies the animal in its natural environment. Where this can not be done, attempts are made to recreate the animal's world, and the models are based on what actually exists in the field. In short, the ethologist studies what the animal is and not what the animal can be made to do.

With the emphasis on the evolutionary factors that govern a stimulus-response situation, Konrad Lorenz and Niko Tinbergen, major thinkers in the ethological school, have provided models of behavior that have surprising applicability in the field of management in particular and to human relations in general. Ethological studies of animals that are lower on the phylogenetic scale indicate that many concepts of organization that apply to man also apply to these animals. For example, the organization of the higher primates approximates that of man. Lower on the phylogenetic scale, among the vertebrates, are found such concepts as authority, hierarchy, status, role, and cooperation in the performance of tasks oriented toward the achievement of objectives.

In common with man, all higher animals have developed societies in which some form of conventionalized competition has been substituted for the direct struggle for food. Some ethologists have defined society as an organization capable of providing conventional competition. From the evolutionary point of view, the colony, the group, the organization, and the society have one aspect in common. Each group is governed by a code of amity that extends mutually from the colony to the individual and from the individual to the group. This code of amity acts to prevent intraspecific aggression among the members of the group. This type of society makes possible a system of cooperation and collaboration in which the attainment of objectives—either programmed or consciously developed—becomes the basic cohesive factor.

A code of enmity also appears to govern the behavior of social animals. This code implies discrimination among groups. In other words, the code of amity governs the domestic affairs of the group, while the code of enmity applies to its "foreign" affairs. Each organization will compete with, and may in some instances engage in conflict with, other groups. In order to prevent extremes of intraspecific aggression and the possible extinction of the species, the territorial rights of social animals are developed, recognized, and respected. Competition, selection, and survival operate on groups of the same species and this may result in a great number of small, separate, and competitive groups within the same species each with its own territory and its own system of cooperation.

This takes us to Exhibit 1-1. The area between the two vertical lines may be viewed as a system of authority, whether we are talking about a society, an organization, a group, or an individual. Cooperation and collaboration in the attainment of objectives cannot take place without authority. Within this system of authority, the code of amity of the group in question prevails and determines the conditions of cooperation under which the group either achieves its objectives or perishes. It is important to remember that the individual must obey the system of authority that governs the group. This obedience, in the more primitive

Exhibit 1-1: **Authority, Needs, and Participation**

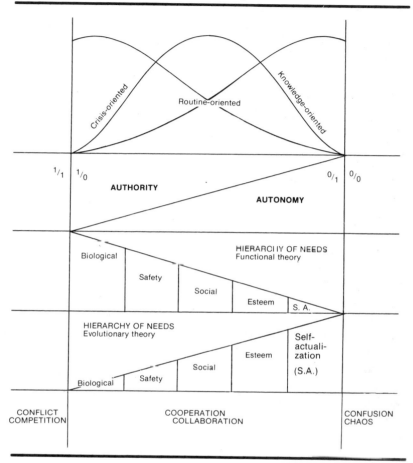

species, is wired into the neural network of each member of the species and behavior conducive to survival is totally instinctive in nature. This formal system of authority is so well developed that the bee colony will, for example, instinctively produce a queen to replace one that has died. The code of amity is an extremely powerful evolutionary force always acting to maximize the probability of survival of the group.

The code of enmity applies to those situations that are governed by competition or conflict. In Exhibit 1-1, this area lies to the left of the left vertical line and is labeled "conflict, competition." In the conflict or competition situation, two or more systems of authority may be distinguished. In this type of authority situation, the code of enmity applies to outside groups, and the code of amity applies within each group. The code of enmity is distinguished by an aversion to strangers of the same species and may range from a mutual physical separation on the part of the individuals belonging to separate groups all the way to the rapid and ferocious slaughter of an individual from another colony, such as occurs in the case of rats.

Exhibit 1-1 also suggests that confusion and even chaos may ensue when authority is either not present or is not exercised. This is illustrated at the right of the right vertical line by 0/0 authority situation.(See Exhibit 1-2 for an explanation of 1/1, 1/0, 0/1, and 0/0.) Every social organization must be governed by objectives and disciplined by a system of authority or else anarchism and nihilism will occur.

The nature of the evolutionary process, in a very simplified form, can be illustrated by drawing part of Exhibit 1-1 as a circle. The area of cooperation and collaboration remains on the outside; the confusion/chaos end joins the conflict/competition end. Now the model, in circular form, tells us that without authority, objectives disappear and the organization perishes (see Exhibit 1-3).

Authority is effective only when it is exercised in accordance with the values of the society. These values may be inherent in the genetic endowment of the particular group, in the case of those species lower on the evolutionary scale, or they may be part of the cultural endowment as in the case of man. Also, for authority to be effective, it must be exercised in accordance with the policies of the

Exhibit 1-2: **Explanation of Authority Situation Designations**

1/1	A situation in which two or more systems of authority are competing with each other; example: organization and union.
1/0	A situation in which one system (society, an organization, a group, or an individual) is highly authoritarian while another is without authority; example: boss retains all the authority and delegates none to subordinates.
0/1	A situation in which one system is highly autonomous; example: members of a group have been delegated all the authority, while the leader has retained none.
0/0	A situation in which authority is either not present or is not exercised.

Exhibit 1-3: **Absence of or Improperly Exercised Authority**

Cooperation
Collaboration

Conflict
Competition

Confusion
Chaos

When cooperation and collaboration
are excluded, organizations (and nations)
end up perishing or falling behind.

organization, the norms of the group, and the needs of individuals. In any event, the group perishes if authority ceases to be exercised or is not reestablished after a period of competition or conflict.

Before following this line further, it is advisable to consider some general aspects of social organization and of organization in general. A fruitful concept is that social organization is an extension of biological organization beyond the limits of the single individual. New and different control mechanisms may be present, but the basic objective always appears to remain the same. The primary objective of an organization is to have a higher probability of survival than that of any of its individual members. From the evolutionary point of view, the survival of the group depends on the survival of the individual member up to and beyond the reproductive stage. This approach places the focus of attention on survival of the species rather than on the individual. Second, it stresses the perpetuation of the information genome—the information encoded in the macromolecules—as the vehicle by which the organization survives and is perpetuated in time.

For biological systems the emphasis is placed on the ability to perpetuate the information genome that specifies the organization of the system. The processes by which information accumulates and the mechanism by which differential reproductive success is accomplished are natural selection and heredity. The information genome cannot escape the mutation and recombination that produce novelty in the genetic message. Also, it cannot escape being processed by natural selection. Thus the mechanism of natural selection does not dictate just what is *essential* for survival. For example, mammalian organization evolved, not because it provided a unique and necessary solution to problems of living on land, but because mammalian features rendered mammals the most efficient reproducers among the alternatives through a historical series of environmental opportunities.

The mechanism by which an organization meets basic objectives is the cooperative action of its components. The nature of this statement may be explained this way: In order for the probability of survival of an organization to be greater than the probability of survival of its subsystems and components, the net behavior of its components must be contingent and not independent. For example, a cell contains structures that have a degree of self-replicability. The mitochondrion has its own DNA content, separate and distinct from nuclear DNA, and is capable of directing some of its own protein synthesis. However, without a normally functioning nucleus, not only does the mitochondrion not function properly, but the cell dies as well. This is a stochastic definition of cooperative action. Implicit is the assumption, which seems obvious, that survival is a function of behavior.

Given the earlier groundwork, it is necessary to differentiate societies in order to extend the theory in terms of differential social control systems. At this point we run into difficulty that is characteristic of the behavioral sciences as they have been applied to the field of organizational theory. The behavioral sciences, other than ethology, have been so space and culture bound that they have virtually neglected man's biological endowment as an animal.

One of the most innovative attempts to integrate the behavioral sciences with biology first happened around 1969.[1] It is Lionel Tiger's contention that much of the development of human organizations can be explained by the process of "male bonding."

Male bonding occurs in vertebrate communities and may be a hominid inheritance from the primates. To put it differently, man's genetic inheritance includes a biological propensity toward male bonding that has come about as a result of the process of human evolution.

The process of male bonding can be traced to the emergence of cooperative hunting behavior patterns in prehistoric man. The scientific evidence suggests that man's hominid ancestors were both meat and plant eaters. Tool (weapon)-using accompanied the development of meat eating, and the combination of the two ultimately resulted in the emergence of all-male groups in which a considerable amount of cooperative behavior was necessary to the attainment of the objectives of the organization.

Cooperative hunting is very closely associated with sexual dimorphism—the set of normal differences that exists between the sexes. Man as the hunter has come to be bigger, stronger, and swifter than the female. He is more aggressive by nature and very deeply concerned with dominance by and over his fellows. The processes of natural selection were of greatest benefit to those cooperative hunting groups that developed a sophisticated code of amity within themselves while directing their aggressive code of enmity toward their animal prey and other outside hominid groups. After a period of time the tools, techniques, and organizations that ultimately emerged from cooperative hunting groups came to be turned to another use, namely that of institutionalized aggression toward the outside hominid groups to which the code of enmity applied. Here we detect the origin of the first human crisis-oriented type of organization. It is more than coincidental that the deployment of the foraging baboon group is virtually identical to that of the infantry platoon of an army when it is engaged in combat operations.

The hierarchy of human organization may be partially viewed as the institutionalization of the primate biogram—the general pattern of specific behaviors—in which the role of dominance plays such an important part. The human male, much like the baboon male, inherits a predisposition to dominate those around him. This pattern of dominance extends initially and with the greatest amount of strength to the males of the group. Furthermore, the satisfaction achieved by being able to dominate is so great that it may frequently override the higher needs that are culturally determined rather than being genetically fixed. The stronger the bonding pattern in effect, the faster and the greater the movement toward status, authority, hierarchy, and organization. Following this line of reasoning, a society based on ascription will tend to be more dominant and hence more authoritarian in nature than one in which ability and performance are the criteria for attaining hierarchical rank.

The male bond may be viewed as being just as important for organizational purposes as the sexual bond is for purposes of reproduction. As previously indicated, meat is associated with male bonding by virtue of the process of evolution. The gathering of animal food provides the milieu in which the male group organizes on a biological basis for purposes of defense in order to support the code of amity. Later, the process of evolution extends the hunting-defense gestalt to the point that the genetic endowment of the group begins to provide for the maintenance of social order. At this point, and obviously with the emergence of a cultural value system, the group becomes a composite of both "man as an animal" and "man as man."

The preceding implies that violence and aggression are perfectly normal activities insofar as food gathering and defensive activities are concerned. Assuming that the pattern of dominance associated with both of these required the passage of hundreds of thousands, if not millions, of years, then it is easy to understand how the concept of authority—the *power* to make decisions that are *obeyed without question* by others—came to be so fundamental to the maintenance of order.

Sexual dimorphism evolved in such a way that the tasks of the human female were performed around the base camp of the group. The period during which human young must be cared for by their elders is far longer than it is for any of the other primates. This results in a natural division of labor in primates and particularly hominids, because the females nurse the young.

Another aspect of sexual dimorphism is perhaps even more important in the evolution of human organizations. The activities of the females tended to become increasingly oriented toward the gathering and later the cultivation of the plants that provide part of the nutritional requirements of the group. These differences in the behaviors of the sexes were accompanied not only by numerous physical distinctions but also by many social changes that were to move the group increasingly away from autonomy and more toward authority. The ethologists suggest that both the reproductive male-female link, the nutritive and social female-offspring relationship, and the hunting male-male bond ultimately came to be programmed into the cycle of man as a species. Given these kinds of genetic programs, the hypothesis can be advanced that organization theory, as it *has* developed during this century, provides an inadequate deductive base as long as it refuses to recognize that man is as much animal as he is man.

The male hunting group is characterized largely by a charismatic system of authority. Leadership is based upon dominance, but this dominance is not stratified in nature. The relationships among individuals tend toward camaraderie, equality, and the lack of a rigid hierarchy. Given the objectives of the group, each individual has considerable freedom and autonomy. Much of anthropological research suggests that nomadic tribes tend to resemble the all-male hunting group in the way that authority is exercised.

The domestication of animals, which probably followed the domestication of plants, moved the male hunting groups back to the base camps. The free and easy camaraderie of the all-male group began to disappear, and charismatic authority began to be replaced by the settled and stratified societies that almost everywhere in the world are highly authoritarian in their modes of organization. The settled group is always fixed to a territory, and this territory must be defended. As hunting became less important, males began to devote more of their time and effort to defense activities and eventually, in many instances, to aggression against those groups that fell within the code of enmity.

The basic aggressive predisposition that accompanied the task of hunting thus became part and parcel of the patterns and activities through which social order was maintained. The social system came to include the military as a crisis-oriented segment. The warrior retained and even enhanced his position of high status within the society. This enhancement was partially, at least, due to the fact that the role of the warrior now required only bravery in battle, because it had been totally purged of all the more menial economic aspects of food gathering.

The exploitative opportunities open to the dominant males increased manifold. In the past, the hunting group had been a force for creativity and innovation. Now the focus was increasingly on the preservation of the dominant group within the society and the expansion of that society at the expense of others. The military became the guardians of the status quo and allied themselves with the males who owned the territory and the priestly class that enforced the code of amity.

The alliance between the owners of territory and the protectors was a natural one that lasted for many centuries. The code of amity was used to convince the many that they were "born to obey" the social order and that dominance by the few who were "born to rule" was thoroughly proper and correct. It is indeed paradoxical that man's increased freedom from the environment came to be associated with a decrease in the amount of social freedom.

The approach to the exercise of authority was one based on rigid hierarchy, command, and status based on ascription. Male bonding was still present but it now excluded the vast majority of males as well as almost all females.

To the extent that the striving for social freedom is *either* biological or cultural in nature—and we need not attempt to settle that argument at this point—a code of enmity will begin to develop within the greater society. This code of enmity will ultimately become firmly established within a society whenever a written language is invented. By the same token, however, the emergence of such a complex behavior as linguistic ability means that ideas can be both stored and disseminated on a continuing basis.

Creativity and innovation may be viewed as processes that are constantly at work insidiously tearing apart the code of amity of the group. Problem solving, concept formation, and linguistic behavior are part and parcel of the processes of creativity and innovation. As we have indicated elsewhere, the satisfaction of higher level needs is directly related to autonomy and freedom.[2] One wonders if the freedom we treasure today may not in part at least be something in our genes that traces back to the campfires of our prehuman hunting ancestors many millenia ago.

Man's instinct for freedom, as we have suggested, is part of his genetic endowment as a hunter. This instinct has been strengthened and reinforced by cultural heritage. Technology has made man economically freer of the environment. Democracy has made man much more autonomous in a social and psychological sense. Those segments of the population that do not share in these freedoms—who reject the code of amity—will resort to violence and aggression to attain them. This is always the pattern of behavior of those who feel they have been cheated and cut adrift by those who comprise the establishment.

A respect for the code of amity will not grow and strengthen when millions of the deprived—the black, the young, the poor, the old, the working-class whites, and the numerous ethnic minorities—feel that they are not satisfying their needs within the society.

The affluent society in recent years has also been the world of the establishment and the institution of the organization man. This world has moved to the right in the scale of authority, needs, and participation (Exhibit 1-1), but it has not shared its freedoms with the many dispossessed minorities. Today is not sufficient to speak only of the "revolution of rising expectations." We now know much more about the nature of man as an animal and as a man, and so we must also speak of the "evolution of advancing aspirations."

ENDNOTES

1. Lionel Tiger, *Men in Groups* (New York: Random House, 1969).

2. Waino W. Suojanen, *The Dynamics of Management* (New York: Holt, Rinehart and Winston, 1966).

REFERENCES

Ardrey, Robert. *African Genesis: A Personal Investigation into the Animal Origins and Nature of Man.* New York: Dell, 1967.
———*The Territorial Imperative: A Personal Inquiry into the Animal Origins of Property and Nations.* A Delta Book. New York: Dell, 1966.
Blau, P.M. and W. R. Scott. *Formal Organizations: A Comparative Approach.* San Francisco: Chandler, 1962.
Brown, Roger, et al. *New Directions in Psychology.* New York: Holt, Rinehart and Winston, 1962.

Clark, W. E. Le Gros. *History of the Primates: An Introduction to the Study of Fossil Man.* Chicago: University of Chicago Press, 1963.

Crile, George, Jr. *A Naturalistic View of Man: The Importance of Early Training in Learning, Living, and the Organization of Society.* New York: World, 1969.

Dahl, Robert A., and Charles E. Lindbloom. *Politics, Economics and Welfare.* New York: Harper & Brothers, 1953.

DeBono, Edward. *New Think: The Use of Lateral Thinking in the Generation of New Ideas.* New York: Basic Books, 1967.

De Uries, Egbert, ed. *Man in Community.* New York: Association Press, 1966.

Dubos, Rene. *So Human an Animal.* New York: Scribner's, 1968.

Ferkiss, Victor C. *Technological Man: The Myth and the Reality.* New York: Braziller, 1969.

Herzberg, Frederick. *Work and the Nature of Man.* New York: World, 1966.

Kardiner, Abram, and Edward Preeble. *They Studied Man.* A Mentor Book. New York: The New American Library, 1963.

Keith, Sir Arthur. *A New Theory of Human Evolution.* New York: The Philosophical Library, 1949.

Koestler, Arthur. *The Act of Creation.* New York: Dell, 1964.

Leonard, George B. *Education and Ecstasy.* New York: Delacorte, 1968.

Lewontin, Richard C., ed. *Population Biology & Evolution.* Syracuse, New York: Syracuse University Press, 1967.

Lorenz, Konrad. *On Aggression.* New York: Harcourt, Brace and World, 1967.

Montagu, F. Ashley. *Man and Aggression.* Oxford: Oxford University Press, 1968.

Morris, Desmond. *The Naked Ape.* New York: McGraw-Hill, 1967.

Nash, Manning. *Primitive and Peasant Economic Systems.* Chandler Publications in Anthropology and Sociology. San Francisco: Chandler Publishing Co., 1966.

Ramo, Simon. *Cure for Chaos: Fresh Solutions to Social Problems Through the Systems Approach.* New York: McKay, 1969.

Storr, Anthony. *Human Aggression.* New York: Atheneum, 1968.

Suojanen, Waino W. *The Dynamics of Management.* New York: Holt, Rinehart and Winston, Inc., 1966.

Syracuse University and the New York State Science and Technology Foundation, edited by Richard C. LeWontin. *Proceedings of the International Symposium, Population Biology and Evolution.* Syracuse, New York: Syracuse University Press, 1968.

Tiger, Lionel. *Men in Groups.* New York: Random House, 1969.

Wylie, Philip. *The Magic Animal.* New York: Doubleday, 1968.

2

Organizational Behavior and the New Biology

Asterios G. Kefalas
Waino W. Suojanen

Although management theorists and practitioners have accepted the model of man that assumes an almost infinite capacity for education and adjustment, recent evidence from ethology studies suggests that this assumption may be misleading and dangerous. It is proposed that there are constraints set by man's genetic endowments that determine educability.

Several years ago, one of the authors of this chapter presented a paper suggesting that "new biology" could provide a ready frame of reference for developing a radically new approach to the study of organizational behavior.[1] Two years later, an article falling in this same genre was published in the *Academy of Management Journal*.[2]

In a similar vein, William G. Scott and D. K. Hart made a plea for a bursting through of the framework of concepts that presently comprises that area of management theory called organizational behavior.[3] They also commented as follows:

> We believe there is a way of thinking about man in organizations that has eluded administrative theorists. For the lack of better language for putting it, we call this "way" metaphysical speculation on the moral nature of man. It

Reprinted with permission from the *Academy of Management Journal*, Vol. 17, No. 3, September 1974.

requires reflection and introspection of the highest ~~~
sophical order—an exercise in which administrative theor~
have not excelled.[4]

This paper represents a speculative excursion that attempts t~
link the "new biology" with what is presently called "organizational"
behavior." The basic question to be explored is: Assuming that
ethology or the new biology can shed new light on the mysteries of
human behavior, what can the value of this new knowledge be in
helping to reassess the assumptions made about man in the study of
organizations?

In reassessing these assumptions, a brief summary of the main
developments of managerial thought may prove useful.

The Development of Management Thought

From the plethora of researching and theorizing about management, it is well known today that what is labeled organization/
management theory constitutes a stream of thought that represents
the aggregation of economic, sociological, psychological, and
political science tributaries. Traditionally these disciplines have
erected their citadel of knowledge on a number of orthodox pillars,
some of which began to reveal their inherent weaknesses fairly
early. For example, the main pillar of the so-called economic-
rational man was fractured under the heavy pressure exerted on it
by the kind of research that began with the Hawthorne Studies.
These studies showed that increased output was due to team work,
cohesiveness, informal organization, interpersonal relations, and
social unity. Although H. M. Parsons has presented new evidence
that suggests that the Hawthorne effect results from "operant
reinforcement contingencies" (information feedback coupled with
financial rewards), the authors believe that the original interpretation of Hawthorne's findings, defining man in organizations as a
social animal rather than as a cold calculator of rewards, has made a
tremendous difference in thinking about man and organizations.[5]
Similarly, classical conditioning (i.e., S-R), as the basic pillar of the
orthodox psychologist, has proven to be an oversimplification.
Comparable developments have taken place in sociology and
political science.

Despite these threats to the foundations of the edifice of knowledge in the social sciences, the basic assumption of man as an infinite learning mechanism remains virtually unchallenged. It is, therefore, understandable that organization/management theory appropriated the assumption of the learning model of man with very little hesitation. It is equally understandable that early ethological signals, hinting at biological limits or invariances to man's educability and plasticity, would have been filtered out of the conceptual frameworks that guided theory formation and/or empirical research on organizations and their management.

Much of the sound and fury that has characterized the attempts to incorporate ethological concepts into the behavioral sciences would have been avoided if the contenders had approached the issue from the basis of a spectrum or continuum rather than from the dualistic, either-or point of view that is basic to all forms of dichotomous thinking. For an example of a continuum, see Exhibit 2-1. It is the very essence of life, as well as of organizational reality, that hardly anything is ever a dualistic black-or-white, but rather that all concepts are composed of a complex series of shades of gray. The habits of dichotomous thinking to which people are prone are difficult to change. Yet they must be drastically modified if theorists are to mine the rich field of ethology and apply these concepts to organizational behavior.

Even a rudimentary search into the management literature will convince one of the abundance of dichotomous thinking. For example, Douglas McGregor postulates that the assumptions that a manager makes about his fellow organizational participants fall into one of two categories: Theory X and Theory Y. Leadership patterns tend to be described as either productivity-oriented or satisfaction-oriented. Organizational structure from the decision-making viewpoint is viewed as being either centralized or decentralized. From the managerial system point of view, organizational behavior tends toward either System 1 or System 4. One notices that the first element of any dichotomy employed in studying organizational behavior represents the "what is," while the second element of the dichotomy sketches the "what ought to be."[6]

To most neophytes, ethology appears to be couched in another dichotomy; is man an animal or is he a man? Professional ethologists advocate a viewpoint that could be summed up in the simple expression—man is both animal and man. Amateur

Exhibit 2-1: **The Aggression Model in Man**

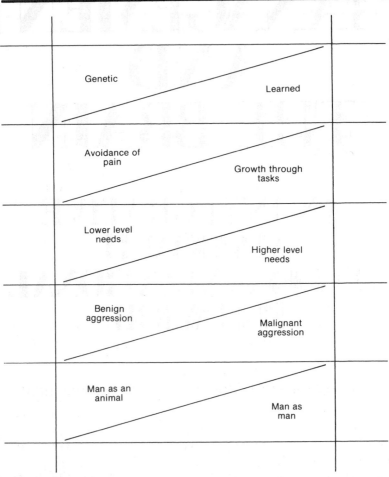

ethologists seem to think that the animal nature of man predominates in his behavior. This posture is in direct contradiction to both that of orthodox social scientists who see no animal in man and that of the scientific ethologists who see the animal characteristics of man as a framework that shapes and even determines the nature of man as man. This latter stance appears to be the more fruitful and is the one that is suggested as having tremendous potential for a new theory about man and his or her behavior in organizations.

The New Biology: Origin and Meaning

The new biology (ethology) emphasizes the study of the development of the total behavior of animals in their natural environment. This is referred to as Ethology I. In recent years, increasing attention has been devoted to the study of the relationship between animal behavior and human behavior. This is called Ethology II.

Ethology I views man as an animal; Ethology II views man as man. Man as man has a culture and a technology, both of which he knowingly exploits in order to satisfy his needs. The link between Ethology I and Ethology II is provided by those species of mammals closely related to man—the apes and the monkeys and, more distantly, the tarsiers, lemurs, and tree shrews.[7]

During the past two decades there has been an outburst of popular books in the area of ethology. The first of these was Robert Ardrey's *African Genesis,* which appeared in 1961. Later he wrote *The Territorial Imperative* (1966) and *The Social Contract* (1970). In *The Social Contract,* Ardrey even devotes a few pages to management theory.

Ardrey may be viewed as the great popularizer of ethology. Sharing almost equal billing with him in the paperback parade are Konrad Lorenz, *On Aggression,* and Desmond Morris with *The Naked Ape, The Human Zoo,* and *Intimate Behavior.* Antony Jay's *Corporate Man* borrows liberally from Lionel Tiger's, *Men in Groups.* Finally, another best-seller has been Lionel Tiger and Robin Fox's, *The Imperial Animal.*

For those who have not yet become acquainted with the popularizers of the new biology, the authors recommend all of the above. A good way to read them is in the order in which they are mentioned here. A few words of warning are in order: Without fail, time and time again, the reader will find himself elated, stunned, triumphant, or horrified, depending on his predilections and biases.

The chasm between the best-seller lists and the scientific literature on ethology can be best appreciated by reading Alexander Alland and Ashley Montagu.[8] The following quotation from Alland is illustrative of the fierce opposition of many behavioral scientists to the attempt to extrapolate deductively from Ethology I to Ethology II:

The last few years have seen a spate of books devoted to proving that human behavior is based either on instinct or on tightly controlled biological principles. Many of these have stressed instinctive aggression or territoriality as the key to an understanding of such social phenomena as war and property relations. Others have attempted to reduce human history to genetic principles or biologically locked sexual differences in behavior which keep men, but not women, in groups. A few have reintroduced racist arguments into scientific discourse. The major effect of these books has been to mislead or confuse those laymen who have little contact with scientific journals and little understanding of the complexities of recent works in such fields as behavioral genetics, ethology, physical anthropology, ethnology, sociology, and physiological psychology.[9]

In an article that appeared in the *New York Times Magazine* another behavioral scientist, David Pilbeam, used the following as the title: "The fashionable view of man as a naked ape is:
1. An insult to apes
2. Simplistic
3. Male-oriented
4. Rubbish"[10]

One of the most extreme arguments against the popularizers of Ethology II, again by a behavioral scientist, is summarized at length in the following:

In the case of man it is possible to say that in spite of all attempts to saddle him with instincts, all such attempts have thus far failed.

The notable thing about *human* behavior is that it is learned. It is nonsense to talk about the genetic determinance of human behavior. Allowing for whatever idiosyncratic contribution the genes may make, everything a human being does as such he has to learn from other human beings. From any dominance of biological or inherited predetermined reactions that may prevail in the behavior of other animals, man has moved into a zone of adaptation in which his behavior is dominated by learned responses. It is within the dimension of culture, the learned, the man-made part of the environment, that man grows, develops, and has his being as a behaving organism. Whatever other recondite elements may be involved in his behavior, and whatever the limits that his genetic constitution may set upon his learning capacities, this is the conclusion of the behavioral sciences—the sciences concerned with the study of the origins and causes of man's behavior. If anyone has any evidence to the contrary, let him bring it forth. That heredity plays a part in all human behavior is patently false, but that heredity plays a role in some human behavior can scarcely be doubted; but this is a very different thing from saying that every form of human behavior is determined by heredity.[11]

Not all behavioral scientists share the views of Montagu and Alland, that heredity makes little contribution to human behavior. In fact one position stands four square with the argument developed in this paper:

The four examples cited to illustrate the operation of heredity fall along a *continuum of indirectness*. Along this continuum are found varying degrees of remoteness of causal links, from the relatively direct and immediate behavioral effects of hereditary metabolic disorders to the more indirect and subtle influence of physical cues that evoke social stereotypes. It should also be noted that, the more indirect the hereditary influence, the greater will be the range of possible behavioral outcomes. This follows from the fact that at each step in the causal chain there is fresh opportunity for other concomitant circumstance to alter the course of development. Thus the more indirect the role of heredity, the greater the feasibility of behavioral modification through environmental manipulation.[12]

As emphasized in the preceding discussion, much of the controversy about the new biology and its application to human behavior has centered around the issue of whether or not man is governed by instinctive behavior patterns. Sometimes it is difficult to determine whether the controversy extends widely enough to include the entire genetic endowment of man as an animal. The aversion to this kind of thinking has been well put by a recent writer:

The total refusal of many sociologists to consider biological evidence is a result of not only the "vested interest" mentioned above nor the feeling on the left that biological considerations are implicitly "racist" but also a reaction to early sociological theorists' reliance on absurd analogies to nature and to the horrors that have been perpetrated in the name of nature. In order to justify slavery, for example, some theorists had hypothesized a biological element that made slavery inevitable despite the fact that the large number of societies that did not have slavery indicated that such a hypothesis was not only uncalled for but obviously incorrect.[13]

Ethology and Human Behavior: The application of ethological concepts to human behavior—or Ethology II—traces back about two decades. One reason for this relatively recent impact is that very little of the early European literature has been translated into English. Many American management scholars do not read languages other than English, with the result that ethological concepts have begun to be incorporated into the literature only as more recent materials have become available in English.

Another, and far more important, reason for the neglect of ethological thought goes back to the eclectic nature of management as a discipline. The behavioral strain in current management thought is based upon anthropology, psychology, and sociology as we currently know them in the American university. One of the basic assumptions of each of these disciplines is that human behavior is learned in nature—that the human being begins life with a clean slate or as a tabula rasa. This means, and the repetition is for emphasis, that acquired knowledge results in learned attitudes that in turn are the cause of systematic and continuing patterns of behavior.

At the present time the systems approach is being used in order to attempt to integrate the operational, quantitative, and behavioral streams of thought into an integrative whole. However, ethology as discussed in this paper has been noticeable by its absence from this integration. Given the present state of the art, the early attempts to introduce it may result in acrimonious and sustained dispute of the kind that continues to characterize the IQ debate.[14]

The very definition of ethology proposed by Niko Tinbergen, that it represents "the objective study of behavior," is enough to raise the hackles of the dedicated nurture-based assumptions of traditional anthropology, psychology, and sociology. This implies that ethology is not only the one existing *objective* behavioral research method, but—much more than this—it once more revives the concept that behavioral characteristics can be genetically transmitted and that, to paraphrase Mark Twain, is an idea whose death has been prematurely announced on an almost scheduled basis.

Why this unyielding and unbending negation of the animal nature of man—of the fact that he is akin to every other species of animal on earth and has codes in his genetic composition that, at least during certain periods in his development, gave him an edge over the other species of animals? Why comments such as those by Montagu and Alland quoted at length in the previous section?

Is it "nonsense to talk about the genetic determination of human behavior" when one of the most humanistic of behavioral scientists admits to the opposite?[15]

> Of course it is true that any impulse or need found in man *and* all other animals is thereby proved to be instinctive beyond the need for any further evidence. This does not however, disprove the possibility that some instinctoid impulses may be found only in human species, or as appears to be the case with the love impulse, in common with chimpanzees alone in the animal world. Homing pigeons, salmon, cats, etc. each have instincts peculiar to the species. Why could not the human species also have characteristics peculiar to it.[16]

Instincts and Ethology: The area of greatest controversy in ethology has revolved around the functions that instinct may or may not play in the behavior of the human being as a species. There appears to be no disagreement about the role of instincts in the behavior of such species as ants and bees. Here there is almost universal agreement that the behavior patterns are part of the neural network of the species. As soon as it is alive, the ant or bee can perform effectively and efficiently in its ecological niche. In other words, the behavioral attributes of these species are completely programmed as a part of the genetic endowment and no learning of any kind is necessary. Not even the most unbending of behavioral scientists would argue with this explanation.

Advances during the past two decades in brain research and the interpretation of brain functions suggest that the learning processes of the human being are both biologically and environmentally related in a systematic fashion.[17] Although the data are insufficient to draw firm conclusions, any number of intriguing hypotheses can be drawn that suggest that behavioral scientists go out on a biological limb when they deny the presence of instincts or innate behavior in *Homo sapiens*.

In the move up the evolutionary ladder, nurture or "new brain" behavior increases in importance and nature or "old brain" behavior patterns become less important until, in the case of man, all behavior has come to be viewed as learned. This, in essence, is the way the arguments and the assumptions of behavioral and social scientists have developed in recent decades. This is in contrast to the views of geneticists who feel that nature and nurture are mutually reinforcing as, for example, in the following:

> What is most remarkable of all is that, while all other organisms become masters of their environments by changing their genes, man does so mostly by changing his culture, which he acquires by learning and transmits by teaching. Indeed, many animals have become adapted to living in cold climates by growing warm fur or by becoming dormant when the weather is cold; man has conquered cold by building fires and by wearing garments. Adaptation by culture is enormously more rapid and efficient than genetic adaptation; a new thought or a new invention made by one man can become a part of the patrimony of all mankind in a relatively short time. Let us not forget, however, that is it the human genotype that enabled man to invent fire and clothing. Genetic and cultural adaptations are not alternative or mutually exclusive; they are mutually reinforcing. Human genes and human culture are connected by what is known as a circular feedback relationship; in other words, human genes stimulate the development of culture, and the development of culture stimulates genetic changes which facilitate further developments of culture. To say that natural selection has built man's culture is a misleading over-simplification; natural selection has, however, built the genetic endowment that made culture possible.[18]

Another intriguing hypothesis suggests that tool-using primates and the technologies that they employ have evolved together as symbiotic, coupled systems in which a change in one induces a change in the other.[19] Part of this thesis indicates that selection operates on the total system as a unit. This tends to reinforce Theodosious Dobzhansky's argument and to suggest that organizational behavior theory as we know it today will have to be considerably modified as we learn more in the areas of Ethology I and Ethology II.[20]

To put it differently, the issue of nurture versus nature appears to be far broader than the existing assumptions of the behavioral sciences. The current approach assumes that the brain of man is static—a tabula rasa at birth—and that the environment is dynamic. Whatever is necessary for individualization and socialization can be learned. For example, if aggression is bad for the person and the society, it can be eliminated by learning that it is undesirable.

The ethological approach is based on the assumption that both the brain and the environment are constantly evolving in an interrelated fashion. From this point of view, there probably is nothing that can be defined as instinctive or innate behavior in the naked ape. As the human primate has evolved, and man's realm of consciousness has moved more and more to the forebrain, man's total behavior has tended to become less instinctive, less innate, even less impulsive. But that is only part of the answer.

Each individual human being at birth carries a particular combination of genes in his cells. This is known as a *genotype*. In management terms, this is comparable to a standard or a potential. Each individual also represents a *phenotype,* which is the product of the interactions between the genotype and the environment. In management terms, the phenotype may be viewed as actual performance with demophora serving as a corrective feedback system between the phenotype and the genotype.

Granted the plausibility of the evolving brain of man, it appears to be simplistic to argue that human behavior is totally determined by genetic environment just as it is equally ingenuous to claim that it is decided by the external environment. Instead, if the two work together as a coupled system, then much organizational behavior can be better understood than has been the case in the past. For one example, the IQ controversy referred to earlier may ultimately yield to demophoric analysis, in line with Dobzhansky's thesis that differences are not deficits. For another example, much clearer insights may be gained into controversies such as the one now enveloping the legal and ethical implications of behavior modification. In a general sense, the list of problems that can be attacked, given this hypothesis, is virtually endless.

Animal Behavior or Ethology I: Prior to the development of ethology, the only discipline concerned with animal behavior was zoology. Ethology, as a science, has grown to maturity only during the past quarter century. That ethology now occupies a coign of vantage among the sciences is evidenced by the fact that three ethologists won the Nobel prize in medicine in 1973.[21] The early scientific development of ethology took place mainly in Europe and particularly in Germany. In recent years, the public in the United States has become increasingly interested in ethology primarily as a result of the popular works of such people as Ardrey, Lorenz, Morris, Tiger, and Fox.

It is important to remember that ethology attempts to study the behavior of a species before the behavior has been modified by learning in captivity. Obviously the members of a species learn from other members of a species, even when all of this learning occurs in the wild. Ethology I views this kind of learned behavior as important but also tries to study behavior before any learning at all has occurred. No ethologist worth his or her salt will argue that any given pattern of behavior is either totally learned or totally innate. In terms of behavioral physiology, ethology consists of two parts: (1) the behavioral aspect, which may be said to be learned, and (2) the physiological portion, which may be said to be inborn or genetic (Exhibit 2-1).

Ethology II—Animal, Primate, and Man: The investigation of the three dimensions of the human being—as animal, primate, and man—has been inhibited in the past by a number of factors. For many, it is difficult to accept the notion that man does not differ in any significant way from the other animals, and particularly the primates. To the extent that the scholar accepts the concept of Economic Man, it becomes difficult if not impossible to study the human being as Social Man. Only when we study man as a totality do we come to see man in true proportion and perspective, that of "man as man." Man as an animal or as a primate has the overriding goal of avoiding pain and surviving in the environment. A theory of management that views man from this standpoint will tend to emphasize all those assumptions and principles that are the earmark of the functional theory.

When we study "man as man," we come to see him not as a creature solely interested in avoiding pain, but as a human being seeking growth and self-actualization from the work that he does and the kind of person that he is becoming. Only the lower level needs in man are determined by the biological inheritance. When we view man from a total point of view, we see that he is a being whose behavior is characterized by discovery, achievement, self-realization, and progress. It is these higher level needs that summarize the concept of man as man.

The differences between man as animal and primate and man as man can be easily illustrated by two parallel arrows pointing in opposite directions. The arrow on the top shows man's preoccupation with avoiding pain. The bottom arrow depicts man's nature as man. This part of the nature of man is concerned with motivators or the satisfaction of higher level needs through the accomplishment of tasks that enable the individual concerned to grow and to learn, to become more of a total person with the passage of each day of life (see Exhibit 2-1 also).

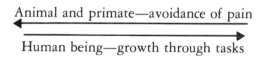

Animal and primate—avoidance of pain

Human being—growth through tasks

Ethology II focuses closely on the relationships that exist between man and the primates. Recent advances in primatology suggest that apes and monkeys possess many attributes that in the past have been used to distinguish man from animals. Ancient tradition says that man is the only creature who uses language. A more recent tradition claims that man has a genetic grammatical capability. Today there is every indication that even this bastion of human superiority is being breached. As the evidence available has increased, behavioral scientists have had to change their opinions about language as the exclusive possession of man.[22] Now it is more plausible to argue that humans have a language with more words and more complex combinations of symbols than the communication processes of the other species of primates.

It is true that a number of those who have devoted their attention to the popularization of the concepts of ethology have tended to lean too heavily on the role played by instincts in human behavior. The thrust of these speculations is that man is nothing but an animal among other animals, a naked ape dominated by his own savage biology and driven by killer instincts. About half a dozen such instincts are said to more or less dominate or even determine human behavior in the form of complex and specific responses that are largely hereditary and unalterable by man in response to environmental stimuli. Such responses do not involve reason, and have as their goal the removal of somatic tensions.

Five of these instincts have been the center of much research and speculation by ethologists. These five basic animal drives have been called the "Fünf Bösen" or five evils by the German-speaking ethologists who have pioneered the discipline. These five instincts are reproduction, hunger, fear, aggression, and grooming. As an aid to memory, they can be called the five "f's"—*flirting, feeding, fleeing, fighting,* and *feeling.* It is the view of numerous social and behavioral scientists that none of these instincts apply to man— that human behavior patterns that are called instincts when referring to other species are not programmed into the neural network of *Homo sapiens.* By the very nature of scholarship we sometimes tend to throw out the baby with the bathwater, and the move on the part of behavioral scientists to deny the animal nature of man may represent one of these continuing dilemmas.

One issue of controversy in Ethology II has been the concept of territoriality. Invariably the opponents of ethology deny the relevance of territoriality by citing a number of species that are not territorial in nature.[23] It may be true that such writers as Ardrey and Lorenz have sometimes resorted to exaggeration and hyperbole in advancing arguments that relate the territorial imperative to malignant aggression in man. That is not the issue here. The fact remains that man does kill his own kind, just as do many other species of animals, so to deny aggression is to deny the very nature of man as an animal.

Benign and Malignant Aggression: Erich Fromm has established a theoretical position that differs considerably from the instinctivism of the popularizers of ethology and the neobehaviorism of B.F. Skinner.[24] Benign aggression, according to Fromm, operates in the interest of the survival of both the individual and the species, is biologically adaptive, and ceases to exist when the threat has disappeared either through fighting or fleeing. Benign aggression is phylogenetically programmed and is an impulse that man shares with all mammals. (Significantly, Fromm uses the word *impulse* rather than *instinct*.) By contrast, Fromm argues, malignant aggression is specific to man, is not phylogenetically programmed, and is not biologically adaptive. Fromm believes that most previous discussions have failed to make the distinction between the two types of aggression that are present in man, and hence the reason for much of the disagreement about the relationship between territoriality and the fighting and fleeing impulse or instinct.

Apparently, the distinction that Fromm draws between benign and malignant aggression will help to reconcile the conflict between the ethologists and their popularizers and those behavioral scientists who still refuse to accept the animal nature of man as far as aggression and territoriality are concerned. Fromm, after all, is highly respected by the humanistic psychologists because he is one of the leaders in the discipline. If, as indicated in Exhibit 2-1, we accept benign aggression as mapping with the concept of man as an animal, how can we refuse to map malignant aggression similarly into the nature of man as man? And once we go this far, then can we continue to deny that aggression and territoriality are basic concepts requiring much more study than has been the case up to the present?

Conclusions and Implications for Organization Theory

Organization theory focuses on the study of man in organizations. Until quite recently, organizations have been viewed as cooperative systems aimed at the efficient transformation of scarce resources into socially desired goods and/or services. The role of man in the organization has been considered as one of coordinating and rationalizing the cooperative activities of organizational participants. This view of the "rational economic organization man" has come under increasing fire as a result of the well-known

Hawthorne studies as well as numerous subsequent developments in the policy arts and the behavioral sciences.

During the past two or three decades, many large-scale attempts have been mounted to develop a more complete and encompassing theory of man and of his behavior in organizations. During this time, most researchers have accepted as axiomatic the statement of the earlier Greek philosophers that man is *by nature a social and political animal*. Unfortunately, primary emphasis has been placed on the meaning of "political and social" while assuming the "by nature" aspect to be self-evident. The theoretical frameworks that have proven most useful in this search have been derived from the policy arts and the behavioral sciences, most notably economics, political science, psychology, and sociology.

In both theory and application, the policy arts and the behavioral sciences still tend to view man in organizations as little more than a learning machine. Provided with the right or appropriate economic, social, political, and psychological incentives (environment), man can be made to learn a preferred pattern of behavior. As a consequence, there are few scholars even today who would question that there is anything in human nature that cannot be fixed or conditioned through proper education or training. In the mid-fifties Ashley Montagu concluded his inquiry into the "Biosocial Nature of Man" by reaffirming this conviction. He stated:

> Indeed, the species character which should be part of the definition of Homo sapiens is educability. Man is the most plastic, the most educable, the most malleable of all creatures on the face of the earth.... Educability is man's most important species trait, overshadowing all others.[25]

Management theorists and practitioners wholeheartedly accepted the model of man that assumes an almost infinite capacity for education and adjustment. This acceptance has been the progenitor of a multiplicity of leadership, motivation, and control theories and techniques ranging from the so-called Human Relations approach, Theories X and Y, Systems 1 through 4, and the Managerial Grid, all the way to the latest applications of Operant Conditioning. Note that nearly all of these schemes are characterized by an overwhelming acceptance of the tabula rasa assumption of man and his unlimited capacity to learn how to change his behavior to fit the requirements imposed by the organization.

The evidence from ethology appears to suggest that the assumptions of infinite educability and plasticity may be both misleading and dangerous. Just as the Hawthorne experiments showed that industrial workers respond not only to economic incentives but also to psychological and social motivators, so the Ethology Effect proposes that there are constraints that determine the educability of man. These limits are set by man's genetic endowments—his inborn nature. These biological limits constitute the parameters that both mold and limit the extent of his learned behavior.

This chapter has attempted to demonstrate the virtual absence of any kind of ethological assumptions in theories purporting to explain and predict the behavior of man in his organizations. This has been rationalized on the grounds that the disciplines from which organization theories originated did not consider ethology to be relevant to the study of human behavior. It is the authors' opinion that the intellectual capital upon which these theories were based appears to be rapidly depleting and that a new approach to the study of human behavior in organizations is in order. When this occurs, organization theory may well develop into a discipline that can both explain and predict much more about organizational behavior than has been the case in the past.

This is, therefore, a very appropriate and opportune time to take a fresh look into the basic assumptions underlying the evaluative base currently used in studying the nature of the organization man. If it is, in fact, proven by ethologists that man's educability and behavioral flexibility or plasticity are constrained by certain innate characteristics, then we face a change in management theory of a significance comparable to that introduced into the discipline by the Hawthorne Studies. For lack of a better name, this has been referred to as the Ethology Effect. That it is important, there can be no doubt, but it cannot be claimed to be new. It was Machiavelli himself who stated many years ago:

> You must know then, that there are two methods of fighting, the one by law, the other by force: the first method is that of men, the second of beasts; but as the first method is often insufficient, one must have a recourse to the second. It is therefore necessary for a prince to know well how to use both the beast and the man.[26]

ENDNOTES

1. Waino W. Suojanen, "Evolution, Ethology, and Organization," *Southern Journal of Business* (October, 1970): 107-116.

2. Dwight E. Robinson, "The Evolutionary Heritage of Corporation Man: Introducing the Organization Theory of Anthony Jay," *Academy of Management Journal*, 15 (1972): 345-353.

3. William G. Scott and D.K. Hart, "The Moral Nature of Man in Organizations: A Comparative Analysis: Reply," *Academy of Management Journal*, 14 (1971): 241-255.

4. Ibid., 538.

5. W. M. Parsons, "What Happened at Hawthorne?" *Science*, 8 March 1974, 922-932.

6. The two-factor theory of motivation would be another likely candidate to be included in the list of dichotomies employed in the management literature. Yet the present listing is far from exhaustive.

7. Alison Jolly, *The Evolution of Primate Behavior* (New York: Macmillan, 1972).

8. Alexander Alland, Jr., *The Human Imperative* (New York: Columbia University Press, 1972); Ashley Montagu, *The Biosocial Nature of Man* (New York: Grove Press, 1956); and Ashley Montagu, ed., *Man and Aggression*, 2nd ed. (New York: Oxford University Press, 1973).

9. Alland, *Imperative*, preface.

10. David Pilbeam, "The Fashionable View of Man...," *New York Times Magazine*, 3 September 1972, 10.

11. Montagu, *Aggression*, xvii.

12. Anne Anastasi, *Common Fallacies about Heredity, Environment, and Human Behavior* (Iowa City, Iowa: The American College Testing Program, 1973), 5.

13. Steven Goldberg, *The Inevitability of Patriarchy* (New York: Morrow, 1973), 77.

14. R.J. Herrnstein, "The Perils of Expounding Meritocracy," *Science*, 6 July 1973, 36-37; and Christopher Jencks, et al., *Inequality* (New York: Basic Books, 1972).

15. Many readers may not be aware that Maslow early in his career was very much interested in ethology. Abraham Maslow, "The Role of Dominance in the Social and Sexual Behavior of Infra-human Primates III: A Theory of the Sexual Behavior of Infra-human Primates," *Journal of Genetic Psychology*, 48 (1936): 310-348.

16. Abraham Maslow, *Motivation and Personality* (New York: Harper, 1954), 139.

17. William C. Gevarter, "Man—His Brain and His Freedom," *Journal of Humanistic Psychology*, 15 (Fall 1975); 79-90; Robert E. Ornstein, *The Psychology of Consciousness* (new York: Viking, 1973); Maya Pines, *The Brain Changers* (New York: Harcourt, Brace, Jovanovich, 1973); and Stevens Rose, *The Conscious Brain* (New York: Knopf, 1973).

18. Theodosious Dobzhansky, *Heredity and the Nature of Man* (New York: New American Library, Small Case, 1966), 145-146.

19. Gevarter, "Man"; Erich Fromm, "Man Would as Soon Flee as Fight," *Psychology Today* (August 1973): 35-45; Ornstein, *Consciousness;* and J.R.Vallentyne and H.L. Tracy, "Demophora: Greeks Had Words for the Interdependence of Biological and Technical Growth," *Science and Public Affairs* (May, 1973): 24.

20. Dobzhansky, *Heredity.*

21 These three Nobel laureates are Konrad Lorenz, Niko Tinbergen, and Karl von Frisch.

22. Jolly, *Primate Behavior.*

23. John H. Crook, "The Nature and Functions of Territorial Aggression," in *Aggression*, 183-220; and Ralph Holloway, "Territory and Aggression in Man: A Look at Ardrey's Territorial Imperative" in *Aggression*, 176-182.

24. Fromm, "Flee as Fight," 35-45.

25. Montagu, *Nature of Man*, 108-109.

26. Niccolo Machiavelli, *The Prince and the Discourses* (New York: Random House, The Modern Library, 1950), 64.

Part II

The Brain and Management
(An Introduction)

3

Management and the Human Mind: On the Three Kinds of Contingencies

Waino W. Suojanen

Some years ago, I tried to reduce the paradigm of managerial situation to three general types—those concerned respectively with crisis, routine, and knowledge.[1] More recently, Paul E. Mott has done the same, and perhaps more importantly, has narrated and verified the usefulness of this three-way paradigm.[2] Mott indicates that the effectiveness of organizations can be measured in terms of three types of circumstances or situations or contingencies. These are, in his own words, the following:

A. Organizing centers of power for routine production (productivity)
   1. The quantity of the product
   2. The quality of the product
   3. The efficiency with which it is produced

B. Organizing centers of power to change routines (adaptability)
   1. Symbolic adaptation

This chapter was originally published in *Energy: Today's Choices, Tomorrow's Opportunities* (World Future Society, 24 April 1974) under the title "Management, the Human Mind, and the Future of Work" and is reprinted with permission.

   a. Anticipating problems in advance and developing satisfactory and timely solutions to them

   b. Staying abreast of new technologies and methods applicable to the activities of the organization

  2. Behavioral adaptation

   a. Prompt acceptance of solutions

   b. Prevalent acceptance of solutions

C. Organizing centers of power to cope with temporarily unpredictable overloads of work (flexibility)[3]

Those who are familiar with my *Dynamics of Management* and subsequent publications will recognize these as analogous to my (1) routine-oriented, (2) knowledge-oriented, and (3) crisis-oriented situations or contingencies, except that I list them in the following order:

(1) Crisis-oriented

(2) Routine-oriented

(3) Knowledge-oriented[4]

About twelve years ago, I presented a paper that discussed the managerial implications of the new biology in terms of man as an animal and man as man.[5] Nearly four years later, A.G. Kefalas of the University of Georgia and I wrote a paper that goes much more deeply into those aspects of the "new biology" that are useful in trying to understand the nature of man as a manager.[6] It has become increasingly evident that those aspects of biology that are relevant to man as a manager are moving ahead very swiftly and that it might now prove very useful to plug into the work being done on the configuration and structure of the human brain and how all of this relates to both the science and the art of management. Two simplified sketches of the human brain are presented in Exhibit 3-1. The reader will profit considerably from a study of this exhibit before proceeding further.

The Three Brains and the Three Human Contingencies

According to biological literature, man is the possessor of three related and yet conceptually separate brains. These consist of the "old" or visceral brain and the two "new" functionally asymmetrical left and right half brains (henceforth referred to as the left and right

Exhibit 3-1: **The Constituents of the Human Brain**

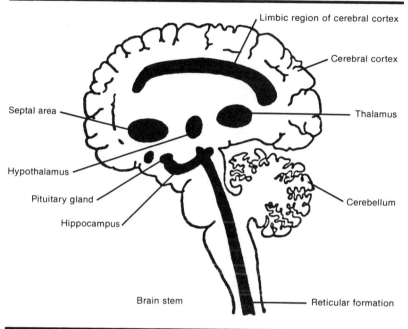

Limbic region of cerebral cortex
Cerebral cortex
Septal area
Thalamus
Hypothalamus
Pituitary gland
Hippocampus
Cerebellum
Brain stem
Reticular formation

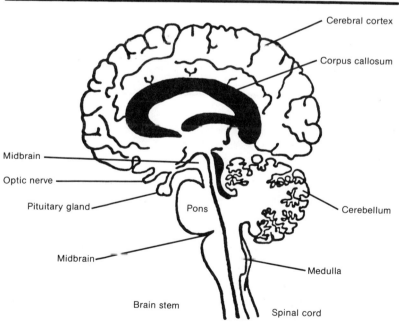

Cerebral cortex
Corpus callosum
Midbrain
Optic nerve
Pituitary gland
Pons
Cerebellum
Midbrain
Medulla
Brain stem
Spinal cord

Exhibit 3-2: **Model of the Minds of Man**

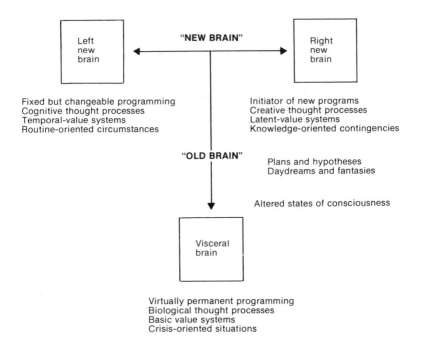

new brains). A simple model of these three minds of man is presented in Exhibit 3-2.

The *hindbrain* of man consists of the *cerebellum,* the *medulla,* and the *reticular formation.* In times of crisis, when adrenalin must be poured into the human system in order to summon the totality of reserves, the cerebellum, the medulla, and the reticular formation work together through the *limbic region* to alert the *forebrain* (consisting of the cerebral cortex, limbic system, thalamus, and hypothalamus) as well as to take care of such elemental aspects of survival as pointing the feet in the right direction to fight, to flee, or to freeze. The medulla serves as the switchboard that enables the reticular formation to alert the forebrain, while the cerebellum functions as a "manager by exception" by determining which situations are worthy of note and which should be ignored. The reticular formation is not a discrete structure but rather a neural network that runs through the medulla and on into parts of the forebrain including the *thalamus* and the *cortex*.[7]

The higher the species, working up say from fish to frog to alligator to shrew and to man, the smaller the relative size of the midbrain. As vertebrate species have evolved, the midbrain has become proportionally smaller, while the forebrain has increased in size and become more important. This might be referred to as a case of optimization within constraint.

The midbrain receives certain impulses from receptors in the eyes and has primary control responsibility for the eye muscles. It also connects the hindbrain to the forebrain, although most of the predominantly sensory functions that it performed in the vertebrate ancestors of man have now been taken over by the forebrain.

Before discussing the cerebral cortex, let's pause for a brief analysis of the *hypothalamus*—a part of the forebrain that is so important that it has been called "a brain within the brain." As one popular writer puts it, "the hypothalamus, which is part of the forebrain and not the midbrain or hindbrain, ... regulates the entire autonomic nervous system, and thus the body's internal environment, including its temperature, chemical balance, and appetites, as well as the emotions."[8]

The hypothalamus is only one part of the limbic region of the forebrain. In addition to the hypothalamus, other parts of this integrated network are the *hippocampus,* the *amygdala,* the *septal area,* and parts of the reticular formation.

The hindbrain, the midbrain, and the limbic region of the forebrain may be viewed in totality as that portion of the nervous system that man shares in common with his vertebrate and primate relatives. These brain areas comprise the hominid equivalent of the brain of other mammals and, taken together, may be viewed as comprising the man as an animal (see visceral brain on the left side of Exhibit 3-3)

In summary, what we have been discussing so far is concerned with the everyday experiences that man as an animal encounters. The hindbrain, midbrain, and limbic system, comprising the visceral brain of man, regulate those kinds of behaviors that have been extensively studied by the ethologists. These behaviors comprise the six "f's"—fight-or-flight, freezing, feeding, feeling, and flirting. The visceral brain expresses itself through organ activity. From the viewpoint of Abraham Maslow, the visceral brain is concerned with the satisfaction of "lower needs" or with Frederick Herzberg's "hygiene factors." By contrast, the cerebral cortex is concerned with two distinct and separate kinds of "man as man," or intellectualized, aspects of experience.

The Cerebral Cortex and the Two New Brains

Any good text on neurobiology or even biology will present the physiology of the human forebrain in whatever detail the reader is interested in pursuing.[9] From the viewpoint of management theory, the most interesting part of the forebrain is the cerebral cortex—defined by Webster as "the expanded anterior portion of the brain that in higher mammals overlies the rest of the brain, consists of cerebral hemispheres and connecting structures, and is held to be the seat of conscious mental processes."

Modern physiological and psychological research has discovered that the cerebral cortex really consists not of two symmetrical hemispheres but of two new brains—the left new brain (LNB) and the right new brain (RNB). These new brains are functionally asymmetrical and therein lies a matter of great significance to both the science and the art of management.[10]

In the left new brain of most people are located what Robert E. Ornstein calls the "linear" functions of man as man—language, rational cognition, analytic capacity, and the sense of time. The right new brain, by contrast, governs the nonlinear or nonverbal functions—spacial relationships, intuition, subjectivity, and the creative potentials of man in such fields as sculpture and painting.

In recent years, management thought has focused more and more on left-new-brain concepts of rationality and system. More than once over the years, during discussions with quantitatively oriented colleagues, I have advanced the tentative concept that there may be a role for intuition in the management discipline and have been pooh-poohed for my lack of understanding of rigor and rationality in decision making and problem solving. I well recall receiving such a reaction from a colleague immediately following a discussion we had had about the management implications of the Watergate affair!

In a broad, philosophical sense, Eastern thought throughout the millenia may be viewed as having been right-new-brain dominated, particularly in such areas as Sufi, Yoga, and Zen. Those of us who grew to maturity in the age of logical positivism tended to view Eastern thought with more amusement than understanding, even though we were sometimes quick to emphasize the role of art and subjectivity in the discipline of management.[11]

The heart of the scientific method is contained in four steps—observation, hypothesis, experiment, induction. Rationality, logical positivism, quantification are the essence of this form of the left-new-brain approach to problem solving—which Edward de Bono calls *vertical thinking*.[12] Vertical thinking, to use de Bono's analogy, consists of digging the same hole deeper. As he puts it, vertical thinking

(1) is a stepwise process—each step follows on from the previous step in an unbroken sequence;

(2) must be correct at every step (this is perhaps the essence of the process);

(3) selects and deals with only what is relevant.[13]

Nonlinear, intuitive, creative thinking tends to be right-new-brain dominated and may be viewed as emphasizing the role of art in the practice of management. This is what de Bono calls *lateral thinking* and is analogous to digging a hole in another place or fashioning a canal between two holes. Lateral thinking is the antithesis of vertical thinking: it is not sequential; it does not have to be correct at each step; it is not restricted to relevant (read left-new-brain) information. In vertical thinking, data are used as a contribution to the development of a structure. In lateral thinking, information is employed provocatively and insightfully to bring about a restructuring.[14]

In recent years, a number of management scientists have begun to experiment with behavior modification techniques. Behavior modification represents an attempt on the part of the experimenter or manager to elicit desired behavior by using aversive conditioning or positive reinforcement. As suggested by Exhibit 3-2, the world of the behavior modifier consists of heredity, environment, and the present situation. To put it differently, behavior modification assumes the virtually permanent programming characteristic of the visceral brain as mediated by the existing circumstances within the left new brain. Clearly, behavior modification represents little more than a continuation of vertical thinking.

Until quite recently, it was assumed that man was at the mercy of his autonomic or so-called involuntary nervous system. On every hand, the evidence is now beginning to mount that this is not the case at all—that, instead, mind can exercise considerable control over body and indeed over mind itself. This technique is known as biofeedback and it represents a step, perhaps one of the most significant in the evolution of man, in the methodological triumph of lateral thinking over vertical thinking. The differences between behavior modification and biofeedback are well expressed in the following:

> In B.F. Skinner's opinion, we have no choice but to use operant conditioning, in one form or another, to change people's behavior. He believes this is the only way to ensure peace without repression. Disagreeing, most of the researchers involved in biofeedback believe that man can change himself through voluntary actions. He can reshape his personality, improve his health, in a sense remake his world through biofeedback.[15]

The Mind of Man and Man the Manufacturer

From the viewpoint of management theory, there is a fascinating relationship between the mind of man and the way people behave in organizations. Without asymmetrical new brains, man would never have become a hunter or a weapon maker or a tool user or a technologist.

Three aspects of the physical configuration of man are of critical importance in the development of man the animal into man the man. These are man's grasping hands, his binocular and stereoscopic vision, and his striding stance. The earliest primates lived in trees and in time became able to grip branches by using the opposable thumb. Fingers enable a species to develop more manual dexterity than is possible with hooves or claws.

A species that lives in the trees must develop accurate depth perception in order to navigate a narrow branch or to jump from one branch to another. In time, the primate face evolved and became flatter so that both eyes faced forward and could focus on a single object in a binocular fashion. Later, stereoscopic vision developed, enabling primates and hominids to see in three dimensions.

Stereoscopic vision ultimately became fused with the cerebral cortex in quite a remarkable way. Nerves from the right eye led not only to the left new brain but also to the right new brain. The left eye became connected to the cerebral cortex in a similar manner. The two new brains acquired the differential functions mentioned earlier; the grasping of hands in man also acquired specialized functions. The *power grip,* for most humans, is found in the right hand (which is controlled by the left new brain) and the *precision grip* is present in the left hand (which is controlled by the right new brain). Think of the implications of this the next time you crack a nut or shoot a bow and arrow.

Logical Positivism and Metaphysics

In the world of experience, Sufi, Yoga, and Zen are viewed by many members of left-new-brain dominated cultures as the outdated mysticism of the East. When members of the younger generation evince an interest in these and in even more esoteric value systems, many in the older generation are unable to accept this "unconventionality."

Those of us who represent the establishment, the power structure, "the man," were adults prior to or early in the 1940-1970 time frame—a period of affluence during which the real per capita income doubled. This is a phenomenon that will probably never happen again. To our generation, left-new-brain rationality was the key that Economic Man used to unlock and ultimately to squander the treasure trove of nature.

This older (left-new-brain dominated) generation continues to govern in this country as well as in many others. This generation favors Theory X over Theory Y, System 1 over System 4, maintenance factors over motivators, animal needs over human needs. Their theory-in-use is a left-new-brain theory—their espoused theory is right-new-brain.

The younger generation has grown to adulthood during the 1940-1980 time period. The espoused theories they learned from their parents, but, as they matured, they became aware of their conflict with the theories-in-use. This situation created the dichotomy of alienation—it was evident to the young that their parents were behaving like children rather than like adults.[16] To put it in their terms, we, their parents, were behaving like hypocrites.

A crisis of enormous proportions came to the fore as the immensity and the implications of this alienation became clearer. As Walter Weisskopf puts it:

> They (people) try to escape this split by union downward or union upward. Both aim in different ways to overcome consciousness. *Union downward* tries to eliminate consciousness through such means as intoxication, drug addiction (which is not an expansion but an extinction of consciousness), sexual stupor, apathetic passivity, "through wine, women and song," on the sensual level. The movements of today which use massage, nudism, sensitivity training, physical touch encounters and so forth are trying to find ways to overcome, by more or less physical means, the estrangement from which we suffer. Sometimes definite elements of *union upward*, with expansion of consciousness, are involved in these activities. Aldous Huxley's mysticism, built on mescaline, is a mixture of both.[17]

As he continues, Weisskopff discusses union upward as antinomic, and yet as part of a continuum, to union downward. According to Weisskopf, left-new-brain scientific and technical knowledge, which is purportedly value-free, places too much emphasis on rationality and tends to derogate intuition, thereby creating a pattern of alienation and separation.[18] This kind of alienation is different from a kind discussed by Karl Marx, Max Weber, and Emile Durkheim and more recently by the behavioral management theorists. Yet, note that a common strain is present in all of them—either workers are not recognized as fully functioning human beings, or they operate under an authoritarian system of hierarchically managed activities, or their work and/or its product lack meaning and significance. In this connection, Weisskopf is critical of some of the behavioral management theories, and those who try to understand the functioning of the human consciousness would undoubtedly tend to agree with him.

Suggestions for Further Research

A study of Exhibits 3-2, 3-3, and 3-4 suggests that management theory in the past has been almost totally focused on the left-new-brain, routine-oriented type of situation. This is just as true of the work of Chester Barnard, Herbert Simon, and Douglas McGregor as it is of Henri Fayol, Frederick W. Taylor, and Max Weber. The 1900-1980 time period, in retrospect, was one with an obsessive concern for efficiency, both as a goal and as an achievement.

This concern with efficiency, as indicated in Exhibit 3-3, operates at the left and the middle ends of the man as an animal/man as man continuum.

Exhibit 3-3: **Management Contingencies and the Minds of Man**

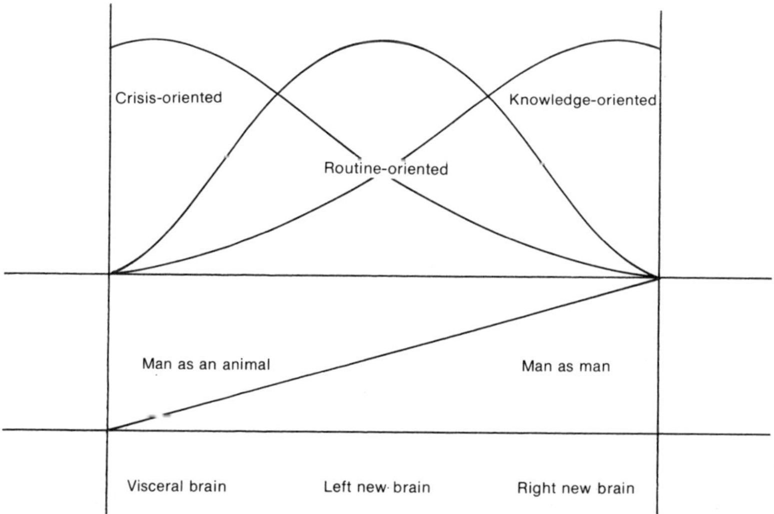

Exhibit 3-4: **Suggestions for Further Research**

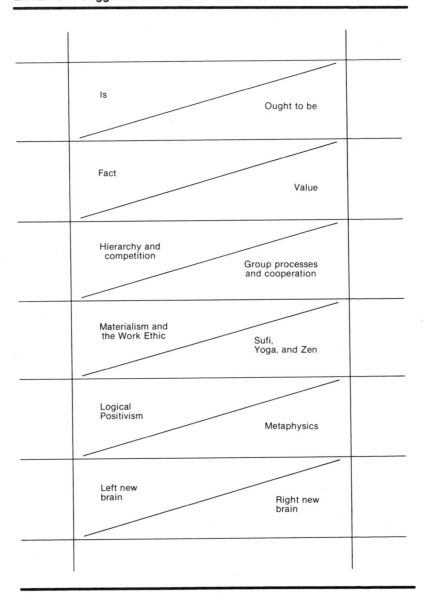

Is — Ought to be

Fact — Value

Hierarchy and competition — Group processes and cooperation

Materialism and the Work Ethic — Sufi, Yoga, and Zen

Logical Positivism — Metaphysics

Left new brain — Right new brain

In the future, management theory and organizational behavior will probably pay more attention to the ethical, the metaphysical, the spiritual, and the creative. The directions of this thought are presented in Exhibit 3-4. Each rectangle in Exhibit 3-4 may be viewed as an addendum to the bottom rectangle in Exhibit 3-3.

Now that industrialized societies are beginning to press the limits of growth, other values will have to be substituted for efficiency and growth. We must learn more about man and how he, as an animal, will react to crisis-oriented situations that threaten his survival. We know next to nothing about the management of emerging situations that tend to be temporary in nature but that extract an enormous human toll in tension and depression. As Exhibit 3-2 suggests, we have much to learn about the visceral brain and how it enables us to cope with situations that pose an immediate threat to the individual, the group, the organization, and the society.

Crises occur because men do not plan or because the plan did not embrace the given crisis as a possible situation. In the latter instance, we must learn more about "old brain" patterns of reactive behavior. In the former case, we must learn even more about the functioning of the right new brain and how its limitless potential can be tapped, not only for us but also for the countless generations yet to be born. In the present state of the art, our knowledge about creativity—its identification, nurture, and utilization—is as primitive as the technology of our Stone Age ancestors.

Planning is of the essence if change is to be deliberately initiated or generated. In the absence of planning, man must react or adapt to sudden change that comes as a surprise. During the next quarter century, man must learn how to utilize his creativity to build a society to replace the one based on nature's bountiful supply of energy. The world of yesterday emphasized growth and gross national product—tomorrow's world will focus just as intensely on a steady state and cooperation and the quality of life. At this point, the past of management thought is mere prologue. As Exhibit 3-2 suggests, it is a long journey from the latent value system of the right new brain through the temporal value system of the left new brain to the basic value system of the visceral brain. If we take the tide at the flood, there is no question that it will lead us to vistas far more exciting than those that marked the 1940-1980 period.

Back in 1974, *Business Week* explored the world of right-new-brain phenomena in an article entitled "Why Scientists Take Psychic Research Seriously."[19] The closing paragraph of this article made the following comments:

Researchers are convinced that everyone possesses some dormant psychic powers that can be tapped. . . . There seems to be a great untapped potential in the human mind. . . . Perhaps we can evolve man and his social structures so that he can cope with the problems we face. . . . Many of our basic concepts may need construction. The image of man himself may have to change.[20]

A few years ago, a cartoon in *Peanuts* put it far better than I have been able to do in this chapter:

Right new brain speaking: "Some morning I'm going to get up real early and watch the sun rise. . . ."

Left new brain speaking: "Actually, as you probably know, the sun doesn't rise, . . . the Earth turns . . ."

Right new brain meditating, perhaps transcendentally. . . .

Right new brain speaking: "Some morning I'm going to get up real early and watch the earth turn. . . ."

ENDNOTES

1. Waino W. Suojanen, *The Dynamics of Management* (New York: Holt, Rinehart and Winston, 1966).

2. *The Characteristics of Effective Organizations* (New York: Harper and Row, 1972).

3. Ibid., 20.

4. Ibid., 102-111.

5. "Evolution, Ethology, and Organization," *Southern Journal of Business* (October, 1970): 107-116. The original paper was presented at the annual meeting of the Southern Academy of Management in 1969.

6. Asterios G. Kefalas and Waino W. Suojanen, "Organizational Behavior and the New Biology," *Academy of Management Journal*, 17, no. 30 (1974): 515.

7. James D. Ebert, et al., *Biology* (New York: Holt, Rinehart and Winston, 1973), 424-426. This an outstanding book and should be in the library of anyone interested in the "new biology." Exhibit 3-1 has been adapted from this volume.

8. Maya Pines, *The Brain Changers: Scientists and the New Mind Control* (New York: Harcourt Brace Jovanovich, 1973), 37.

9. See, for example, Ebert et al., *Biology*, 427-430.

10. For a discussion of the mind of man that is ahead of the state of the art, see Robert E. Ornstein, *The Psychology of Consciousness* (New York: Viking Press, 1972).

11. See, for example, Suojanen, *Dynamics of Management*, 33-42, 55-72.

12. For a discussion of vertical (linear) and lateral (nonlinear) thinking, see Edward de Bono, *New Think* (New York: Basic Books, 1967).

13. Edward de Bono, "The Virtues of Zigzag Thinking," *Think* (May-June 1969): 8.

14. Ibid., 9.

15. Pines, *Brain Changers*, 83. See also Ornstein, *Psychology of Consciosness*, 187-205. Edward Rosenfeld, *The Book of Highs: 250 Methods for Altering Your Consciousness Without Drugs* (New York: Quadrangle/New York Times Book Co., 1973).

16. For more on this, see Thomas A. Harris, *I'm OK-You're OK* (New York: Avon, 1973). In the Suojanen model, it helps to think in terms of child-parent-adult (CPA). This is an easy mnemonic concept for people who teach in schools of business administration.

17. Walter A. Weisskopf, *Alienation and Economics* (New York: Dutton, 1973), 20-21 (italics supplied).

18. Ibid., 21.

19. 26 January 1974, 76-78.

20. Ibid.

4

Star Trek, the Human Central Nervous System, Organizations, and the Role of Management Science

Waino W. Suojanen

Two articles in an issue of *Interface* several years ago presented additional comments on the continuing debate over the proper role of operations research/systems analysis in the broader field of management theory and organizational behavior.[1] One article indicated that a number of proposals for change within the profession have died because of a general lack of interest. A second article by Rick Hesse and Steve Altman suggests that the Star Trek phenomenon may be used to explain to businessmen and managers how management scientists and operations researchers can contribute to the broader goals of organizational purpose.

Star Trek

Hesse and Altman view the decision-making process on board the United Star Ship Enterprise as a responsibility shared jointly by Captain Kirk, Mr. Spock, and Dr. McCoy. In the Hesse-Altman model, Captain Kirk is the decisive managerial mind, Mr. Spock the analytical, management science mind, and Dr. McCoy the intuitive, behavioral science mind. The essence of decision according to this model is triune—three minds combine to select an optimal course of action.

The article points out that "decision-making is not only the province of operations research, management science, or decision science, but is something that everyone is interested in." The authors suggest that "large scale decisions are better made by experts, or that experts can aid the common man in making such decisions." I agree with this analysis as far as this particular point is concerned, but despite the authors' assertion that "we can't see inside of Captain Kirk," I also suggest that we can indeed see inside of the Captain, because Captain Kirk is the average TV spectator, an author of this article, or any human being we care to choose.

As a biogenetic structuralist, I contend that there is no intervening reality between the human central nervous system (CNS) and the environment. Behavior, from this point of view, is the *synthesis* of the dialectic between the brain as *thesis* and environment as *antithesis*. This dialectic is enfolded within another dialectic—that of man as an animal and man as man with the human central nervous system as the synthesis. The latter, however, remains an incomplete synthesis that alternates between old brain and new brain—between the unconscious-preconscious, on the one hand, and the conscious on the other. In this drama, which includes all of life and the larger cosmos, management science and operations research are mere fragments, albeit important ones.

In this chapter I shall follow the Star Trek/management theory paradigm so well developed by Hesse and Altman. View it this way. We have invited Captain Kirk to join us as we discuss the future of human organization, and we look inside his brain as he integrates ship, captain, crew, and staff. We can do this because we bring to the examination the powerful tools of neurophysiology and psychobiology. We also let our imaginations wander, but no more than did Jules Verne when he predicted that men would one day journey to the moon from Florida and return safely.

The Minds of Man

Over the course of the years I have published a number of articles that have tried to couple advances in neurophysiology and psychobiology to an integrative theory of management.[2] As part of this paradigm, Exhibit 3-2, chapter 3, presents a schematic of the human brain that is in accord with the latest neurophysiological evidence.

Simeons argues that many human behaviors are under the control of the diencephalon or visceral brain (VB) rather than the cerebral cortex. Building on the Simeons model, I developed the concept of a visceral brain which is equal in importance, although different in function, from the dual hemispheres of the cortical brain. This visceral brain controls the functions of man as animal—fight-or-flight, freeze, feed, feel, and flirt as indicated in Exhibit 4-1. What is even more important, according to the most recent neurophysiological evidence, is that the seat of decision in man is located in the visceral brain.

We must remember that the left new brain (like Mr. Spock) and the right new brain (like Dr. McCoy) are staff elements in the decision-making process. These brains are computers and tape decks that represent "the elaboration of the function of censorship [that] led to all the complicated processes of conscious perception, memory, association, learning, and reasoning."[3]

In Exhibit 3-2, Captain Kirk may be viewed as the visceral brain (VB), Mr. Spock as the left new brain (LNB), and Dr. McCoy as the right new brain (RNB). In contrast to popular opinion—and this includes management scientists as well as members of the television audience with an average IQ of 80—the decisive mind of Captain Kirk is located in the old or visceral brain rather than in the new brain which consists of the left new brain and the right new brain.

In Exhibit 4-1, the functions of the human brain are viewed in terms of the acronym A QUIVER SCANS 6 F's. The left new brain is, as Hesse and Altman suggest, a Mr. Spock—Analytical, QUantitative, Intellectual, VErbal, Rational. Similarly, the right new brain is a Dr. McCoy—Synthesizing, Creative, Artistic, Normative, Spatial. These two disparate functions of the new brain are illustrated in Exhibit 4-2. The functioning of the visceral brain will be discussed later.

Decision and consciousness do not appear to be qualities that are confined to man alone. Chimpanzees not only have the power of language but also "swear, invent names, learn signs from each other, have demonstrated syntactic capabilities, have translated from spoken to sign language, and have used words to express

Exhibit 4-1: **Acronym of the Functions of the Three Minds of Man**

A QUIVER SCANS 6'Fs'

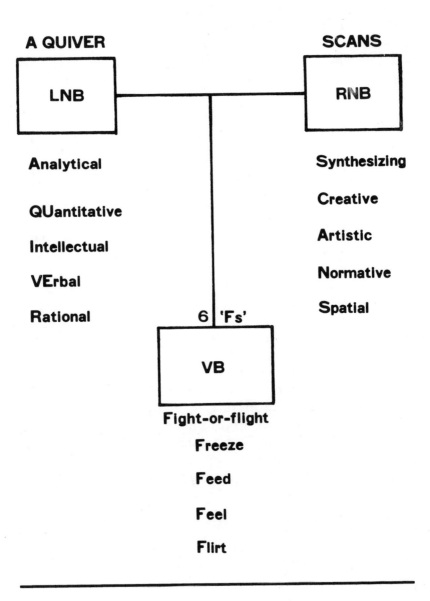

A QUIVER

| LNB |

Analytical

QUantitative

Intellectual

VErbal

Rational

SCANS

| RNB |

Synthesizing

Creative

Artistic

Normative

Spatial

6 'Fs'

| VB |

Fight-or-flight

Freeze

Feed

Feel

Flirt

Exhibit 4-2: **The New Brain**

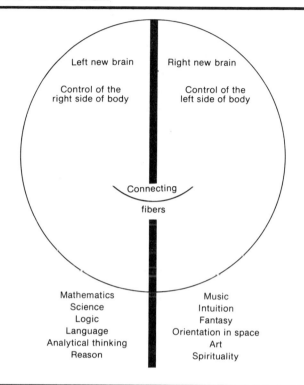

Left new brain

Control of the
right side of body

Right new brain

Control of the
left side of body

Connecting

fibers

Mathematics
Science
Logic
Language
Analytical thinking
Reason

Music
Intuition
Fantasy
Orientation in space
Art
Spirituality

Note: In this Exhibit language is presented as a function of the left new brain. Research literature indicates that cerebral asymmetry is much more pronounced in the human male than it is in the human female. Females tend to have speech control centers in both the right and left new brains. Other recent research seems to indicate that bilinguals may be more bilateral than monolinguals.

emotion, to joke, to converse, to lie."[4]

Man can now communicate with chimpanzees, and it is evident that this primate relative of ours can reason and make decisions. As Linden points out: "If chimps and other animals share our gifts of reason and language, what then happens to our prerogatives in nature?" [5]

Those who remain prisoners of the "environment only" school will disagree with the contention that consciousness, free will, the power of decision—call it what you will—is located in the visceral or "old" brain. If one agrees that the seat of decision is the brain stem, then chimpanzees and man lie at one end of the social animal continuum and ants and bees at the other.[6] From the viewpoint of sociobiology, man as an animal *exists* in nature rather than ruling it. One can even go a step further along the line of thought (as I do) and posit the existence of consciousness in all the higher vertebrates—they all have brain stems.

Shortly before he died, Wilder Penfield, the greatest neurosurgeon of the mid-twentieth century, published a book that greatly strengthens the thesis of Albert Simeons.[7] Penfield, however, goes far beyond Simeons and anatomically locates the *seat of consciousness* in the visceral brain rather than in the cortical brain. According to Penfield, the left new brain and the right new brain do not control the visceral brain but vice-versa!

If one accepts the Simeons-Penfield hypothesis, then the Captain Kirk in the mind of the human being is in the visceral brain rather than in the cerebral hemispheres. If this is the case, then both the left new brain and the right new brain may be viewed as giant computer tape decks that evolved in response to the drive of our early ancestors to survive and reproduce. Note carefully that Penfield has located the decisive mind and that it is in the visceral brain. Exhibit 4-3 shows how the decisive mind relates to the pleasure areas (to be discussed) and to the left new brain and right new brain.

The Chemistry of Choice

The Captain Kirk in the visceral brain is under the close influence of the pleasure areas of the reptilian brain. According to H. J. Campbell, a British physiologist, the behavior of man as an animal is dominated by the search for pleasure.[8]

As indicated in Exhibit 4-3, the pleasure areas send chemical "yes" messages to the decisive mind. By contrast, the new brain sends chemical "no" messages. When these plus and minus impulses are in balance, Captain Kirk makes realistic decisions. When the pleasure areas dominate the decision, the end result is characterized by the kind of hedonism that destroys the pleasure seeker as well as his or her cultural fabric. When the left new brain dominates the decision, we get the rationality of Economic Man, which emphasizes the decision rather than the decision's impact on man.

In this connection, we must remember that the combined output

Exhibit 4-3: **Central Nervous System Processing Model**

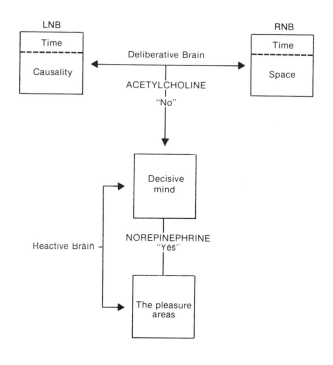

of the left new brain and right new brain is a "no" message to the decisive mind. Taken singly, the left new brain produces "no" messages in the normal state of consciousness whereas the right new brain produces "yes" messages.[9]

If the left new brain (Mr. Spock in the Hesse-Altman model) is temporarily rendered quiescent, the yes messages from the right new brain will reinforce those of the pleasure areas and we get an altered state of consciousness.

During an altered state of consciousness, the human brain fantasizes, daydreams, forms hypotheses—call them what you will. Hypothesis is the very essence of conceptual variation. Without it creativity and innovation are nothing but product and process improvements rather than a trek through the stars.

Time, space, and causality are distorted in any altered state of consciousness because the left new brain does not perform the judging or censorship function that is the very essence of the left new brain in the normal state of consciousness. The outlines of this type of distortion can be perceived by referring to Exhibit 4-3. If one covers the left new brain in this Exhibit, it is evident that time, space and causality are processed quite differently in the decisive mind when it receives only "yes" messages from the right new brain and the pleasure areas. Clearly, Mr. Spock plays as important a censorship role in the minds of man as he does aboard the USS Enterprise.

In a similar way, intellectual selection is essential to the advancement of knowledge. Without the "no" messages of the left new brain, wings would not be necessary for flight in the atmosphere. Censorship is needed—choice always requires an "it won't fly, Wilbur" to every fantasy or daydream or hypothesis. The process of censorship—of experiment and induction in scientific method—serves to assure Captain Kirk of the feasibility of the alternatives that he has either generated himself or that have been proferred to him by his staff assistants.

If we now turn to Exhibit 4-4, we can see that each of the minds of man performs functions that are analogous to the Hesse-Altman model of the USS Enterprise. Let's amplify the model by viewing the crew as the analog of the pleasure areas and the ship as the analog of the human skull. This system may now be viewed as the central nervous system. Continuing this line of reasoning leads us to Exhibit 4-5 that suggests strongly that Star Trek portrays well the analogies between the human nervous system and organization and management theory as they are studied in schools of business administration.

Planning, Intention, and Fixed Action Patterns

In an article titled "Planning on the Left Side and Managing on the Right," Henry Mintzberg located the decisive mind in the right new brain.[10] As I have tried to point out in earlier sections of this chapter, Captain Kirk the decider lives in the visceral brain, not in the right new brain. In this section, I shall attempt to prove that both Mr. Spock (left new brain) and Dr. McCoy (right new brain) are involved in the planning function—that planning is located in the frontal lobes of both hemispheres—not the left new brain alone as Mintzberg suggests. However, in the section that follows this, I shall try to show that management science and operations research do tend to reflect left-new-brain functioning.

The essence of managerial activity is to work successively through a series of actions in order to achieve a goal. The anticipation inherent in this kind of activity may be viewed as planning.

Planning appears to be localized in the frontal lobes of both the hemispheres of the new brain, although the evidence bearing on this is still on the sparse side. The evidence available indicates that the frontal lobes of both hemispheres operate jointly when "expectancy" is involved. The presence of evoked reponses or evoked potentials may be signs that the left new brain and the right new brain are preparing for "synchronous and joint action."

Exhibit 4-4: **Planning and the Minds of Man**

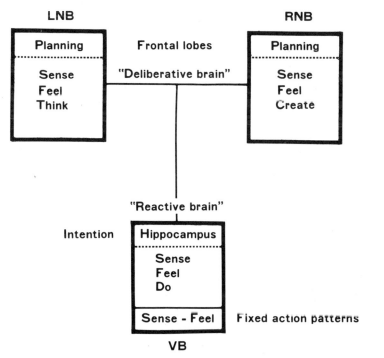

Exhibit 4-5: Star Trek, the Central Nervous System, and Human Organization

Star Trek	Nervous System Elements	Functions	Duties
U.S.S. Enterprise	Nervous System	Mission Accomplished	Organization
Crew	Pleasure Areas	Sense-Feel-Do	Workers
Captain Kirk	Decisive Mind	Sense-Feel-Decide	Manager
Mr. Spock	LNB	Sense-Feel-Think	Management Scientist
Dr. McCoy	RNB	Sense-Feel-Create	Behavioral Scientist

In summarizing his discussion of the functioning of the frontal lobes, Calder concludes that:

> We need not suppose that the frontal lobes are where we actually make decisions. That may occur, if indeed it can be said to happen anywhere in particular, deep in the mid-brain. The front of the brain is perhaps more like a trusted adviser who handles public relations and planning.[11]

In a vein similar to that of Calder, Howard Gardner points out that the frontal lobes

> seem to be less involved with an individual's ability to handle delimited problems and tasks than with the capacity to plan ahead, to monitor.... The frontal lobes in man are the last to develop in a physiological sense and presumably are also the last to be integrally involved in the mental life of man. They seem to assume crucial importance for just those aspects of thought which emerge only in adolescence or adulthood: the ability to think about oneself as a separate individual, to make elaborate plans and to see that they are carried out, to alter goals when that seems appropriate, to form a model of the world and one's relationships to it, to behave and respond appropriately across diverse social situations, to mediate between the pressures of the outer world and one's own inner prompting.[12]

The visceral brain processes the stream of consciousness—the relationship between past, present, and future—within which planning takes place. Those who would assign consciousness to the new brain have misinterpreted the physiological facts now available to us. The mediation between the frontal lobes of the new brain and the stream of consciousness in the visceral brain is performed by the hippocampus. As evidence of this, Penfield points out that any major removal of the anterior portion of the frontal lobe causes malfunctioning of the person's "capacity for planned initiative."[13]

Short-term memory, of course, is a basic ingredient to long-range planning. The events connected with short-term memory appear to be associated, not at all with the left new brain and the right new brain, but with the hippocampus. Each hippocampus is a curved flap of gray matter that lies tucked under the appropriate cortical hemispheres. The word *hippocampus* means "sea horse" and suggests a resemblance to its marine counterpart. As Penfield has indicated, when the hippocampus on each side of man's brain is removed, the ability to reactivate the stream of consciousness, both voluntarily or automatically, is lost. The hippocampi may be viewed as links between the frontal lobes of their respective hemispheres and the data processing mechanisms of long-range memory throughout the entire brain.[14]

The hippocampus is a neurophysiological computer with an input (sensory) register, a memory register, and an output (motor) register. Olds points out that "there are not enough middle register neurons to take down the inscription of the life history of the animal so it would be necessary to assume that these memories did not last very long, and that these memory registers became available for reuse after several hours or days."[15]

The hippocampus orders the stream of consciousness viewed as a process. This process extends from the immediate past through the present and into the immediate future. Without this continuum, there can be no recent memory. Neither can there be formulation of intention based on past experience combined with perception of the present environment. One hippocampus in the visceral brain matches respectively with both the left new brain and the right new brain and serves as the keeper of the keys that unlock the stream of consciousness when prompted by the decisive mind. Recent evidence also indicates that the route from short-term memory to the long-term memory of the new brain is through the left-new-brain and right-new-brain hippocampi: "N. Butlers and L. Cermak find the hippocampus of that side 'the left new brain' involved in retention of verbal materials, that of the opposite side 'the right new brain' in nonverbal memories."[16]

Both the right new brain and the left new brain are involved in the planning process. The right new brain provides the SCANS type hypothesis and the left new brain provides the A QUIVER type experiment and induction through which the brain produces and evaluates any number of possible courses of action and ultimately settles on that which appears to be potentially the most productive. The processing takes place, as indicated above, in such a way that relevant experiences are integrated into long-range chemical memory during rapid eye movement—dreaming deep while irrelevant experiences are purged from the memory registers of the hippocampi. The dreaming state of consciousness thus serves as a process for clearing out old programs in the hippocampi and for debugging the new programs in the new brain.

Apparently the manager's brain—Captain Kirk in this instance—functions in three planning-operations-control modes, and each of these modes is related by situation to the three discrete brains I have described. These functions, are presented in Exhibit 4-4.

The pleasure areas (See Exhibit 4-3) process fixed-action patterns that are stimulus-response sequences of coordinated motor actions. The motor actions are "learned without learning" and are relatively constant in form. These patterns, which are genetic in nature, program the individual for survival and reproduction in the classical evolutionary mold. All of us, for example, become frightened when we are crossing the street and a speeding automobile veers toward us This fright requires no conscious reaction to a plan, simply because any extended scanning of alternatives might well mean death. However, the fright does indicate awareness and causes a rapid stimulus-response behavior.

Note that the decisive mind controls intentions that may be defined as the products of attention directed toward an object of attention. Once we have jumped out of the way of the speeding automobile, our awareness turns to attention and we, for example, attempt to remember the license tag number and a description of the erring vehicle. Action becomes intention through hippocampal processing. The effective manager or commander does not panic because his decisive mind remains unflappable or unfreakable, even in those emergencies that threaten his life.

Many experienced managers, such as Captain Kirk, display an uncanny capacity to make sound decisions in the most turbulent of environments. They keep their heads when those around them are losing theirs. The essence of the way they make decisions is that they treat the crisis-oriented situation as a routine-oriented contingency. Only a very few people possess the individual competence to deal with crisis in this cold-blooded, dispassionate way. Very little, if any, effort in management education or training curricula is devoted to inculcating the competence of "coolness under fire." The first year of the MBA program at Harvard probably focuses more closely on developing fixed-action patterns that are appropriate to the crisis-oriented milieu encountered by the line manager than does any MBA program known to the writer.

In the jargon of the street, the manager who "has his act together" is "unfreakable." Captain Kirk does not "freak out" because he never becomes so upset as to be incapable of responding appropriately to the requirements of any situation that the USS Enterprise may encounter. Captain Kirk knows well how to play the inner game of command because he knows that "there is no need to give any sight or sound the power to upset him. He can choose to see the disturbance as stemming from his mind and not from the event. Then he can find a solution."[17] In many instances we might well remember that "if I am not the problem, then there is no solution."

The inner game of command applies equally to the frontal lobe process of *planning activities* by the two hemispheres of the new brain. For purposes of neural functioning, planning may be defined as an ordered arrangement in space and time designed causally to attain an overall objective. In this connection, it is important to note that the planning function encompasses all aspects of the new brain. Equally important to bear in mind is that plans become intentions during the period of execution.

Captain Kirk, as commander or manager, understands that the essence of decision making exists in the here-and-now. Mr. Spock is able to solve quantitative problems or to serve as a prosthetic left-new-brain supplement to Captain Kirk's own A QUIVER competence. Similarly, Dr. McCoy can solve behavioral problems and provide on-the-spot advice to Captain Kirk. However, only Captain Kirk has both the formal authority and the acceptance authority of the commander of the USS Enterprise as a going concern in which rules have to be made, formulas revised, and plans recast—as demanded by the very act of being—while attempting to achieve the objectives of the mission. In every sense of the concept, Captain Kirk is a hunter and line manager whereas Mr. Spock and Dr. McCoy are planners of the hunt—important staff people each in his own way but not pivotal in the moment-to-moment, decision-making operations of the organization.

Hunters and Planners of the Hunt

Sir Arthur Keith, the first of the primatologists, and Robert Ardrey, the popularizer of ethology, have used the hunting hypothesis to explain many aspects of human anatomical, neurophysiological, and behavioral evolution. I am in total agreement with this hypothesis and have tried with some success to apply concepts from ethology to the functioning of present-day organization.

In *Men in Groups,* Lionel Tiger argues that the male hunting group is the prototype of modern organization. I would go a step further and hypothesize that organized hunting groups, which predated *homo* among our prehominid ancestors, determined the nature of man as man in an evolutionary sense as he exists today.

In agreement with Jerre Levy, I would argue that fifteen million or so years ago there were two main jobs to be performed by our male, prehominid ancestors—hunting and planning the hunt. As she puts it:

> It is obvious that an optimal troop will have many able hunters and a few able planners. If hunters plan, the probability of a successful hunt is lessened. In either case, the net result for the troop will be less meat. If this is consciously recognized, the planners will be left at the home site while the hunters, following a plan they have been given, will seek their prey.... In the evolution of man it is clearly reasonable that the group of *Hominids* would survive best in which the majority of its members were generalists but in which some ideal minority were specialists.... The laterally specialised person is in this sense a generalist while the laterally non-specialised person is a specialist.[18]

Captain Kirk may be viewed as the hunter/commander/decision maker with maximal asymmetry between the left new brain and the right new brain combined with the unfreakable visceral brain, as illustrated in Figure 4-4 and discussed in the previous section. The asymmetry between the left new brain and the right new brain of the line manager, or what Jerre Levy calls the "hunter," is illustrated in Exhibit 4-6.

In contrast to Captain Kirk, Mr. Spock may be viewed as a person whose left new brain dominates the right new brain. In essence, he can be viewed as a person with two left new brain's as illustrated in Exhibit 4-7.

In opposition to Mr. Spock, who is the "compleat" management scientist, Dr. McCoy is a behavioral scientist with two right new

---

Exhibit 4-6: **Cerebral Equality**

Two "separate", cortical brains

Each brain operates "independently" / Sense-feel-<u>do</u> behavior pattern
Person concerned is a generalist / Has evolved advantage for <u>line</u>
management / The manager who gets things <u>done</u> / The generalist with
two "new" brains / Makes decisions and finds opportunities

---

brains as developed in Exhibit 4-8.

Evidence that managers are both born and made and that some of us are at an evolved disadvantage in the art of management is increasingly apparent in neurophysiological literature. To quote Levy again:

> Those *Hominids* with functionally symmetric hemispheres may be the most able planners, but being deficient in depth perception, visual memory, Gestalt closure, and directional discrimination of movement...the present percentage of people with left and right manual and cerebral dominance can be accounted for in terms of the cognitive-behavioral implications of various types of cerebral organizations and the biological fitnesses of those with these, organizations during man's evolutionary history.[19]

Summary

Operations research/systems analysis, as exemplified by Mr. Spock in Star Trek, represents only the left-new-brain aspect of the problem-solving process in organizational affairs. The right new brain, or behavioral science aspect of organizational problem solving, is illustrated by Dr. McCoy. The commander or the manager is one who utilizes both left-new-brain and right-new-brain counsel and advice as his visceral brain zeroes in on the decision.

We must remember that command or line-management or decision making, as epitomized by Captain Kirk in the case of the USS Enterprise, is an activity that is unique unto itself. Decision

---

Exhibit 4-7: **LNB Dominates RNB**

Both new brains work as "one" LNB

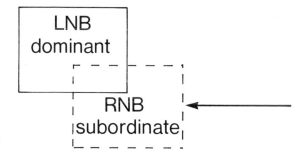

Cortical brain favors A QUIVER functions
Sense-feel-think behavior pattern
Person concerned is a specialist
Performs best in such positions as:
  o Staff functionary
  o Planner
  o Management scientist
  o Operations researcher
Solves problems

Exhibit 4-8: **LNB Subservient to RNB**

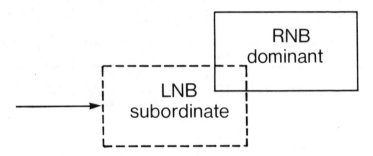

Both new brains operate as "one" RNB

RNB
dominant

LNB
subordinate

Cortical brain leans toward SCANS functions
Sense-feel-create behavior patterns
Favor creative pursuits such as:

o Art and sculpture
o Poetry and literature
o Architecture
o Music

Finds problems

making, in contrast to problem solving, is concerned with the here
and now. Therefore, the commander or manager must possess far
better than average control over his visceral brain functioning at
the fixed-action, pattern-intention levels than is the case with the
adviser or the staff assistant.

Organizational behavior literature has been unable to fill in the
void between management theory and administrative practice
despite continuing efforts to do so. A few efforts have been made to
explain administrative practice by resorting to the neurophysiological literature that discusses the cerebral asymmetry of the new
brain. The article by Henry Mintzberg, cited earlier in this chapter,
falls into this category.

Recent advances in neurophysiology and psychobiology suggest that the decisive mind is located in the visceral brain. If we accept this concept and apply it to management theory and organizational behavior, a good many pieces of the administrative puzzle fall into place almost as if by magic. Not the least of these pieces is the role that operations research/systems analysis should play in the overall pattern of how organizations such as the USS Enterprise achieve their missions.

ENDNOTES

1. Dieter Klein and Paul Butkovich, "Can the Professions of Operations Research/Management Science Change and Survive?" (May 1976): 47-51; and Rich Hesse and Steve Altman, "Star Trek: An Optimum Decision Making Model" (May 1976): 60-62.

2. See for example, my paper "The Minds of Man and The Uses of Management Science," *Clemson University Review of Industrial Management and Textile Science* (Spring 1975): 51-66.

3. A. T. W. Simeons, *Man's Presumptuous Brain* (New York: E. P. Dutton, 1961), 34. I recommend that the reader's odyssey through the minds of man begin with this volume—it is breathtaking in its prescience.

4. Eugene Linden, "Man Talks So Oddly," *New York Times*, 20 April 1976.

5. On April 23, 1976, Grace H. Yeni-Komshian and Dennis A. Benson reported in *Science*, "Anatomical Study of Cerebral Asymmetry in the Temporal Lobe of Humans, Chimpanzees, and Rhesus Monkeys," (387-389) that chimpanzees as well as human beings do indeed share common physical features for communication in the left new brain but that these are absent in the rhesus monkey.

6. For the complete argument on this, see Edward P. Wilson, *Sociobiology: The New Synthesis* (Cambridge: Harvard University Press, 1975). By the way, this volume has engendered heated scholarly debate.

7. Wilbur Penfield, et al., *The Mystery of the Mind: A Critical Study of Consciousness and the Human Brain* (Princeton, N.J.: Princeton University Press, 1975).

8. H. J. Campbell, *The Pleasure Areas: A New Theory of Behavior* (New York: Delacorte Press, 1973).

9. For the account of the chemistry of the minds of man that I have used here, see James Olds, "The Neuropsychology of Motivation" in *Brain Mechanisms and the Control of Behavior*, ed. W. Ross Adey et al. (London: Heinemann Educational Books, 1974), 483-500.

10. *Harvard Business Review* (July-August 1976): 49-58.

11. Nigel Calder, *The Mind of Man: An Investigation into Current Research on the Brain and Human Nature* (New York: Viking, 1970), 190.

12. Howard Gardner, *The Shattered Mind: The Person after Brain Damage* (New York: Knopf, 1975), 267-268.

13. Penfield, *Mystery of the Mind*, 35-36, 58-59, 65-66.

14. In this discussion, I have relied greatly on the chapter by James Olds, "Behavior Theory and the Brain," in Adey et al., *Brain Mechanisms*, 343-360. Management scientists interested in computer/central nervous system analogs will find reading this chapter a thrilling experience.

15. Ibid., 356-357.

16. W. J. H. Nauta, "Brain-Behavior Relationships," *Science* (24 September 1976): 1236.

17. W. Timothy Gallwey, *The Inner Game of Tennis* (New York: Random House, 1974), 134-135.

18. Jerre Levy, "Psychobiological Implications of Bilateral Asymmetry," in *Hemisphere Function in the Human Brain* Stuart J. Dimont and J. Graham Beaumont, ed. (New York: Halsted, 1974), 173.

19. Ibid., 174.

Part III

Addictive Personal
and Management Behavior

5

Addiction and the Minds of Man

Waino W. Suojanen

In the course of his lifetime, every American ingests a wide variety of drugs for one of two principal purposes. Many of us are on drug regimens that have been set up for us by our physicians. Perhaps a larger number are on "medical" programs that we have set up for ourselves, using over-the-counter drugs to treat illness, whether real or fancied. When the chemical suits the disease and the patient, no matter who the "physician," we can define the person concerned as using the drug for a medical purpose.

A number of us employ alcohol or other chemical substances for another purpose—to obtain a sense of pleasure. One recent volume defines chemicals of this kind as "sensual drugs."[1] Hardin and Helen Jones refer to such chemicals as sensual drugs because they activate the pleasure centers in the visceral brain.

The Minds of Man

As we saw in Chapter 4, Exhibit 4-1, the functions of the human brain are viewed in terms of the acronymn, A QUIVER SCANS 6Fs. The left new brain is A QUIVER brain—*A*nalytical, *QU*antitative, *I*ntellectual, *VE*rbal, *R*ational. Similarly, the right new brain is a SCANS brain—*S*ynthesizing, *C*reative, *A*rtistic, *N*ormative, *S*patial. These two different minds are located in the new brain. But let's take a closer look at the old, or visceral, brain (VB).

The visceral brain regulates our subconscious behavior. These behaviors are what I call the "six f's"—*F*ight-or-*F*light, *F*reeze,

Feed, Feel and *Flirt.* The behavior of animals, and the behavior of man when he is satisfying his lower-level or animal needs, are virtually identical.

The visceral brain consists of the hindbrain, the midbrain, and that part of the forebrain known as the limbic region. In terms of function, the visceral brain consists of the decisive mind, the pain areas, and the pleasure areas. In order to understand addiction, let us take a look at how the pain areas and the pleasure areas are related to the decisive mind. The relationships between the three minds of the visceral brain, and the relationship of the visceral brain to the new brain during the normal state of consciousness (NSOC) are shown in Exhibit 5-1.

H. J. Campbell argues that all vertebrate behavior is directed toward avoiding pain and seeking pleasure.[2] Behavior must be changed from time to time because the animal becomes satiated from any given sensory input. Obviously, the behavior pattern for pain is different from that for pleasure. The fight-or-flight response, for example, tends to move the animal away from pain rapidly because the old brain interprets pain as a threat to survival. Pleasure behavior tends to be more prolonged, but here also, in time, the satiation principle begins to operate and the animal turns to other desired stimuli.

Given the present state of our knowledge about the differences between man and the other animals, we can argue that man both knows, and knows that he knows. What we tend to say about other animals is that they know, but we, as human beings, do not yet know whether they know that they know. In the primates, for example, the pain and the pleasure areas appear to be activated by nerve impulses that orginate in the left new brain and the right new brain as well as those that are mediated by the pain areas and the pleasure areas. As our knowledge about animal behavior has advanced in recent years, however, it has become evident that other "animals" are far more intelligent than we had previously assumed.

The human animal worries about the past, for example, and this causes sorrow; he anticipates the future and this results in joy. It is as if the pain areas of the visceral brain were linked to the "sorrow" areas of the left new brain—the criticizing brain—and the pleasure areas were wired into the "joy" areas of the right new brain—the euphoric brain. As I shall try to demonstrate later, this appears to be

Exhibit 5-1: **The Minds of Man, Normal State of Consciousness (NSOC)**

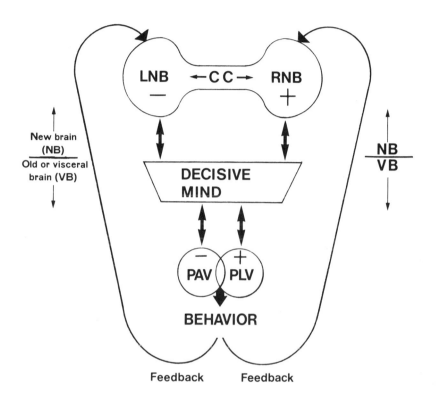

Schematic diagram showing the relationships between the decisive mind and the new and old brains. Shown are the two minds in the new brain, the left new brain (LNB) and the right new brain (RNB), as well as the pain areas (PAV) and the pleasure areas (PLV) of the visceral brain (VB). The corpus callosum (CC) is a bundle of nerve fibers that connects the LNB and the RNB.

the case. I believe we can understand the process of addiction much better when we understand that the right new brain and the pleasure areas together comprise a "euphoria" subsystem. When satiation occurs, the decisive mind tries to move the minds of man to homeostasis or equiphoria. Because of chemical changes, overshoot occurs. Overshoot causes dysphoria-pain in the pain areas and sorrow in the left new brain.

Censorship between Old and New Brain

The dictionary defines censorship as the agency in the mind that represses unacceptable notions before they reach consciousness. One of the unique aspects of the development of human reason is the evolution of such a process. In order to understand behavior, let us think of the censoring process as operating or being inserted between incoming stimuli and those parts of the brain that used to cause automatic responses in our reptilian ancestors at an earlier stage in evolution. As these reptilian ancestors moved into the trees, mechanisms had to be developed to suppress incoming messages to the brain that would have called for the automatic behavior that promoted survival in an earlier stage of evolution. Those individuals who continued behaviors that were optimal for reptilian behavior but disadvantageous to life in the trees died early. Those who survived did so because the genetic makeup that selected for censorship was vastly extended to cover all of the senses including movement, and ultimately certain hormonal and instinctual stimuli.[3]

As evolution continued, some of our reptilian ancestors began to change into the tree-living, primate ancestors of the species that we now call man. The primitive, fight-or-flight response of such a mammal might be to run away and hide when it perceived a large bird circling high above the forest. In time, censorship operated to hold this behavior in abeyance until it became perfectly clear that the visitor in the sky was indeed a predator—a bird that enjoyed making meals out of tree-living primates. In time, most birds were ignored, and any specific threatening bird was "tracked" until the fact of predatorship became evident. At this point, the alert stage of the fight-or-flight response was elicited. Blood pressure rose, the heart began to beat faster, and the muscles tensed along with a number of other changes, as the creature hastened for cover.

At the moment that the predator bird began its swooping attack, censorship moved our hominid ancestor from the alert stage to the activate state. Perhaps all that happened initially was a pause between the alert (epinephrine) state and the activate (norepinephrine) state. The fight-or-flight reponse then took over and continued until the censorship processes of the decisive mind terminated the behavior.

The Decisive Mind

We can begin our study of the decisive mind by assuming that the left new brain and the right new brain should be viewed as staff assistants to the decisive mind located in the brain stem of the visceral brain. These two brains are really nothing more than computers and tape decks that represent "the elaboration of the function of censorship (that) led to all the complicated processes of conscious perception, memory, association, learning and reasoning."[4]

A. T. W. Simeons argues that many human behaviors are under the control of the decisive mind located in the diencephalon. Building on the Simeons model, I have developed the concept of a visceral brain that is both superior in function and central in location to the dual hemispheres of the cortical brain. As I have suggested earlier, the visceral brain controls the functions of man as an animal—fight-or-flight, freeze, feel, feed, and flirt. What is even more important, the most recent neurophysiological evidence supports the Simeons hypothesis—that *the seat of decision in the human being is located in the visceral brain.*

Shortly before he died, Wilder Penfield, one of the great neurosurgeons of the mid-twentieth century, published a book that greatly strengthens the Simeons thesis.[5] As previously discussed, Wilder Penfield went beyond Simeons and anatomically located the *seat of consciousness* in that part of the visceral brain that I term the decisive mind. According to Penfield, the left new brain and the right new brain do not control the decisive mind, but vice versa!

If one accepts the Simeons-Penfield hypothesis, then the seat of consciousness of the human being is in the decisive mind rather than in the cerebral hemispheres. If this is the case, then both the left new brain and the right new brain should be viewed as two giant computer tape decks that evolved to control the censorship mechanism of our early ancestors. Exhibit 5-1 shows how the decisive mind relates to the pain and the pleasure areas and to the left new brain and right new brain.

What About the New Brain?

A lot of people, even at the present time, refuse to accept the evidence that there are two brains and two minds in the cerebral cortex. A number of times, when delivering papers at professional meetings, I have been told point-blank that the concept of a "split-brain" is utter nonsense—that any deficit in the functioning of the left new brain can be made up in the right new brain or vice versa. This, by people with doctorates in the behavioral sciences!

Despite the fact that the bilateral asymmetry of the new brain was discovered more than a hundred years ago, many people cannot accept the fact that each of the cerebral hemispheres is a brain in itself—not a part of a whole but a subsystem within a larger system. Even fewer people are aware of the fact that each hemisphere has a mind of its own—that "schizophrenia" in both structure and functioning is the very essence of humanity.

The two hemispheres of the new brain are joined by an enormous bundle of connecting fibers called the corpus callosum (CC). Messages flash back and forth through these fibers from one hemisphere to the other. Obviously, it makes no sense to have a right new brain and an left new brain in the new brain if the decisive mind cannot utilize them as staff assistants in an integrative fashion to work for the ultimate benefit of the organism as a whole.

The existence of a split brain, of an A QUIVER, left new brain and a SCANS, right new brain, linked by the corpus callosum, became established through the brilliant research work of Roger Sperry and his colleagues at the California Institute of Technology almost twenty years ago.[6]

Sperry and his colleagues discovered the existence of the left new brain and the right new brain as a result of experimental work they were doing with patients who had had their corpus callosums severed. Why severed? Some patients suffer from a severe form of epilepsy that originates in one hemisphere and then migrates to the other through the corpus callosum. When the corpus callosum is severed in the operation, the seizure is confined to the originative hemisphere alone, with the result that the attack does far less damage than it did when it affected both hemispheres.

Split-brain patients have no more difficulty coping with the problems of everyday life than do so-called normal people. In experimental situations, however, these patients appear to behave as two completely different persons. For example, if a pencil is shown to a split-brain person in an experimental situation so that the image registers only in the right new brain, the person will answer "nothing" or "I don't know what you're talking about" to the questions "What do you see?" The important point here is that the image of the pencil was processed by the right new brain which is not specialized for speech. In a split-brain patient, because the corpus callosum has been transected, the right new brain cannot "talk" with the left new brain and so no words come forth. If the same pencil is placed on a tray with a number of other items, and the patient is asked to grasp with his left hand what he has just seen, he will pick up the pencil. However, he will be unable to explain why he chose the pencil instead of some other object on the tray.

The split-brain patient tends to behave in a confused manner and the experiment continues. The reasons for this confusion have continued to elude investigators. One reason for the confusion becomes evident if we compare Exhibits 5-1 and 5-2. As indicated in Exhibit 5-2, the corpus callosum serves as the feedback channel between the hemispheres of a normal person during the normal state of consciousness. By contrast, as shown in Exhibit 5-2, the decisive mind serves as the feedback channel in the split-brain patient. This poses few problems in the normal state of consciousness. However, the load on the decisive mind of the split-brain subject becomes unbearable during the experimental situation because it cannot integrate an incomplete stream of sensory data.

In a normal state of consciousness, the functioning of the two hemispheres of the new brain is integrated by the decisive mind. How does this take place? Exhibit 5-2 shows how the minds of the split-brain patient are coordinated in the normal state of consciousness. The feedback loop connecting the pain areas and the pleasure areas with the left new brain and the right new brain is incomplete because the corpus callosum has been severed and information no longer can be processed back and forth by the hemisphere at the new brain level. However, this is not evident in the normal state of consciousness because the decisive mind continues to serve as a substitute for the corpus callosum. In the split-brain person, it is evident that feedback orginating in the separate hemispheres and that coming from the pain areas and pleasure areas is integrated at

Exhibit 5-2: **Impaired Feedback Model, Split-Brain Patient**

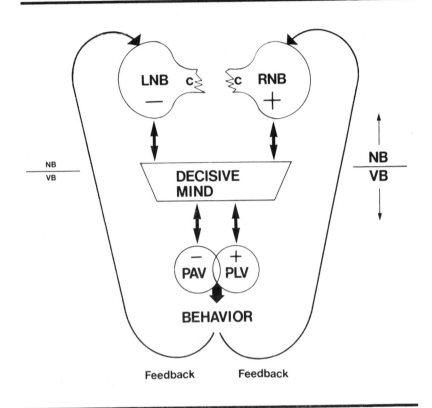

the decisive mind level, rather than at the new brain level.

In the experimental situation the behavior of the split-brain patient is quite different from the normal state of consciousness. If we refer again to Exhibit 5-2, we can replicate the experiment discussed earlier by doing the following: First, we cover the left new brain in Exhibit 5-2 with a piece of paper. Now, we track what takes place when the image of the pencil is projected to the right hemisphere only. In this case the right new brain sees the pencil but it processes the visual information only and cannot identify it by its correct name. Some students say that the right new brain is mute— that it has no language-processing capability. This is correct only in the split-brain situation. In the normal state of consciousness situation, when the corpus callosum is intact, the right new brain processes a rudimentary language processing competence—enough to communicate with the left new brain, which is all that is necessary. After all, the brain, like the well-structured organization, works best when all of its parts divide the labor. However, again like a well-managed organization, the brain, through its built-in redundancy, can make up for its "absent" member.

Euphoria and Addiction

As I indicated earlier, many people seek to activate the pleasure areas experimentally by resort to sensual drugs. The subject, in this situation, seeks to move from the equiphoria of the normal state of consciousness to a euphoric state of consciousness, using drugs or alcohol as the medium toward this end. I have diagrammed the feedback circuits of chemically induced, trophotropic reponse in Exhibit 5-3. Exhibit 5-3 is a simplified version of Exhibit 5-1. It shows pleasure and joy as pluses and pain and sorrow as minuses. In the normal state of consciousness, the two pluses and the two minuses cancel, so that we feel neither high nor low but just normal or equiphoric.

Exhibits 5-4 and 5-5 can be viewed together as a representation of the search of the subject for a euphoric or nutritive state of consciousness. Trophotropic stands for "acting nutritionally." Thus, sleep, as an altered state of consciousness, acts nutritively by "knitting the raveled sleeves of care." The only difference between Exhibits 5-4 and 5-5 is that Exhibit 5-4 shows the feedback circuits in the minds of man in more detail than does Exhibit 5-5. Exhibit 5-4 may be converted into Exhibit 5-5 simply by covering the left side with a piece of paper.

Exhibits 5-6 and 5-7, viewed together, present addictive or ergotropic phenomena. "Ergo-" stands for work, and there is little question that every addict has to "work" hard to maintain his habit even though he may long ago have passed the stage where he receives any pleasure from it. As Exhibit 5-7 illustrates, the addict by now probably is "sick and tired" at the new brain level of being "sick and tired" at the level of the old brain.

(*Text continued on page 90.*)

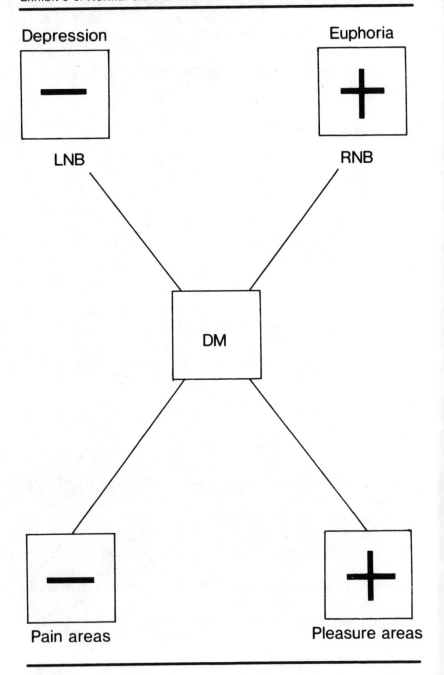

Exhibit 5-3: **Normal State of Consciousness**

Depression

LNB

Euphoria

RNB

DM

Pain areas

Pleasure areas

Exhibit 5-4: **The Minds of Man, Trophotropic Reactions**

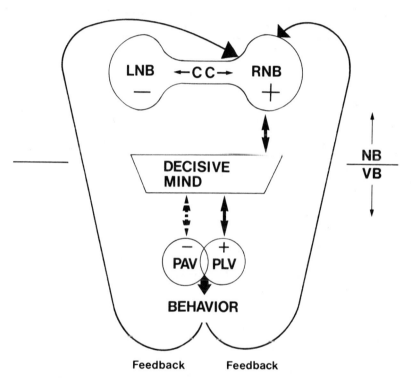

Simplified schematic of those areas of the minds of man which are dominant
in euphoria, experimental drug use, positive addiction, and manic behavior.

Exhibit 5-5: **Altered State of Consciousness**

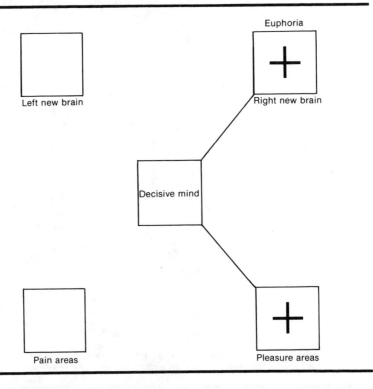

Euphoria

Left new brain

Right new brain

Decisive mind

Pain areas

Pleasure areas

Exhibit 5-6: **The Minds of Man, Ergotropic Phenomena**

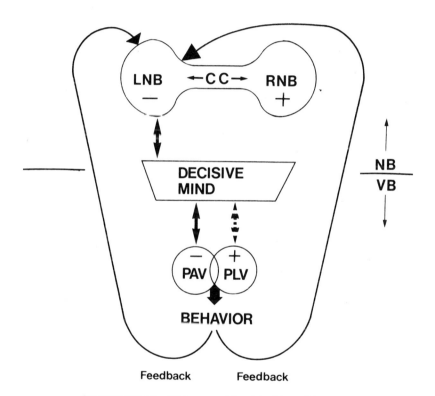

Simplified schematic of those areas of the minds of man which are dominant in addictive, depressive, and ACORN behavior.

Exhibit 5-7: **Addictive Stage of Consciousness**

Depression

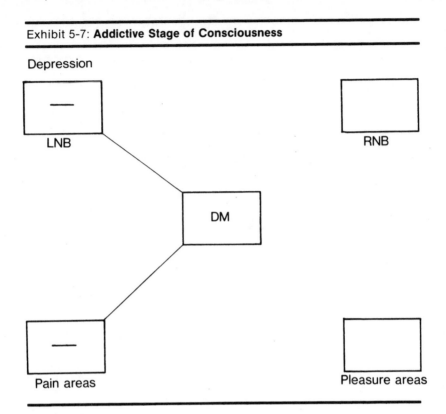

Conclusion

For a number of years, I have been attempting to show that the addition of a visceral brain, both as an entity and as a concept, provides much better answers to problems of social, organizational, group, and individual behavior than does the more prevalent concept that the left new brain and the right new brain are the seat of both decision making and consciousness. In this chapter, I have tried to demonstrate that a number of models can be made by combining the constructs of the new brain and the old brain, which show how the minds of man function in the various states of consciousness that have been discussed in the literature. These models also explain the functioning of the various components of subsystems of the brain in the various states of consciousness.

NOTE:

In this article reference is made to the right new brain's possession of a rudimentary language processing competence. This is consistent with the findings of split-brain patients (mostly male) at that time. As indicated in Exhibit 4-2, chapter 4, more recent research points out that females and bilinguals seem to be more bilateral than are monolingual males.

ENDNOTES

1. Hardin B. Jones and Helen C. Jones, *Sensual Drugs: Deprivation and Rehabilitation of the Mind* (New York: Cambridge University Press, 1977), 2.

2. H. J. Campbell, *The Pleasure Areas: A New Theory of Behavior* (New York: Delacorte, 1973), 63-87.

3. A. T. W. Simeons, *Man's Presumptuous Brain* (New York· E.P. Dutton, 1961). I recommend that the reader's odyssey through the minds of man begin with this volume—it is breathtaking in its prescience.

4. Ibid., 34.

5. Wilder Penfield, *The Mystery of the Mind: A Critical Study of Consciousness and the Human Brain* (Princeton, N J · Princeton University Press, 1975).

6. R. W. Sperry, "The Great Cerebral Commissure," *Scientific American*, January 1964, 42-52.

6

Addictions—Negative and Positive

Waino W. Suojanen

Over fifteen years ago I developed the integrative model that since then has become the basis for much of my writing in the fields of organizational behavior and management theory.[1] About nine years ago I was lecturing on management, using the integrative model, when a student pointed out to me that exactly the same model was being used by another author to describe the process of experimentation, addiction, and recovery in the field of alcoholism.[2] With just a few changes in wording, the models used by Vernon Johnson to analyze alcoholism as an addiction and the one developed by myself to describe the processes of management can be modified to describe any habit or syndrome that initially may provide people with pleasure but that ultimately becomes an addiction and makes their lives unmanageable.

Exhibits 6-1 through 6-4 represent my condensation of the various stages of alcoholism that Johnson describes in his book *I'll Quit Tomorrow*. These four figures, in conjunction with models explained in chapter 5, "Addiction and the Minds of Man," can be used to explain how a habit or problem syndrome can become an addiction. In many such cases the person concerned wishes to change behavior, despite the feeling that his or her behavior has not yet reached the stage where life has become unmanageable.

People with addictive leanings live both in the affluent suburbs as well as in the poverty-stricken ghettoes. Addictively inclined people, as indicated in Exhibit 6-1, tend to have varying hover points in their normal state of consciousness. The hover point is the

Exhibit 6-1: **Varying Hover Points**

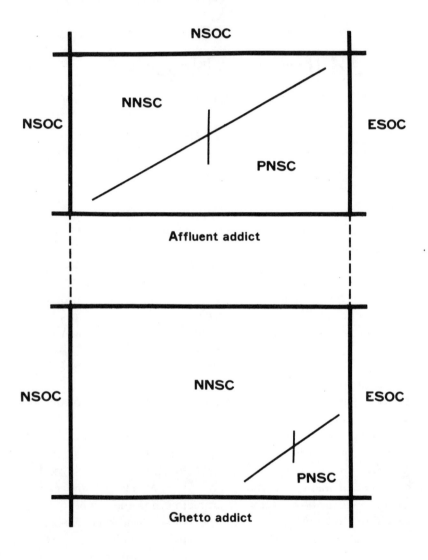

Note:
NSOC = Normal State of Consciousness
NNSC = Negative Normal State of Consciousness
PNSC = Positive Normal State of Consciousness
ESOC = Euphoric State of Consciousness

balance point or the point around which the processes of homeostasis adjust during the normal state of consciousness. The top panel of Exhibit 6-1 shows the hover point for an affluent subject. Where the positive normal state of consciousness is greater than or equal to the negative normal state of consciousness, as it is with those who are in higher income brackets, the need for a euphoric state of consciousness appears to be less compelling than for those whose negative normal state of consciousness is much greater than the positive normal state of consciousness. The latter situation is illustrated in the bottom panel of Exhibit 6-1. Where life is nasty, brutish, short, and demeaning, highs are more avidly sought and more vividly experienced.

Exhibit 6-2 indicates that most addicts start from a normal state of consciousness and experience the "highs" of the altered state of consciousness during the early or experimental stages. As I suggested in the preceding paragraph, the normal state of consciousness has both positive and negative elements. The negative normal state of consciousness and the positive normal state of consciousness make up the normal state of consciousness. The negative normal state of consciousness and the positive normal state of consciousness cancel each other at the hover point. This point is indicated by a slash in Exhibits 6-1, 6-2, 6-3, and 6-4.

Exhibit 6-2 provides a narrative of the various stages that the person undergoes as he experiments with alcohol or other mind-altering, sensuous drugs. Other trophotropic phenomena, such as positive addiction and manic behaviors, tend to follow a similar pattern. During the experimental stages of drug use, the "researcher" frequently achieves euphoria—the "high" of the altered state of consciousness, which is the goal of every person who has ever searched for "better things for better living though biochemistry."

Exhibit 6-3 illustrates the various unpleasant stages or steps that occur in the process of either alcoholism or drug addiction. There is no need to confine this model to substance abuse alone: it can also be used to illustrate the steps through which the so-called "neurotic," (a term no longer found in the diagnostic vocabularies of the American Psychiatric Association) individual and the ACORN move as their lives become increasingly unmanageable. For those who may wonder what I mean by ACORN: it is an acronym that

Exhibit 6-2: **Experimental Stages of Drug Use**

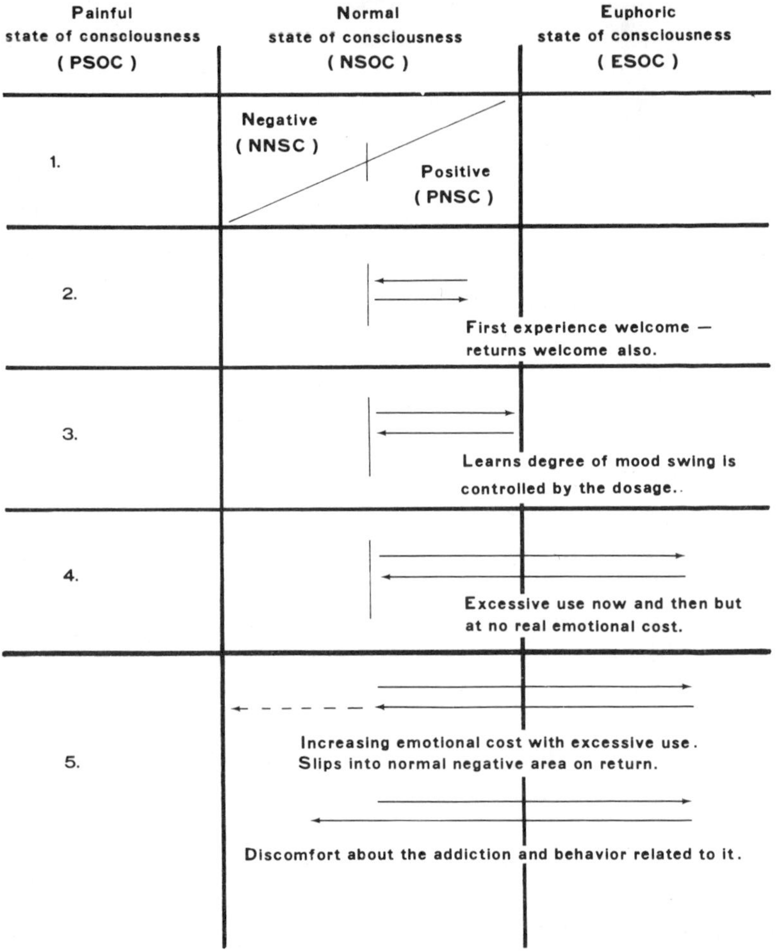

Painful state of consciousness (PSOC)	Normal state of consciousness (NSOC)	Euphoric state of consciousness (ESOC)
1.	Negative (NNSC) Positive (PNSC)	
2.		First experience welcome — returns welcome also.
3.		Learns degree of mood swing is controlled by the dosage..
4.		Excessive use now and then but at no real emotional cost.
5.		Increasing emotional cost with excessive use. Slips into normal negative area on return. Discomfort about the addiction and behavior related to it.

stands for *A*ddictive, *C*ompulsive, *O*bsessive, *R*eally *N*utty behavior. It makes no difference whether or not the ACORN behavior is induced by substance abuse or whether it is what the traditional theory labeled as neurosis or even psychosis. In all of these behavior patterns, the panels show that pain is the earmark of negative addiction. This pain may continue for months and years and goes away only when the person concerned takes the first step.

This is often called "being sick and tired" (at the new brain level) of being "sick and tired" (at the visceral brain level). In Exhibit 6-4, the panels illustrate the major steps on the road to recovery. The two basic elements to recovery are (1) individual responsibility, and (2) positive peer pressure and support.

The world is full of people who suffer. In order to end this suffering, they seek chemical relief. This relief, by the way, need not

Exhibit 6-3: **Unpleasant Stages of Drug Addiction**

Painful state of consciousness (PSOC)	Normal state of consciousness (NSOC)	Euphoric state of consciousness (ESOC)

Negative (NNSC)

Positive (PNSC)

6.   Progressive **NNSC** causes waning feelings of self worth and chronic loss of ego strength.

7.   Progressive deterioration of self—image. Chronic phases of self—destructive and finally suicidal tendencies.

8.   Free floating mass of negative feelings about self. Rational defenses lock in causing mental mismanagement.

9.   Starts off at PSOC and comes off to a worse PSOC   No longer able to start here and arrive at ESOC.

10.   Projection causes guilt , re: school, family, society, anxiety, guilt, shame, remorse, self—hatred, desperation, hopelessness, etc.

be in the form of sensual drugs alone but includes alcohol, over-the-counter drugs, and prescription drugs as the chemical substance of choice. As I plan to demonstrate later, one can also seek and obtain relief through positive addiction. Positive addiction has the advantage that it does not cause the harmful after-effects of chemical substances. Additionally, positive addiction has a number of other benefits in terms of improving the quality of one's life in many different dimensions.

Exhibit 6-4: **Recovery from Addiction**

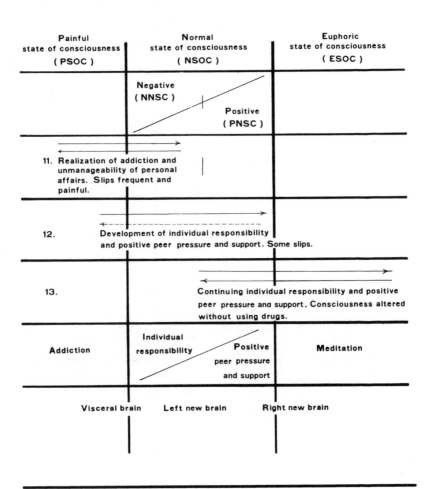

People who suffer have never learned how to live one day at a time. Instead, they continue their nutty behavior, unaware that just as chemistry determines behavior in the case of negative addiction, so can behavior determine chemistry in the case of positive addiction.

Positive Addiction

In the book, *Positive Addiction,* which was published in 1976, William Glasser develops a theory of increased inner strength through a procedure he calls "positive addiction" (PA).[3] Simply stated, a positive addiction is an activity undertaken for forty minutes to an hour daily that requires little or no conscious mental effort. The person undertaking the activity should feel it is beneficial to him physically, mentally, or spiritually. The activity is usually done alone, is noncompetitive, and is noncritical. To reach the state of positive addiction, one must continue the activity for six months to a year. During the positive addiction state, the person will experience periods of inability to recall events that take place around him. A fairly long period of abstinence from scheduled, positively-addicted activity will cause the person to suffer all the symptoms of withdrawal from chemical substances. Although Glasser discusses two major areas of positive addiction, meditation (mental) and running (physical), he indicates that as long as certain criteria are met, almost any activity can become positively addictive.

The following six steps describe positive addiction:

1. It is something noncompetitive that one chooses to do and to which one can devote an hour (approximately).

2. It is possible for one to do it easily and it doesn't take a great deal of mental effort to do it well.

3. One can do it alone or (rarely) with others, but it does not depend upon others to do it.

4. One believes that it has some value (physical, mental, and/or spiritual) for the addict.

5. The practitioner believes that persistence results in improvement, but this is completely subjective—the practitioner is the only one who measures that improvement.

6. The activity must be one that a person can do without

criticizing himself. If one can't accept oneself during time of involvement, the activity will not become addictive.

In developing the positive addiction model outlined in Exhibit 6-5, it was necessary to alter slightly the negative addiction models (Exhibits 6-2, 6-3, and 6-4). In negative addiction, the addictive activity causes both the move from the normal state of consciousness to the euphoric state of consciousness, and later to the painful state of consciousness. In positive addiction the practice of the activity moves the person concerned from the normal state of consciousness to the euphoric state of consciousness, whereas nonpractice of the activity moves the individual from the normal state of consciousness to the painful state of consciousness, and results in withdrawal symptoms. The straight-line indicator (the dotted line to the right of the hover point in Exhibit 6-5) suggests that positive addiction is very similar in effect to chemical or negative addiction.

In the management of behavior change, positive addiction has proven to be very useful. William Glasser reports that most positively addicted persons cut down on such negatively addictive behaviors as the consumption of alcohol and nicotine. He also reports a significant lessening of stress. Herbert Benson reports that another form of positive addiction, the relaxation response, has effects similar to those cited by Glasser. Benson presents evidence to indicate that the practice of the relaxation response, which I view as another form of positive addiction, results in dramatic reduction in drug use and in many instances recovery from drug addiction. The same applies to smoking as well as to alcohol abuse and alcoholism.[4]

At the root of most forms of negative addiction is the attempt to cope with stress—the negative normal state of consciousness elements in our daily life—by chemical resort to relaxation. The ultimate result is negative addiction with all of its gruesome physical, mental, and spiritual consequences to the addict and his family. Hans Selye, one of the world's leading authorities on stress, suggests that "diversion from one activity to another is more relaxing than complete rest" but that "few things are as frustrating as complete inactivity, the absence of any stimulus, any challenge, to which you could react."[5] We should listen to Selye and pay attention

Exhibit 6-5: **Positive Addiction Model**

Painful state of consciousness (PSOC)	Normal state of consciousness (NSOC)	Euphoric state of consciousness (ESOC)
	Negative (NNSC) / Positive (PNSC)	
	|←----→|	Begin activity that can become PA.
	|←-------→|	Brief lapses into PA state but not enough to become addicted.
Non-activity causes some discomfort, mostly guilt.	|←--------→|	Occasional lapses for longer periods more frequently.
Non-activity causes discomfort, guilt caused by missing possible state.	|←--------→|	Longer periods of PA state.
Non-activity causes discomfort caused by missed PA state.	|←--------→|	Periods of PA generally during most activity.
Non-activity of alternative PA causes discomfort.	|←--------→|	Alternative PA causes lessened PA experiences.

- - - - - - - non-activity
————— activity

to his caveat—any single form of positive addiction holds the potential of becoming a stressor in itself with all of the bad consequences that flow from that. Each of us should be aware that a sound personal program of living and loving offers far more hope than any single positive addiction technique. In essence, what we all need is both a program and a kit of tools—not just one or two selected instruments or techniques.[6]

Positive Addiction and Neurotransmitter Biochemistry

The concept of positive addiction presents us with a uniquely different way of viewing such problems as substance abuse and addiction along with such ACORN-type, subjectively-induced, addictive syndromes as the Type A Behavior Pattern and the Executive Stress Syndrome. Research data indicate that a lowered level of the catecholamine metabolites in the urine is accompanied by depression and that an increased level of these chemicals in the urine is an indicator of hyperactivity or mania. The "catecholamine hypothesis of affective disorders postulates that endogenous depression is due to a functional deficiency of brain catecholamines, and that mania is due to a contrasting overactivity."[7] Mania is often marked by euphoria, excitement, and enthusiasm, very much like the aftermath of a positive addiction experience.

Although no correlation has been established between catecholamine levels and positive addiction, we can hypothesize that positive addiction experiences result in heightened norepinephrine and epinephrine levels. If this can be biochemically verified, it would appear that the possibilities of improved mental health through positive addiction are virtually boundless.

Glasser states that a positive addiction increases mental strength. If we assume that a human being has three brains, the visceral (old brain controlling the animal value system), the left new brain (cognitive thought processes), and the right new brain (spiritual thought processes), then additional theories of positive addiction can be formulated.[8] Norepinephrine is the neurotransmitter in the median forebrain bundle that connects the visceral, the left new brain, and the right new brain. Additional amounts of norepinephrine may result in increased linkage among neurons and thus result in increased mental capacity. Here again a possible link between positive addiction and brain level norepinephrine exists.[9]

Findings in Sweden suggest that the levels of catecholamine metabolites present in human urine can be used to determine the stress to which human beings have been exposed.[10] Just as researchers have begun to understand the roles played by the catecholamines in human behavior, other researchers have discovered another family of neurotransmitters that are of interest to students of addictive behavior. These neurotransmitters are the endorphins.

Endorphins and Altered States of Consciousness

To some, the relationship between the catecholamines and altered states of consciousness may come as somewhat of a surprise. However, research on neurophysiopharmacology is moving ahead on many fronts these days.

What are the endorphins? First, they are called endorphins because they are *end*ogenous mor*phine*-like substances. They occur naturally in the brain or the pituitary gland and they mimic the effects of opiates such as morphine and heroin. Or perhaps it would be more accurate to say that opiates mimic endorphins. Neuro scientists think that the endorphins may be a new class of neurotransmitters, such as the catecholamines which were discovered much earlier.[11] The endorphins are of significance in the study of both negative and positive addiction because their characteristic effect in humans "is less a specific blunting of pain sensation than the production of a peculiar state of indifference, an emotional detachment from the experience of suffering."[12]

At the time this was being written, an article appeared in the *New York Times Magazine* discussing the endorphins at length.[13] As Cherry puts it: "Some investigators suggest in private that natural painkillers such as anodynin or enkephalin may be at the heart of the mystery of painless people."[14] It is no far leap to go one step beyond this to suggest that the endorphins may provide a clue that in time may help to explain why some people become hooked to a substance in a very short period of time whereas others continue to use the same substance for years without developing either psychological or physiological addiction.

A story in *Science News* titled "An LSD Competitor" discusses the discovery of a neurotransmitter called DMT (dimethyltryptamine).[15] According to the discoverers, who are at the University of Alabama Medical Center, DMT appears to bind to the same site to which the hallucinogen LSD binds. This observation suggests that LSD may exert its action by displacing DMT from its binding site. Even more provocative, they have discovered that DMT levels in the brain increase considerably when a person or experimental animal is placed in a situation of extreme stress. Since studies in other labs have linked schizophrenic episodes with stress in some cases, there might be a link between DMT levels and schizophrenic episodes.[16]

More specifically, how can the endorphins help to explain the positive addiction behavior pattern? The January 22, 1977 issue of *Science News* had an interesting letter by Joseph Barranco (p. 51) that provides a clue. Barranco pointed out that acupuncture releases endorphin, a pain suppressant, when nerve cells deep inside a muscle are stimulated. A similar response mechanism may well underlie the neurophysiology of positive addiction. Let us quote Barranco directly since he discusses this issue so well:

> Consider several well-known observations from an activity which might exhibit such effects in their purest and most intense form—training and competition in endurance athletic events. Bicycle racers and distance runners need a warm-up before they feel right. They *know* that the "second wind" exists. They can fall during a race and not even notice they have just broken bones or lost skin. They tell you they are addicted to their sport. And they become almost euphoric merely talking about 'putting in the miles' during training.
>
> It would not be unexpected if large amounts of endorphin were released during such efforts. Such a mechanism would have much wider benefits to a species than providing some members with a natural high. Surely there is great survival value in automatic reinforcement for practicing some strenuous and possibly exhausting and painful activities, such as chasing or fleeing or even standing around chewing your food. All this, of course, in addition to the switching off of unneeded and disabling pain from traumatic wounds. A simple assay for endorphins would tell us how severe or prolonged this natural stimulation need be, and how close it is to opiate addictions.

The drug naloxone has no discernible effects of its own but is extremely effective in blocking the effects of such opiate narcotics as heroin and morphine. For this reason, naloxone is used in the detoxification of patients who are suffering from an opiate overdose. Its effects, in these situations, are nothing less than dramatic.

For some time, the Chinese method of relieving pain, called acupuncture, has been under study in Canada and the United States. Interestingly, and in complete agreement with my theories about the minds of man, studies have shown that the effects of acupuncture are abolished by naloxone.[17] One states the results of Dr. Bruce Pomeranz's research on acupuncture as follows: "Remarkably, the effects of acupuncture in Pomerantz's experiments were abolished by naloxone. This suggests strongly that the hormone released by acupuncture acts upon opiate receptors, i.e., that acupuncture triggers the release of endorphins, which in turn block the pain stimuli just as morphine would."[18]

At the present time, our knowledge about the endorphins remains sketchy. The fact that they exist and that there are a number of them suggests that they play important roles in neural functioning. One role they may play is to make the process of dying a pleasant rather than a painful experience and thereby to suggest "life after life" as one of the rites of passage. In addition, I have examined a number of other possible uses in this chapter.

In any event, the ability of the brain to produce endorphins provides a simple neurophysiological explanation of why addicts become addicted to the chemical of their choice. I feel it is time that we drop the pointless Freudian search for the reasons why people drink or why they use drugs. People use chemicals to achieve euphoria. Later the brain and the body rebel—or as reformed drunks like to put it: "Alcohol gave me wings to fly—then it took away the sky."

I also feel it is time that we quit viewing addiction as a moral problem. The addict is powerless to exert willpower or self-control against neurophysiological mechanisms that "blow his mind." Clearly, exhortations to someone who is addicted to a substance—or to an activity such as compulsive gambling or obsessive overeating—won't take us very far. Much more important in this area is a better understanding of how the minds of man function and how they interface with his soma.

Neuroendocrinology

The sciences of neurophysiology and psychobiology are so new in origin that their findings still remain virtually unknown in the social, and even in the behavioral, sciences. Neuroendocrinology emerged as an offshoot of endocrinology in the 1960s. Prior to that time, endocrine functioning was viewed as a closed system—one in which chemistry determined behavior. Because it was a closed system, the hormones, circulating through the bloodstream, served as transducers to link the various endocrine glands. Hormones are powerful chemical messengers produced by glands in the endocrine system that act upon receptor cells located in the tissues of the various organs of the body. According to this older and now discarded theory, any involvement of the endocrine system with the nervous system was minimal.[19]

During the past fifteen years or so the older theory, which assumed hormone-to-hormone transduction in the endocrine system, has yielded to the newer theory, which states that the hypothalamus converts nervous system signals to endocrine system signals. To put it differently, the older theory argued that hormonal characteristics serve as a causal factor in influencing behavior. The newer theory looks upon the relationship between hormones and behavior as interactive and, in reliance on this assumption, neuroendocrinologists today study the influence of social and psychological factors on hormonal secretion just as they trace the influence of hormones on behavior.

In the past, the relationship was one in which:

Chemistry determines *Behavior*

The current approach to neuroendocrinology reserves the above relationship:

Behavior determines *Chemistry*

If both of the above are correct, then it is possible to write the relationship of the two combined as:

Behavior determines *Behavior*, or conversely as:

Chemistry determines *Chemistry*

Summary

Every day as I read the newspapers or watch television, I run into people who are very much concerned with proving that life after life exists or that mind is more powerful than matter. The world appears to be full of people who desperately want to believe that permanent altered states of consciousness exist and that if these states are discovered, they will serve as esoteric substitutes for the grubbiness of the straight world, which is governed, almost in its entirety, by the laws and rules of the normal state of consciousness.

My hypothesis is a much simpler one. All it requires is a recognition that there are at least three brains and as many as five minds inside the human skull. For about five centuries, men could not study the functioning of the brains and the minds of man because of a pact that existed between organized religion on the one hand and organized medicine on the other.[20] The church had given organized medicine the right to dissect the human body in exchange for recognition of the church's preeminence in matters affecting the soul. Now, that pact no longer is in effect.

NOTE

On page 102 of this chapter Dr. Suojanen states that, "Although no correlation has been established between catecholamine levels and positive addiction, we can hypothesize that positive addiction experiences result in heightened norepinephrine and epinephrine levels." Since this material was originally wirtten and presented at the third annual Southeast Drug Education Conference in 1977, numerous studies on long distance runners and other endurance athletes has indeed shown an increased level of catecholamines and endorphins in the body after physical participation in strenuous activities.

ENDNOTES

1. Waino W. Suojanen, *The Dynamics of Management* (New York: Holt, Rinehart and Winston, 1966), 104.

2. Vernon E. Johnson, *I'll Quit Tomorrow* (New York: Harper & Row, 1973), 7-31.

3. William Glasser, *Positive Addiction* (New York: Harper & Row, 1976).

4. Herbert Benson and Miriam Z. Klipper, *The Relaxation Response* (New York: Avon Books, 1976), 149-157.

5. Hans Selye, *Stress Without Distress* (New York: Signet, 1974), 137.

6. Chapter 8, "Coping with Stress and Addictive Behavior," covers two of these techniques in detail.

7. Robert A. Levitt, *Psychopharmacology: A Biological Approach* (New York: John Wiley, 1975), 83.

8. See chapter 5, "Addiction and the Minds of Man," for a discussion of the triune brain.

9. Carolyn Adams Kicey, "Catecholamines and Depression: A Physiological Theory of Depression," *American Journal of Nursing* (November 1974): 2018-2020.

10. Ulf Lundberg, "Urban Commuting Crowdedness and Catecholamine Excretion," *Journal of Human Stress* (September 1976): 26-32; Marianne Frankenhaeuser and Bertil Gardell, "Underload and Overload in Working Life: Outline of a Multidisciplinary Approach," ibid., 35-46.

11. For a discussion of the endorphins that is easy to understand, the reader is referred to Jean L. Marx, "Neurobiology: Researchers High on Endogenous Opiates," *Science* (24 September 1976): 1227-1229.

12. Avram Goldstein, "Opioid Peptides (Endorphins) in Pituitary and Brain," *Science* (17 September 1976): 1081.

13. Laurence Cherry, "Solving the Mysteries of Pain," 30 January 1977, 12.

14. Ibid., 52.

15. 5 February 1977, 88.

16. Ibid.

17. Avram Goldstein, HIH "HIGH on Research," *U.S. Journal of Drug and Alcohol Dependence* (April 1977): 8. In this article, Dr. Goldstein reviews the acupuncture research of Dr. Bruce Pomerantz of the University of Toronto.

18. Ibid.

19. For an interesting discussion of the application of neuroendocrinology to behavioral science, see Alice S. Rossi, "A Biosocial Perspective on Parenting," *Daedalus* (Spring 1977): 1-31.

20. George L. Engel, "The Need for a New Medical Model: A Challenge for Biomedicine," *Science* (8 April 1977): 131.

7

Management, Addiction, and Coming to Be

Waino W. Suojanen

My approach to management is situationist in its orientation. This approach originated with Mary Parker Follet long before World War II. A simple model of her definition of leadership is that it must be governed by the logic of the situation. According to her, a leader:

1. Understands the situation.
2. Understands the requirements of the situation.
3. Acts or decides according to the logic of the situation.

If a person is to function as a leader, he or she must provide insight, inspiration, and incentive for those people who suffer. The true leader helps the addict to realize that his life has become unmanageable and that he must do something about his problem.

Insight means that the supervisor or teacher has an understanding of the process of addiction and of the physical, mental, and social behavior associated with it. Insight means compassion rather than sympathy. Compassion is empathy and understanding; sympathy is personal identification. The troubled worker or addict can use a lot of compassion, but sympathy should be avoided like the plague.

Inspiration may be viewed as the activating or essential principle influencing a person. The teacher or the supervisor is often in a position to inspire the subject because those close to him or her tend to be unaware of, sympathetic to, or covering up his problem. The person who is compassionate understands that therapy cannot begin as long as the subject, his family, and his friends are busily engaged in covering up his problem.

Incentive derives from the Latin words for stimulating and setting the tune. In later use, *incentive* means having the quality of kindling. The teacher or supervisor is in a position to provide incentives of both the negative and the positive kinds by virtue of the authority he possesses over the subject. So it's more than a mere matter of setting the tune or starting the fire. Even more important is continuing pressure and support. The subject may use addiction as an explanation for his aberrant behavior, but that never makes it an excuse. Furthermore, there is no problem that people have that goes away if the irresponsible behavior is continued. As a matter of fact, any problem gets worse if the addictive and irresponsible behavior is continued.

If insight, inspiration, and incentive are missing, the odds are very high that the addict will end up insane, incarcerated, or in infinity. Clearly, the teacher and the supervisor have a personal obligation to help the addict achieve individual responsibility. After this step, positive peer pressure and support can be substituted for the negative peer culture that was instrumental in getting the person interested in "better things for better living through biochemistry." Finally, after the addiction has been arrested, the person can begin to experiment with the different methods of altering consciousness without using drugs. In order to acquire additional understanding about compulsive behavior, let us next turn to the neurophysiology of the minds of man. It is becoming increasingly evident that addiction, like the human brain, operates on a physical, a mental, and a spiritual level.

The Visceral Brain and the Limbic Region

Recent research findings about the structure and the functioning of the human brain strongly suggest that it is a much more complex organism than we have been able to imagine even in our wildest dreams.

The visceral brain regulates the behaviors of "man as an animal." Among the most important of these behaviors are what I have previously described as the "six f's"—fight, flight, freeze, feed, feel, and flirt. Those of you who have watched the television program, "Wild, Wild World of Animals" on a regular basis may have noticed the similarities between the behavior of animals and the behavior of man when he is satisfying his lower level or animal needs.

The study of animal behavior is known as ethology. A number of books have appeared in recent years that have drawn analogies between animal behavior and human behavior. For obvious reasons, these attempts have been surrounded by an enormous amount of controversy. I do not wish to get involved in that controversy here, although I did write the first journal article to appear on the relationship between the behavior of social animals and the behavior of people in organizations. What I do wish to point out is the important role played by the visceral or "old" brain of man in the processes of initial pleasure and ultimate addictions.

The visceral brain consists of the hindbrain, the midbrain, and that part of the forebrain known as the limbic region. It may help you to remember that limbic means edge or border. Even better, when the addict is in *limbo* he is in "a region on the border of Hell" as one of my dictionaries defines it.

The limbic system is a very old part of the visceral brain and, from the viewpoint of the study of addiction, perhaps the most important region in the minds of man because it includes what H. J. Campbell calls the "pleasure areas."[1]

In "subhuman animals," the activity state of the pleasure areas is preserved by nerve impulses originating from the situation of peripheral sensory receptors. Human animals are unique in that the pleasure areas can be activated by nerve impulses that originate in the thinking parts of the brain—the "new brain."

Campbell argues that all vertebrate behavior is directed at seeking pleasure and avoiding displeasure. Behavior must be changed from time to time because the pleasure areas become satiated from the effect of any one given sensory input. Human beings, in contrast to other animals, obtain pleasure by (1) using subhuman mechanisms of sensory stimulation, (2) combining cortical stimulation with subhuman, sensory modalities, and (3) using the thinking regions either alone or in combination with prosthetic systems. Because the neural mechanisms that are concerned with the activation of the pleasure areas constitute the basic machinery for all behavior, the normal, abnormal, and addictive behaviors can all be considered as variants of neural functioning. The neural mechanisms of behavior are influenced by many factors and especially by such drugs as narcotics, hallucinogens, stimulants, and depressants.

The Left New Brain and the Right New Brain

To review, modern neurophysiology tells us that the "new" or cortical brain of man consists of two structurally symmetrical but functionally asymmetrical hemispheres. This means that the left new brain and right new brain look alike but have quite different tasks to perform. The relationships between the left new brain and the right new brain and how they relate to the visceral brain are discussed below.

In the left new brain are located the quantitative, intellectual, verbal, and rational capacities of the typical manager. I say typical because left-handed people sometimes are different—the right new brain rather than the left new brain is dominant in them. The sense of time is located in the analytical and cognitive left new brain. As an aside, when we measure IQ, which usually measures quantitative and verbal skills, we are concerned with the left new brain, ignoring almost totally the visceral brain and the right new brain.

The right new brain is quite different in functions. It governs those actions of man that are nonverbal and nonlinear in nature. These functions include the *S*ynthesizing, the *C*reative, the *A*rtistic, the *N*ormative, and the *S*patial. I use the acronym SCANS to remember these right new-brain functions as opposed to the left new-brain functions, for which I use A QUIVER—*A*nalytical, *QU*antitative, *I*ntellectual, *VE*rbal, and *R*ational.

The normal state of consciousness is largely a product of the thinking regions of the "new brain" or what Ornstein calls the left half brain (remember I use the term *new* to distinguish between the old and new brain).[2] When we think of euphoric states of consciousness, we are in the province of the right new brain. Many of us, as a result, tend to view such Eastern religions as Sufi, Yoga, and Zen as relevant only to out-of-date mysticism. Others of us recognize that we know next to nothing as yet about the ultimate potential of the right new brain to experience altered states of consciousness. We do, however, know enough about the right new brain to argue that there are a number of ways for man to experience "pleasures" of the kind that are fundamental to vertebrates and are probably the reasons for being of the minds of man.

Campbell mentions that people can be divided into the three categories of (1) feeling-doers, (2) thinkers-doers, and (3) those who obtain their pleasure from the employment of higher mental processes.[3] I prefer to use the three categories of (1) feel-do, (2) think-do, and (3) think-create, which correspond to the functions of the visceral brain, left new brain, and right new brain, respectively.

The "pleasure areas" of the visceral include the amygdala, the septum, and the hypothalamus. The latter, in turn, controls the pituitary, which is often called the master gland. In the case of addicts, the pleasure areas operate at unacceptably low levels and the pleasures that are sought are those at the subhuman, feeling-doing, visceral brain levels.[4] Whether stimulant, depressant, narcotic, or hallucinogen, the addiction makes the life of the subject as a human being unmanageable. Another way of phrasing the above is to say that being hooked by an addiction is the substitution of medication for meditation.

From Compulsion to Coming to Be

Our actions can be controlled by another person, by ourselves, or by a group. The troubled worker always has a supervisor, and much of the impetus—both negative and positive—to begin to treat an addiction can originate with that person. A student is in a similar position—if the teachers understand the processes and the therapies for addiction, they can inform the student about the nature of the illness and encourage him or her to seek assistance.

When we are discussing control of our actions by others, we frequently make reference to the institution. In these situations, the addict is normally in a situation wherein his or her actions are almost totally controlled by others. For example, the penitentiary may be viewed as lying at one end of a continuum in which almost total authority over the "cons" is exercised by the "cops" and the "counselors." The school lies at the other end of the continuum—

partial control is exercised by the system for only part of the day. The custodial penitentiary seeks changes in behavior by utilizing the "club outside the head." By contrast, the enlightened school tries to modify behavior by relying on the "club inside the head."

I view the club inside the head as discipline—an internalized system of values. One of the principal objectives of the public school system is to inculcate concepts of responsible citizenship in the student. Individual responsibility is the same as mental health, just as individual responsibility is a measure of mental ill-health.

Individual responsibility is a necessary but not a sufficient condition if the addict is to move from compulsion to cure. A necessary step is the attack on the illness of addiction—and this is a problem that only the physician is qualified to solve. Once medical help has been enlisted, the person is in a position to begin therapy. From my viewpoint, the next step is based on individual responsibility.

Irresponsibility, Addiction, and Responsibility

Once a person has become an addict, he lives in a world that can neither be envisioned nor understood by one who has not been a citizen of that society himself. As Donald J. Ottenberg has pointed out, it is helpful to remember that when we deal with addiction that "it's almost as though there are three persons involved in the therapeutic relationship, whereas we are used to dealing with two, ourselves and the patient or client."[5]

Neither the manager nor the teacher can change the attitudes or the behaviors of the troubled worker or the student. Remember that addiction is the "third party" present on the scene, and unless the subject can be brought to this realization, the problem will continue to impair his performance. The principal reason Alcoholics Anonymous is successful where professional therapists fail is that their members know well about this third party—having lived with this "person" for extended periods of time. Unfortunately, many professionals lack this insight, and I say unfortunately not because I feel they should pay the high initiation fees that addicts pay, but because they have never come to understand how forcefully that third party governs the behavior of the troubled worker or the addict.

The troubled worker and the addict are irresponsible in their behavior because they have never become deeply enough involved with other people to learn how to relate to them and to learn to help them instead of hurting them. Probably the worst part of addiction is the impact that it has on those who live or work or go to school with the person who still suffers.

When a person acts in such a way that he feels he is worthwhile to himself and others and learns to love himself as well as other people, his behavior is right or moral or responsible. Another way of putting this is to substitute *responsible* for *mental health* and *irresponsible* for *mental illness*. Included in irresponsibility are the problems faced by the troubled worker and the addict—marital and financial troubles, emotional problems, drug addiction, and alcohoilism. An excellent discussion of the above concepts is provided in a volume written by the developer of reality therapy.[6]

Individual responsibility is the essential first step if the individual is to resume management of his own life. The supervisor or the teacher can help tremendously by understanding that reality therapy is quite different from conventional psychotherapy. I shall cover the basic differences between the two approaches in the ensuing paragraphs.

1. *Conventional psychiatry* argues that mental illness exists, that such illnesses can be usefully classified, and that the mental illness can then be treated according to this diagnostic classification. *Reality therapy* does not accept the notion of mental illness. Therefore, the manager or the teacher cannot become involved with a person until that person has become responsible in his or her behavior.

2. *Conventional psychiatry* requires that we probe into the past life of the person, because only by understanding what caused the troubled behavior can we change it. *Reality therapy*, by contrast, works in the present and toward the future. There is no point in getting involved in the past because, although it may provide an explanation of what happened, this should never serve as an excuse for irresponsible behavior. The past is history and the future is a mystery—so reality therapy, as the manager or the teacher utilizes it, should concentrate on the here and now. To put it differently, the supervisor or teacher can have an impact on a person's attitudes or behaviors only if that individual behaves responsibly.

3. *Conventional psychiatry* maintains that the patient must

transfer to the therapist the attitudes he has toward important people in his past life. The patient, through this process of *transference*, gains insights into his past. This enables him to give up his old attitudes and thus changes his behavior so that he can better relate to other people. *Reality therapy* tells us that we relate to employees or students as ourselves, not as transference figures.

4. *Conventional psychiatry* emphasizes that the therapist helps the patient to gain insight and understanding into his unconscious mind. Unconscious problems are considered to be more important than the conscious and free association, dream analysis, interpretation of transference, and educated guessing of the psychotherapist and are the ingredients of successful therapy. *Reality therapy* does not search for unconscious conflicts or the reasons for their existence. A good simple rule in this connection is *utilize—don't analyze*. Reality therapy begins when the person concerned accepts individual responsibility, and this has to take place at the conscious, "new brain" levels.

5. *Conventional psychiatry* completely avoids the problem of morality—deciding whether the behavior of the person is right or responsible. Undesirable behavior is a result of mental illness and can be cured only by rigorous adherence to steps 2, 3, and 4 as just outlined. Once this is done, the behavior should become socially acceptable. *Reality therapy* emphasizes individual responsibility. The manager or teacher or parent must face the issue of wrong or right squarely. Until the person himself faces the fact that his behavior has made his life unmanageable and that this is hurting other people, there can be no progress.

6. *Conventional psychiatry* is not interested in teaching people how to behave better and to satisfy their needs. Rather, it holds that people will behave better once they understand the historical and unconscious sources of their problems. *Reality therapy* teaches people how to fulfill their needs. The school or business organization should have a policy covering addiction, and this policy should call for a confrontation when the problem begins to impair performance. If the condition continues, the person should be offered unhesitating support in seeking assistance on condition of cooperation. Finally, if the preliminary steps fail, strict disciplinary methods should be used. These methods will utilize separation as a final penalty. Unless the threat of final separation remains real, the

addict will discount the danger and any therapy will fail. Remember that the policies we employ should be based on compassion, not sympathy.

Positive Peer Pressure and Support

Positive peer pressure and support is the next step on the therapy ladder after the assumption of individual responsibility. The assumptions underlying positive peer pressure and support are simple, but each is extremely important:[7]

1. People can behave responsibly when they choose to do so.
2. People know what they are doing and why.
3. All people want respect and recognition from others.
4. Every person experiences deep personal satisfaction from helping others.

Within the framework of positive peer pressure and support, as within other group-focused peer support and peer pressure organizations, authority figures do not govern—they serve instead as teachers-leaders-counselors or TLC. I like to think of TLC also in its popular context of tender loving care. The tasks of faculty in a school setting where positive peer pressure and support is employed are simply to:

1. Make sure that groups deal with their responsibilities.
2. Make experimenters and addicts question their former negative normal state of consciousness and positive state of consciousness values.
3. Provide TLC to people caring about one another. Obviously, people who are individually responsible are in a good position to love themselves and hence to love others.

In contrast to popular opinion, positive peer pressure and support works as well within the institutional environment as it does in the outside world. One example of positive peer pressure and support within the institutional context is positive peer culture (PPC).[8] I have followed positive peer culture for several years and it works—within youth-serving agencies and schools.

Any form of positive peer pressure and support, such as positive peer culture, is based on the assumption that problem or addictive behavior can be contained and changed by giving the individual a positive role in a group process and subculture in which he can learn to know himself and to relate to other people. Although pressure or punishment may sometimes be employed in positive peer pressure and support, its use should be avoided to the maximum extent possible.

The important point to bear in mind is that punishment only makes people avoid treatment—it is an inhibitor. People try to avoid punishment by not getting caught—it develops neither personal responsibility nor individual growth. It does not make people want to change themselves or help others. People learn to change only when they are being ostracized by their group for hurting themselves and others. Positive peer pressure and support enables people to grow and become responsible by helping, not hurting.

A negative peer culture of the kind found among addicts in minimum security institutions has two basic injunctions—"don't be close" and "don't make it." It hurts others. A positive peer culture reverses this process. It rebuilds a person's internal system of values and shows him that *helping*, not hurting, takes real courage. As the old sayings put it, "I came to take, but I stayed to give," and "you can't keep it unless you give it away."

The important point about positive peer pressure and support of any kind is that it provides a supportive and loving environment that comes to constitute the positive normal state of consciousness of the people who "make" the program. Positive peer pressure and support becomes a healthy and permanent substitute for the positive normal state of consciousness and the euphoric state of consciousness that the person was seeking during the experimental stages of drug or alcohol use. Some become positive-peer-pressure-and-support addicts and provide leadership in the program. Others arrest their addiction through membership in the program.

An important aspect of positive peer pressure and support and positive peer culture is the emphasis on the theme "every member a counselor." This form of group therapy does not depend on or need professional assistance. For example, the eighth tradition of Alcoholics Anonymous states that the organization "should remain forever nonprofessional"—which is about as long a period of time as most of us can envision. In addition to the wide variety of positive peer pressure and support programs, there are yet other ways of combating addiction—these are discussed in the next section.

Meditation and Other Altered States of Consciousness

Addiction may be viewed as the degeneration of a euphoric state of consciousness into a painful state of consciousness. Addiction, as Weisskopf puts it, represents *union downward*. In order to arrest addiction—it is doubtful if there is a cure—we must search for and substitute *union upward*.

Frequently, the addict has a hover point, a point of balance, in which negative normal state of consciousness elements far outweigh the positive normal state of consciousness elements. Situations of this kind are most frequently found in individuals who are poor and in members of minority groups. Such situations also result in alienation and attempts to escape the situation. As Weiskopf explains:

> They (people) try to escape this split by union downward or union upward. Both aim in different ways to overcome consciousness. *Union downward* tries to eliminate consciousness through such means as intoxication, drug addiction (which is not an expansion but an extinction of consciousness), sexual stupor, apathetic passivity, "through wine, woman and song," on the sensual level. The movements of today which use massage, nudism, sensitivity training, physical touch encounters and so forth are trying to find ways to overcome, by more or less physical means, the estrangement from which we suffer. Sometimes definite elements of *union upward*, with expansion of consciousness, are involved in these activities. Aldous Huxley's mysticism, built on mescaline, is a mixture of both.[9]

Weisskopf is far too harsh and pessimistic in his listing of the techniques of union upward—at least in today's milieu. Twelve years ago, to indicate how rapidly our knowledge and understanding have grown, a person with whom I used to work on the management development circuit was dropped from a speakers' list because he advocated Zen as a method of meditation, the euphoric state of consciousness. Four years later, such an august publication of establishment management thought as the *Harvard Business Review* had a widely quoted article advocating meditation as man's innate asset for combating stress.[10]

Altered states of consciousness, including the euphoric state of consciousness, are a product of the right new brain. Consider this. Animals know but only man knows that he knows. Man knows that he knows in his normal state of consciousness, which is governed mainly by the left new brain. Much more important, however, is that man now knows that he has many ways of knowing the altered state of consciousness without the use of drugs. For example, in my library I have a volume with the title of *The Book of Highs: 250 Ways to Alter Consciousness Without Drugs*, published by none other than the New York Times Book Company.[11]

Not only are there many approaches to altered states of consciousness, but meditation, for one, provides an excellent substitute for drugs. Let's take a look at what transcendental meditation has done for a number of addicts, not only for those on narcotics, hallucinogens, stimulants, and depressants, but also for the users of "hard liquor" and cigarettes. Note that this research was performed by Dr. Herbert Benson and others at the Harvard Medical School. He is the person who wrote the *Harvard Business Review* article mentioned earlier.

As a part of my research into altered states of consciousness, I have come to practice a number of them. They work. A good program, which all of us can follow, is presented in the *Harvard Business Review* article by Herbert Benson. From that point forward, you're on your own. It's a lot of fun on a purely personal basis in addition to permitting you to experience altered states of consciousness to the point that you have been there personally when you discuss them with your troubled or addicted people.[12]

Conclusion

The path from addiction to a normal state of consciousness is long and difficult. In time, the addict can, however, move from the lull of compulsion to the world of the earth people, provided he is willing to acknowledge that his life has become unmanageable and that he himself must acknowledge his powerlessness over his addiction. The first step is the assumption of individual responsibility or surrender—call it what you wish—only the addict himself can take this step. As I have indicated, a compassionate teacher or supervisor will understand this and avoid the sympathy that merely serves to cover up or to excuse the irresponsible behavior of the addict.

Once the first step has been taken, the addict is ready for detoxification. Because detoxification falls into the province of the physician, that's about all we can say about it here.

The addict who has been through detoxification is ready to embark on a program of positive peer pressure and support. Fortunately, there are a number of such programs available in large metropolitan areas. For example, matching up the trouble and the program we have:

Financial	Gamblers Anonymous
Marital	Divorces Anonymous
Mental Emotions	Emotions Anonymous
Alcoholism	Alcoholics Anonymous
Drugs	Narcotics Anonymous

Usually we think of positive peer culture as solely rehabilitative in nature. We should, however, be aware that its truly great contribution will ultimately occur in the preventive area—where it serves as a substitute for the negative peer culture in which addicts begin their experimentation. One of the most famous of modern-day psychiatrists puts it as follows:

> Children in trouble, the lonely, the angry, the withdrawn, and children with character disturbances—who later in life become both a threat and/or a burden to our society—can be reached best by their peers, especially if a cured [sic] addict is stressing the miserable and humiliating experiences of an addict. The group as a whole or a few individuals of the group generally generates more rapport or greater power of pulling problem children into an active participation than do parents or teachers. As a rule, when a rejected or deprived child feels to be accepted by his group or as soon as he wins group respect,

he generally begins to cooperate and work along with the group.[13]

The positive peer culture should be based on the concept that each member learn to serve as the discussion leader of the group. We have enough experience with this philosophy to know that it works. More than this, the tradition of nonprofessional therapy provides a means by which any group relying only on its own resources can immediately begin to function. This is not to say that the group does not have access to concerned leaders or special teachers or experienced counselors—merely that the basic thrust be internal, experiential, and existential.

Finally, there are ways of seeking euphoria or altered states of consciousness which do not rely on drugs. As I have indicated earlier, meditation works. Many other approaches also work— ultimately the only limitation, and it is far from being met, is the capacity and ingenuity of the minds of man.

ENDNOTES

1. H. J. Campbell, *The Pleasure Areas: A New Theory of Behavior* (New York: Delacorte, 1973), 63-87. This book is must reading for anyone interested in the processes of addiction.

2. Robert E. Ornstein, *The Psychology of Consciousness* (New York: Viking, 1972). This volume is the pioneering study in psychology of the differences between the functioning of the left half brain and the right half brain.

3. Campbell, *Pleasure Areas*, 80.

4. Ibid., 190.

5. Donald J. Ottenberg, "Addiction as Metaphor," *Alcohol Health and Research World* (Fall 1974): 20.

6. William Glasser, *Reality Therapy: A New Approach to Psychiatry* (New York: Harper & Row, 1965).

7. Two books that discuss a number of group therapy methods are Henrik Ruitenbeek, *The New Group Therapies* (New York: Discus Books/Avon, 1970) and Jerome Liss, *Free to Feel: Finding Your Way Through the New*

Therapies (New York: Praeger, 1975). Two other books, both paperbacks, that I have found personally very useful are Jess Lair, *I Ain't Much Baby— But I'm All I've Got* (Garden City, N.Y.: Doubleday, 1972), and Mildred Newman and Bernard Berkowitz with Jean Owen, *How to Be Your Own Best Friend* (New York: Ballantine, 1974).

8. Harry H. Vorrath, *Positive Peer Culture: Content-Structure-Process* (Michigan Center for Group Studies, 400 N. Pennsylvania Avenue, Lansing, Michigan), 1972.

9. Walter A. Weisskopf, *Alienation and Economics* (New York: Dutton, 1971), 20-21. Italics supplied.

10. Herbert Benson, "Your Innate Asset for Combating Stress," *Harvard Business Review* (July-August 1974): 49-60.

11. Edward Rosenfeld (New York: Quadrangle/New York Times Book Company, 1973).

12. Two paperbacks that I have found to be illuminating are Jhan Robbins and David Fisher, *Tranquility Without Pills: All About Transcendental Meditation* (New York: Bantam Books, 1972), and Maharesh Mahesh Yogi, *Transcendental Meditation: Serenity Without Drugs* (New York: New American Library, 1968).

13. Arnold A. Hutschnecker, *The Drive for Power* (New York: M. Evans and Company, 1974), 326-327. When he was vice president, Richard M. Nixon was a patient of this author.

8

Coping with Stress and Addictive Work Behavior

Waino W. Suojanen
Donald R. Hudson

A mounting body of evidence from the biological sciences and medicine suggests that many aspects of management behavior are analogous to those found in drug addiction. If the individual concerned is the kind of hard-driving, competitive perfectionist whom many organizations prize, and if the strain of coping with work demands is chronic, he may become a victim of the Executive Stress Syndrome (ESS). It is our contention that the chronic strain of the Executive Stress Syndrome must be diagnosed and treated at the level of the individual manager before programs of Organizational Development (OD) and Management by Objectives (MBO) can be effectively instituted at the level of the enterprise.

Stress researchers suggest that the "man in the gray flannel suit" reacts to the strains of managerial work in exactly the same chemical way as did his primordial ancestor when life and limb were threatened by a predator recognized as an enemy by his visceral brain. This chemical reaction to threat is known as the fight-or-flight response. Its relationship to the Executive Stress Syndrome is so important that we discuss it at length in the section that follows.

Under normal environmental conditions, including everyday work loads, the body tends to maintain a fairly fixed internal

Reprinted with permission from *BUSINESS*, January-February 1981. The authors are indebted to James N. Suojanen, M.D., for inculcating us with the subtleties and nuances of endocrinology contained in this article.

environment known as *homeostasis.* In this state, pulse rate, temperature, blood pressure, and respiration fall into well-defined "normal" patterns. Homeostasis applies to the normal rhythm of sleeping, dreaming, and being awake. These physiological and consciousness states remain in equilibrium under "normal" conditions. When we become involved in high stress or distress situations, however, many of our neural, hormonal, and physiological functions undergo dramatic changes.

Each human being is the present-day heir of a primordial fight-or-flight response to external threat or danger. This response is *genetically* imprinted or embedded into the visceral brain of man. In any emergency which constitutes a threat to life, this fight-or-flight response taps those bodily reserves of extra energy that are required to cope with the crisis.

As the body prepares for vigorous exertion, immediate and dramatic changes take place. The pulse quickens. The pupils of the eyes dilate. The lungs inhale more oxygen in order to fuel the muscles for additional, strenuous work. The ears prick up and the hearing improves. Blood clotting agents build up rapidly as a guard against possible bleeding. Digestive processes slow down and virtually stop.

This gamut of responses is ideal if the body is to ward off an assailant, get out of the way of a car, shoot a deer, or run the 100-yard dash. Without the fight-or-flight response, none of these acts would be possible.

During the fight-or-flight response, the body recognizes the stressor, and the endocrine system responds by producing the arousal hormone *epinephrine,* commonly known as *adrenalin.* A little later, the nervous system releases a neurotransmitter called *norepinephrine* or *noradrenalin,* a chemical that acts principally to maintain blood pressure. Its chemical composition differs only slightly from that of epinephrine. Whereas epinephrine serves to alert and arouse the entire body by mobilizing sugar into the blood and redistributing it to the potential action centers, norepinephrine acts to dilate the blood vessels and promote the action of the heart.

The distinction in the way epinephrine and norepinephrine affect bodily functions has been discussed by Edward O. Wilson, a noted biologist, who observes:

A curious effect discovered in human beings is that violent participation in aggressive encounters induces the release of relatively large quantities of norepinephrine together with only moderate amounts of epinephrine, while the *anticipation* of aggressive interaction, in the form of anger or fear, favors only the release of epinephrine. Professional hockey players on the bench, for example, secrete only epinephrine at the same time their teammates playing on the floor are secreting mostly norepinephrine.[1]

In the literature, the fight-or-flight response is sometimes called the fright-flight-fight response. This term is more descriptive of the Executive Stress Syndrome than is the shorter fight-or-flight response because it brings the stressor (fright) into the total picture. This is important, as John W. Mason has pointed out, because *psychological events,* as much as physiological, can trigger the Executive Stress Syndrome.[2] In other words, although there is *no* physical danger whatsoever, the visceral brain may interpret the psychological situation just as if there were a critical threat to life and limb. This causes "the adrenalin to flow," as we have indicated earlier, and the visceral brain assumes dominance over the cortical brain for the period of the emergency.

Mason's evidence suggests that *many managers react to psychological distress just as if it were physiological stress.* The work environment provides the psychological stimulus that, in each of its manifestations, is the behavioral analog of the actual fight-or-flight situation. Although there is no physical danger whatsoever, the visceral brain interprets the situation just as if there were a threat to life or limb and the relevant defense mechanisms are placed on alert.

This alert status is damaging to the individual both physically and psychologically. The body chemicals (catecholamines and glucocorticoids) produced under such alert conditions have served throughout the period of human evolution the very important function of increasing the probability of survival of the individual. Now, under the stress conditions of modern management, they create a "dis-ease" which can rapidly be transformed into a disease.

Here we have a baffling paradox. On the one hand, the fight-or-flight response has a high physiological value because it increases the probability of survival. On the other hand, it is highly dysfunctional because the central nervous system responds to many stressful and distressful psychological situations as if life and limb were at stake when they actually are not. This latter response, as Mason's work suggests, is unhealthy in that it creates bodily conditions that may result in mental and physical illness. Whatever the answer to the paradox, the question remains: What implications does the fight-or-flight response have for organizational behavior and management theory?

It is our contention that "distress" type situations in organizations frequently are the result of compulsive or addictive behavior on the part of managers. We further contend that much of such dysfunctional behavior on the part of managers is the result of their attempts, unknowingly, to satisfy their needs for a "high" from work or crisis management that is physiologically exactly the same as that sought by the alcoholic and the drug addict. In the next section, we will look briefly at the nature of both the chemical and the psychological "high" and how behaviors aimed at satisfying a need for such highs tend to become addictive.

Chemical Aspects of Behavior

The catecholamines produced by the body under conditions of physical and psychological stress—epinephrine and norepinephrine—have a chemical composition which closely resembles that of the amphetamines. One official study made the following point a few years ago:

"Amphetamines are synthetic amines which are in many ways similar to the body's own adrenalin (epinephrine). These drugs normally evoke an arousal or activating response not unlike one's normal reaction to emergency or stress."[3]

In the parlance of the street, the amphetamines go by the collective name of "speed." All of us have heard of "speed freaks" whose behavior, as indicated in the *Interim Report,* "is usually characterized by action, power, arrogance and physical pleasure ('kicks'), and regularly leads to suspicion, paranoia, hostility, and often aggression."[4]

Significantly, the workaholic personality and the Type A Behavior Pattern, which we shall discuss later, also are characterized by "action, power, and arrogance" that often result in "suspicion, paranoia, hostility, and aggression" on the part of the manager and the people who work for him.

The attempts of people to achieve pleasure or avoid pain will be examined in the next section as an analog to the behavior of the manager who has become compulsive and obsessive about the role of work in his or her life. Without realizing it, many of us are "workaholics"—we are just as dependent on the "high" we get from earning our daily bread as the "speed freak" is on his pills. The only difference is that the drug abuser seeks "better things for better living through biochemistry" by popping pills, whereas the workaholic creates his chemical (catecholamines) in his own mind.

The Work Ethic

All of us know that one of the best ways to cut down on stress and stimulus overload is to take a long vacation each year rather than a number of short ones. Despite this, according to the Institute of Life Insurance, top managers who can easily afford the best vacations—and who probably need them the most—now tend to avoid long, uninterrupted annual holidays.[5] Instead, they use their vacation time in short increments—adding them to weekends and business trips. This can be counterproductive because the resulting continued and prolonged stress increases the risk of heart attacks and ulcers while reducing the manager's ability to think creatively in his work role.

What accounts for the compulsion or obsession to keep working night and day and taking vacations in short periods? Does this kind of behavior represent what is necessary if one is to prove himself ready for the responsibilities of high rank in the organization? Or does it represent something else—a dysfunctional pattern of behavior that is bad and perhaps even potentially catastrophic to the individual, his family, his organization, and the society? Perhaps the latter lies at the heart of the case.

Origins of the Work Ethic: Before the Protestant Reformation, the idea of a vocation and the concept of a calling applied only to the clergy. The clergy lived in monasteries, separated from the rest of society. This separation was unacceptable to Martin Luther for two reasons. It placed the responsibility for living the gospel on a mere handful of the people, and it separated the religious existence from sectarian life. In order to obtain support for his opposition to the church structure, Luther called on laymen to fulfill their secular calling for Christian service through their daily labors. By integrating the concept of calling with the sanctity of toil, Luther transformed the popular idea of work from a way of providing the material needs into a strategic position for the expression of personal religious responsibility.

John Calvin built on the ideas of Martin Luther and developed the basic outlines of the Puritan Ethic—now known as the Work Ethic. Calvin insisted that every occupation, no matter how humble, could be a "calling" worthy of its full reward in this world and the next, providing it was practiced in the stern discipline of monastic rule. The person who brought to any task the qualities of industry, thrift, honesty, abstinence, and sobriety, and in addition prayed and attended church regularly, promoted the glory of God and the virtue of "vocation" as much as any cleric. Calvin argued that this person also proved that he was a member of that small "elect" company predestined by God for eternal salvation. Thus hard work and life hereafter became jointly and symbiotically one and the same.

The Calvinist view of life and work, and the Puritan or Protestant Ethic that sprang from it, were very stimulating and comforting philosophies to all those who had to work hard for a living—and that included almost everybody. Those who worked hard, and had wondered why this was necessary, were now in a position to tie work and religion together. The aims and methods of hard work served both God and Mammon. Furthermore, if one's labors yielded a goodly income, if one's values denied one the pleasure of wasting it in riotous living, and if one became wealthy, then all this was indeed an example of virtue as its own reward.

A professor of theology summarizes the Protestant Work Ethic as follows:

> A universal taboo is placed on *idleness* and *industriousness* is considered a religious ideal; *waste* is a vice, and *frugality* a virtue; complacency and failure are outlawed, and *ambition* and success are taken as sure signs of God's favor; the universal

sign of sin is *poverty,* and the crowning sign of God's favor is
wealth.[6]

The Luther-Calvin model of the sanctity of work has become so
embedded into the value system of the United States that it now
reaches into and often dominates the political, economic, social, and
technical aspects of our life. One criticizes the Work Ethic at his
own risk. It is part of our thesis, however, that a compulsive and
obsessive preoccupation with the sanctity of work helps to explain
why the behavior of top managers so often ends up being
counterproductive, not only to themselves individually but to their
organizations and the society as well. Even more tragically, many
die of coronary heart disease because they live lives through which
they are continuously pouring high-voltage chemicals into their
bodies as a result of low-voltage (stress) situations. Such compulsive and obsessive work behavior is known as "workaholism."

Workaholism: The word "workaholic" is a semihumorous,
invented word that avers that the person concerned is as dependent
on overwork for his "kicks" or "highs" as is the speed freak on his
amphetamines or the heroin addict on his opiate narcotic. If we
were to view the workaholic as we do the alcoholic, we would say
that he is a person whose craving for work has become so obsessive
that it disturbs or interferes with his bodily health, his personal
happiness, his interpersonal relations, and his smooth social
functioning.

We must, however, make a big distinction between workaholism
and alcohol and drug addiction because of the different ways in
which the community and culture view them. The person who
overworks compulsively and obsessively is held in high esteem in
the United States. By contrast, the alcoholic and the drug addict are
viewed with scorn and contempt and frequently are even treated as
criminals. The public attitude toward workaholics is different
because they are under the influence of the Work Ethic and their
behavior is viewed very positively.

Compulsion, Obsession, and Type A Behavior: A book by two heart
specialists (cardiologists) has been widely publicized in the management literature.[7] This study develops the relationship between

Type A Behavior—a psychological concept—and heart disease. Those factors that are commonly accepted as leading to heart disease—overweight, lack of exercise, excessive smoking, high-fat dietary habits—are evaluated at length.

From our point of view, one of the most interesting comments made by the authors is the following, which appears in the preface:

> In the absence of Type A Behavior Pattern, coronary heart disease almost never occurs before seventy years of age, regardless of the fatty foods eaten, the cigarettes smoked, or the lack of exercise. But when this behavior pattern is present, coronary heart disease can easily erupt in one's thirties and forties.[8]

What is the Type A Behavior pattern that is associated with a high incidence of coronary heart disease among managers? How does it differ from the Type B Behavior pattern? Again, the similarity of Type A Behavior to the type of stressful and distressful behavior we have discussed earlier is more than coincidental. As we shall try to indicate later, a number of successful managers appear to be stimulus addicts who apparently induce the equivalent of the "high" of the dependent drug user in their own minds by creating crises at work that cause a number of variants of the fight-or-flight syndrome on the part of themselves, their associates, and their subordinates.

The Type A Behavior pattern, from a behavioral standpoint, coincides virtually point for point with the behavior of the workaholic on the job. Both are compulsive in their perfectionism, whatever the task undertaken. Subordinates cannot be trusted to do as good a job as the work-obsessed manager, hence the briefcase goes home full every night. Mastery, thoroughness, and peak performance elicit a glow of self-satisfaction with one's own competence. Subordinates obviously are less than competent—if not incompetent. Because they are lazy and irresponsible, they have to be closely supervised—shades of Theory X and Douglas McGregor! Only the superior epitomizes total personal commitment to the achievement of the goals of the organization. The loyalty of others has to be bought, using such inducements as shorter hours, higher pay, and better working conditions—features which Frederick Herzberg labels as hygiene or maintenance factors.

All of us are familiar with the boast of the hard-driving Type A executive who "doesn't get ulcers but gives them." In every large organization, there are managers whose behavior can be described by the comment, "they build fires just to put them out!" The "crisis," the "fire fight," the "flap" are familiar terms used to describe the obsession and compulsion that are found in profusion wherever the Type A manager leaves his trail of workaholic traits.

Friedman and Rosenman point out that the Type A Behavior pattern characterizes roughly 60% of American managers. The addictive pattern of the workaholic executive is well illustrated in the following quote from their study:

> The great difficulty the Type A subject experiences in delegating work to others is only in part due to his "hurry sickness." It is also due to his belief that *all* his activities require his right hand and only *his* right hand. Nothing can be delegated to anyone else. This chronic refusal grows out of the basic insecurity of the Type A subject. He fears that even the slightest error in performing a task may topple his total structure of past achievements. Each task to be done appears to be too important to risk failure—and trusting an associate or subordinate simply increases the risk to an unacceptable point.[9]

Is it possible for the Type A person—and the chances are high that he is a male—to change his addictive behavior pattern? Friedman and Rosenman answer in the affirmative, as does Oates.

Oates, following Harry M. Tiebout, compares the behavior pattern of the workaholic to that of the alcoholic. Both patterns, like Type A Behavior, can be described as:

> Tense, depressed, aggressive or at least quietly stubborn, oppressed with feelings of inferiority and at the same time acting quite superior, perfectionistic and rigid, overpowered with a sense of loneliness, basically self-centered, defiant in a world apart from others. I have said that work as well as alcohol aids and abets these tendencies and when pursued compulsively will produce a similar personality profile.[10]

The Organization

There is increasing evidence that suggests that the Work Ethic may have highly unfavorable effects on the performance and behavior of both manager and workers in many of our most highly regarded organizations. In far too many instances, the General Adjustment Syndrome—a broader term for the fight-or-flight response—manifests itself, not as a mechanism for coping with crisis and stress, but as a vehicle for producing long-lasting organizational distress. Because of the behavior of so many workaholic Type A managers, the organizations in which they serve in top-management and middle-management positions also tend to become institutions for producing troubled workers by the hundreds and thousands.

It is our contention that workaholic, Type A behavior on the part of management creates any number of syndromes that are highly dysfunctional as far as organizational effectiveness and efficiency are concerned. We list only a few possibilities that fit into a broader General Adjustment Syndrome acronym, as follows:

1. General Addiction Syndrome
2. General Adrenalin Syndrome
3. General Attack Syndrome
4. General Alcohol Syndrome
5. General Anxiety Syndrome
6. General Apathy Syndrome

It is important to remember that each General Adjustment Syndrome listed here is dysfunctional at every relevant level of the organization. In other words, the behavior of both the superior and subordinate can be addictive, and this can repeat itself all the way down from the level of chief executive officer of the organization to that of the most junior supervisor. If we bear in mind the fact that the behavior of top management dictates the behavior of the other members of the organization and if this behavior is addictive, then the end result often will be an enterprise in which members appear to be "busy" in every respect but that is falling down totally on overall performance.

This type of organizational behavior is difficult to correct. The addictive members of top management will hardly acknowledge that their behavior pattern is abnormal when it is they, with their obsession with work, who are responsible for the success of the organization. Any participant who attacks the behavior of top management in this type of situation will be viewed as disloyal, and his services may even be terminated. Participants realize this—after all, the essence of the General Apathy State is epitomized in the old saying "to get along, go along."

Outside criticism will be countered in a similar way. Addictive behavior reinforces the concept of the Work Ethic, and the American image of the successful executive is that of one who is aggressive and competitive. The ideal of the rational manager in today's milieu is one whose on-the-job behavior is governed by an obsession with both time and numbers. The fact that this "ideal type" of rational manager also describes the compulsive attitudes of the workaholic and the Type A Behavior pattern—both of which are highly irrational—is regarded as beside the point. That the manager in question behaves obnoxiously is ascribed to the pressures of office, not to symptoms of personally addictive behavior.

Can a program of Organizational Development help to correct an organization in which the behavior of participants has gradually been synchronized to a General Addictive Syndrome on the part of top management? Hardly. Just as the spouse of the alcoholic mate adjusts to addiction with cover-up and kindness, so does the participant in this type of organization make his own work life bearable by developing his own General Adjustment Syndrome. Any attempt to install an organizational-development program before the General Addictive Syndrome of top management has been corrected will be highly counterproductive.

In practice, an Organizational Development or MBO program will prove ineffective. Why? The answer is simple—yet one that most present-day behavioral scientists do not recognize. The changes in knowledge, attitude, or behavior that Organizational Development or MBO induces at lower levels will be more or less out-of-step with the General Addictive Syndrome stemming from the top of the organization. The Organizational Development or MBO program destroys the General Adjustment Syndrome that each participant has carefully constructed over time as his mechanism for coping—for making life bearable—in an otherwise unbearable situation. Were it not for this subjective General

Adjustment Syndrome, many participants would find it impossible to continue their lives of quiet desperation.

The point here is an extremely important one. Any kind of addictive behavior by an individual results in addictive behavior on the part of those trying to adjust to it. The two go together, and to attempt to change at only one end is pointless and even counter-productive. To change addictive behavior requires that the addict take the first step—"we admitted we were powerless over our addiction—that our behavior was wrecking the organization." The addictive senior manager must admit and accept the fact that his behavior must be changed before any program of changing the behavior of the organization can begin.

In the case of many organizations, the problem is compounded because most or even all of the members of top management have workaholic Type A Behavior patterns. Until the senior manager takes the first step, the other members of top management cannot take it. Organizational behavior change must wait until all members of the top management have begun their individual programs of change. It is indeed ironic that to increase productivity it may be necessary to do a 180-degree turn from the prevailing philosophy if the efficiency criterion is to prevail.

Reengineering Behavior

The Type A workaholic can alter his obsessive behavior if he takes the first step and subsequently adopts a forgiving attitude, develops a sense of humor, experiences a feeling of wonder and awe, and de-programs his attitude of corporate worship. This sounds like a simple order, but it implies a profound change in personality of the kind suggested by Friedman and Rosenman, who present a detailed program explaining how to cope with the Type A Behavior pattern.[11] They suggest a philosophical variant of the twelve steps that have proved useful in helping people change their behavior in self-help and mutual aid programs such as Alcoholics Anonymous and Gamblers Anonymous.

Among their human reengineering procedures, Friedman and Rosenman have found the following steps to be useful:

1. Reengineer "hurry sickness" and hostility.

2. Try to work in a milieu that promotes serenity and peace of mind.

3. Reduce the amount of time devoted to talking.

4. Devote the noon hour to contemplation and relaxation.

5. Forget five o'clock frenzy.

6. Search for aloneness.

7. Focus on the things worth being rather than on those worth having.

8. Practice self-appraisal.

9. Emphasize the broader satisfactions of living and loving.

10. Establish life goals.

11. Devote more time to myth, ritual, and tradition.

12. Delegate.

13. Let the means justify the end.

14. Live life one day at a time.

The Relaxation Response

In recent years, Transcendental Meditation (TM) has been vigorously marketed as a method that can be used to overcome some of the undesirable effects of the fight-or-flight response. One book, which was on the best-selling lists in hardback and is now a paperback, devotes over 260 pages to extolling the virtues of TM.[12]

A word of caution, however. Nowhere in the book by Bloomfield's battalion is there a single word on how to practice TM. If the reader wants to learn TM, he will have to sign up at a center or a retreat for a price ranging from $125 for an adult to $55 for a junior-high student. One must join the "in" group—and pay his dues—because then he receives his *own* mantra (a Sanskrit word to be repeated 20 minutes at a time twice daily). Why does the mantra particularly suit the needs of a unique individual? The teacher knows. How does the teacher know? All TM teachers are trained by Maharishi Mahesh Yogi and *he* knows. He probably laughs all the way to the bank.

We believe in and practice the relaxation response. We are convinced that such meditation aids busy managers to relax and thus better cope with the pressures we have discussed earlier. A little research should convince anyone that meditation has (1) been around for centuries and (2) there is no one right way to relax.

For the manager who is interested in the benefits of meditation without paying a monopolistic rent, we recommend the relaxation response as described by Harvard cardiologist, Herbert Benson.[13] Basically, the relaxation response is simple to elicit. The following steps are sufficient to get you started:

1. Sit in a comfortable position with your eyes closed; wear loose-fitting clothing.

2. Relax your muscles, starting at the feet and working toward the head.

3. As you inhale, mentally follow the air as it moves into your lungs.

4. As you exhale, repeat to yourself some neutral word, such as "one" or a simple prayer of your own.

5. Expect distracting thoughts. When they occur, merely say "oh, well" to yourself and return to the repetition.

6. Continue the exercise for 10 to 20 minutes. Do not use an alarm. When you finish, sit quietly with your eyes closed, then open them slowly before getting up.

It is worth noting that Benson used to refer to the relaxation response as transcendental meditation (no capital letters—no asterisk) in his earlier writing. He now uses the term "mental device" for the mantra of TM. At a recent seminar, attended by one of us, Benson suggested that the repetition of a neutral word such as "one" closes the loop between the visceral brain and the left-half brain and thus minimizes the production of distracting thoughts. In any event, we can personally attest to the effectiveness of the relaxation response—we both practice it.

There is considerable question as to whether transcendental meditation or the relaxation response constitutes a state of consciousness different from the normal. TM advocates advance all kinds of "evidence" to this effect. Benson, although much less enthusiastic, argues very much in the same view. However, a recent study raises a serious question as to whether TM differs at all from sleep. According to this report:

> The range of states observed during meditation does not
> support the view that meditation produces a single, unique

state of consciousness.... The results of Younger, et al., of Wada and Hamm, and of this experiment raise the question of whether the beneficial effects reported for meditation are due to the sleep that occurs during meditation or to some other feature of that process.[14]

There is little doubt that the controversy as to whether TM and the relaxation response are one and the same process will continue for years to come. Similarly, Pagano and his colleagues have dropped a big bombshell into the enclave of the altered-state-of-consciousness advocates. Neither of these controversies needs to concern one at this point except in the way of caveat.

Even if the relaxation response, as advocated by Benson, is nothing more than a self-induced placebo effect that does not differ physiologically from a good nap, it does work. The point to remember is that the fight-or-flight response is controlled by the old or visceral brain. The same is true of the Executive Stress Syndrome.

When the manager takes the first step, he comes to the realization that the old brain need not control the new brain. As Gevarter puts it:

> If we understand that the old brain response to stimuli is determined by knowledge of the situation and internal psychological stress, as well as by the old brain value system and programming, then we can utilize the new brain with its awareness and ability for conscious rational thought and interpretation, to maneuver the situation to elicit a favorable old brain response.[15]

The manager who suffers from the Executive Stress Syndrome as we have described it in this study got where he is by using his new brain to solve problems and make decisions for the organization. Why can't he behave the same way as far as his own behavior is concerned? We see no reason why he can't do this. The relaxation response is only one of the self-help therapies available to the manager who must cope with the Executive Stress Syndrome at work while trying to live a fulfilling personal life.

In this section, we have focused on the relaxation response as a counter to the fight-or-flight response, which is an integral aspect of the Executive Stress Syndrome. Our reason for doing so is both scholarly and personal. It is scholarly in the sense that a change in behavior requires that we become individually responsible.[16] Eliciting the relaxation response can become a most satisfying first step in this direction. It is personal in that both of us now enjoy a new freedom from stress that has made our own lives much more meaningful and satisfying than they used to be. Although we are both Type A workaholics, we have found that there is as much enjoyment in reengineering our behavior to conform to the Type B syndrome as there is in practicing the relaxation response. And for this we are grateful.

ENDNOTES

1. Edward O. Wilson, *Sociobiology: The New Synthesis* (Cambridge, Massachusetts, Harvard University Press, 1975), 253.

2. Robert J. Trotter, "Stress—Confusion and Controversy," *Science News* 31 May 1975, 357-358; and Franklin G. Shontz, *The Psychological Aspects of Physical Illness and Disability* (New York: Macmillan, 1975), 131-155.

3. *Interim Report of the Canadian Government's Commission of Inquiry, The Non-Medical Use of Drugs* (Baltimore, Maryland: Penguin Books, 1970), 45.

4. Ibid., 46.

5. Institute of Life Insurance, *Trend Analysis Program,* Trend Report No. 11 (New York: Institute of Life Insurance, Spring 1975), 21.

6. Wayne E. Oates, *Confessions of a Workaholic: The Facts About Work Addiction* (New York: Abingdon Press, 1972), 84.

7. Meyer Friedman and Ray H. Rosenman, *Type A Behavior and Your Heart* (New York: Knopf, 1974).

8. Ibid., viii.

9. Ibid., 202.

10. Oates, *Confessions*, 92-93.

11. Friedman and Rosenman, *Type A Behavior*, 180-240.

12. Harold H. Bloomfield, M.P. Cain, and D.T. Jaffe, *T.M.—Discovering Inner Energy and Overcoming Stress* (New York: Delacorte Press, 1975).

13. Herbert Benson, "Your Innate Asset for Combating Stress," *Harvard Business Review* (July-August 1974): 49-60; and Herbert Benson with Miriam Klipper, *The Relaxation Response* (New York: Morrow, 1975).

14. Robert R. Pagano, et al., "Sleep During Transcendental Meditation," *Science,* 23 January 1976, 308-309.

15. William B. Gevarter, "Humans: Their Brain and Their Freedom," *Journal of Humanistic Psychology,* Fall 1975, 89.

16. For an excellent study on how to go about changing one's behavior by becoming individually responsible, see William Glasser, *Reality Therapy* (New York: Harper & Row, 1965).

NOTE
From Waino W. Suojanen, January 1981

In 1977 the Committee on Substance Abuse and Habitual Behavior, Assembly of Behavioral and Social Sciences, National Research Council, National Academy of Sciences, published a monograph entitled Common Processes in Habitual Substance Use: A Research Agenda. *One of the key points in this report was the comment:*

> The opponent-process theory may be useful in analyzing various forms of addiction: to opiates, hallucinogens, drugs such as alcohol and tobacco, work, gambling, sports, or sexual activity.[1]

Earlier in this same report, the Committee suggests:

> Patterns of behavior—in eating, taking drugs, work, or play— reflect a person's style of life. Such patterns may be protective, essential to coping with daily routines of life, but they can also lead to problems: organic diseases; behavior disorders; interpersonal difficulties with family, colleagues at work, or members of social groups; and social problems, such as unemployment and crime. Behavior patterns may be shaped by social and peer group pressures. Those that fit societal norms are accepted, while those that do not may be considered deviant. In effect, habit formation can be viewed as social influences modulating individual motivations.[2]

Friedman and Rosenman have established the fact that coronary heart disease and Type A Behavior have a common etiology. Totman points out that "the Type A style is a much researched special case of a more general disposition to set oneself high and rigid standards."[3] I am in total agreement with the concept that the search for perfection is as addictive as being hooked on alcohol, as is well illustrated in the book by Michael Maccoby, The Gamesman.[4] *I highly recommend that the reader acquaint him or herself with the behavior profiles of the "jungle fighter" and the "gamesman" as Maccoby describes them. Type A Behavior describes the "jungle fighter" as an ACORN and the "gamesman" as a Type B, OAK. The ACORN is an Addictive, Compulsive, Obsessive, Really Nutty person; the OAK is an Open, Adaptive, Knowledgeable human being.*

It has become obvious to me since publication of the original article that any manager who behaves like an ACORN may act like a nut for the rest of his or her life, as Maccoby so well documents in the case of the managers he studied.[5] I have also discovered that an ACORN who takes the first step can become an OAK one day at a time. I don't worry about yesterday—yesterday is history; I don't worry about tomorrow—tomorrow is a mystery. If I have one eye fixed on yesterday and the other eye focused on tomorrow, I will look on today cross-eyed. On the other hand, if I am happy today, I will never be unhappy again because it is always today.

ENDNOTES

1. Committee on Substance Abuse and Habitual Behavior, Assembly of Behavioral and Social Sciences, National Research Council, National Academy of Sciences, *Common Processes in Habitual Substance Use: A Research Agenda* (Washington, D.C., National Academy of Sciences, Printing and Publishing Offices, 1977), 3.

2. Ibid., 2.

3. Richard Totman, *Social Causes of Illness* (New York, Pantheon Books, 1979), 136.

4. Michael Maccoby, *The Gamesman* (New York, Simon & Schuster, 1976).

5. Ibid., 173-209.

9

Organizational Development, Power, and Addictive Managerial Behavior

Waino W. Suojanen
Richard Groepper
R. Carlton Bessinger

One of the basic concepts of management theory is that people always behave rationally and that they always operate in a normal state of consciousness. Given this assumption, a manager will change her or his behavior once it is evident that what is currently being done is either ineffective or inefficient or both. From our studies, it is evident that a number of people in the workplace are chemically dependent, substance abusers—that is, they are hooked on mind-altering drugs (MAD). Others suffer from maladaptive addictive disorders (MAD behaviors). Addiction to MAD chemicals and/or MAD behaviors results in impaired performance.

In this chapter we define *addiction* and *maladaptive addictive disorders* as dependence on a chemical or a behavior pattern that is so excessive that it noticeably interferes with the (1) physical health, cognitive functioning, and organizational performance of the individual; or, (2) if the addict is a manager, he or she produces workers with these same health, cognitive functioning, and organizational performance problems. (See chapter 8 for an explanation of the general adjustment syndrome.) In most instances the person is "hooked" on a MAD chemical or on a MAD behavior. Changing this kind of ACORN (*A*ddictive, *C*ompulsive, *O*bsessive, *R*eally *N*utty) behavior requires either outside intervention or "hitting a personal bottom" and can occur only if the suffering individual "takes the first step."

Hitting bottom and outside intervention both operate from the assumption that the individual who is "hooked" is in an altered state of consciousness, a situation in which brain chemistry determines behavior. Among the brain chemicals that control MAD behavior in the altered state of consciousness are catecholamines and endorphins. Of the catecholamines, the one most familiar to the lay reader is adrenalin or epinephrine.[1]

It is important that the reader understand that addiction and the altered state of consciousness can be induced just as much by a MAD behavior as by a MAD chemical. In our work with recovering compulsive gamblers, for example, we have come to appreciate how much they are prisoners of the "bug" induced by the "action." The "high" that the compulsive gambler experiences when involved in gambling is every bit as addictive as the chemical dependency of the alcoholic. The "denial" that the addict expresses is just as pronounced in the operating, compulsive gambler as it is in the practicing drunk. Invariably, denial and the altered state of consciousness go together in the practicing addict, just as do surrender and the normal state of consciousness in the recovering individual.

It is also important that the reader understand the exact context in which we use the term *denial.* One dictionary definition of *denial* is "to disclaim responsibility for." Dictionary definitions are normal state of consciousness concepts—the "denial" of the addict in altered state of consciousness terms means that the MAD chemical or the MAD behavior are part of the "normal" behavior pattern of the individual. In the altered state of consciousness chemistry determines behavior—the addict can move to the normal state of consciousness only by abstaining from the MAD chemical or the MAD behavior.

The Minds of Man

The normal state of consciousness and the altered state of consciousness can be understood better if we assign as much importance to the old, or visceral brain as we do to the new brain. As indicated in Exhibit 4-1, chapter 4, the new brain consists of the left new brain (LNB) and the right new brain (RNB). The visceral brain (VB) is shown at the bottom of this Exhibit.

Exhibit 4-1 also presents the functions of the three brains in the acronym: A QUIVER SCANS 6Fs. The left new brain is an A QUIVER brain—*A*nalytical, *QU*antitative, *I*ntellectual, *VE*rbal, *R*ational. Similarly, the right new brain is a SCANS brain—*S*ynthesizing, *C*reative, *A*rtistic, *N*ormative, *S*patial.

During the process of evolution, the new brain developed a censoring mechanism that was inserted

> between the incoming stimuli and those parts of the brain that reacted to such stimuli... Thus when an important sensory or hormonal message called for an appropriate action, the action itself was screened through the censorship, making a choice from among several possible forms of action possible.[2]

Simeons points out that the new brain "censors" the old brain during the normal state of consciousness. Choice in the S↔O↔R (stimulus—organism—response) sense is possible because the right new brain develops the various courses of action that are possible (conceptual variation) and the left new brain makes the choices (intellectual selection). Logical thought and judgment are the essence of the normal state of consciousness—the intellectual (new brain) governs the emotional (old brain).

The visceral brain. The visceral brain, in evolutionary terms, is much older than the cortical brain. The new brain is around twenty million years old—the visceral brain is about two hundred million years old.

As has been discussed in previous chapters, the visceral brain controls the behaviors of "man as an animal." The two most important animal behaviors are survival and reproduction. These behaviors are shown in Exhibit 4-1 as the 6Fs--*F*ight-or-*F*light, *F*reeze, *F*eed, *F*eel, and *F*lirt. Those readers who are regular viewers of the nature programs on television may have noticed that many 6Fs human behaviors originate in the animal kingdom rather than in human society. This is particularly true of those behaviors that are concerned with survival and reproduction.

The visceral, or "old," brain of man consists of the hindbrain, the midbrain, and the limbic region of the forebrain. It will be helpful if we remember that limbic means edge or border.

The limbic system is that part of the visceral brain that regulates intentional, emotional, and motivational behavior. Included in the limbic region are the decisive mind as well as the pleasure areas (PLV), and the pain areas (PAV), of the visceral brain as shown in Exhibit 5-1, Chapter 5. In subhuman animals, stimulation of the PLV and the PAV originates almost totally from the receptors of the five senses. Human animals are different in that their pleasure and their pain areas can also be activated by nerve impulses that originate in the A QUIVER and SCANS areas of the new brain.

Pleasure-seeking behavior, at the level of the animal, must be changed from time to time because the pleasure areas become satiated, turn painful, and warn the animal that its survival is in jeopardy. This is quite in accord with the ideas of Weil, who argues that the visceral brain seeks pleasure and avoids pain.[3]

During the normal state of consciousness, the intellectual brain governs or censors the emotional brain. However, the emotional or visceral brain always takes charge when the survival of the organism is threatened or when the old brain perceives survival to be threatened. The name given to this reaction is the fight-or-flight response. During the fight-or-flight response, chemistry determines behavior; the animal functions in a stimulus-determines-response mode.

The basic structures that motivate human behavior at the level of feeling or emotion are all located in the visceral brain. The most important of these structures are the pleasure and pain areas. Altered states of consciousness are controlled by the pleasure and pain areas and their associated structures. These motivational mechanisms of behavior are influenced by MAD chemical and MAD behaviors that function as central nervous system (CNS) stimulants or depressants. These include not only illegal drugs but also alcohol, prescription, and over-the-counter drugs as well as nicotine and caffeine. MAD behaviors include compulsive gambling and compulsive overeating as well as workaholic and Type A behavior. The visceral brain is basically a chemical organ; its functioning can be tilted from the normal state of consciousness to an altered state of consciousness by any substance that can penetrate the blood-brain barrier—but more of this later.

Addiction and Training Models Compared

In recent years, the sensitivity training and encounter group movement has gone into eclipse. During this same time period, employee assistance and executive fitness programs have been proliferating all over the United States. The addiction treatment model, which is utilized by every successful treatment center and employee assistance program in the United States, succeeds where the encounter group model failed. The addiction model recognizes that the person who is suffering cannot recover until he or she takes the first step. Another way of saying this in the jargon of alcoholics is "that any form of therapy works with alcoholics as long as it is combined with Alcoholics Anonymous."

The first step of Alcoholics Anonymous reads as follows: "We admitted we were powerless over alcohol; that our lives had become unmanageable."[4] In the case of alcoholism, the first step requires that the individual abstain from the use of alcohol. Given abstinence, the individual reaches the point in time where chemistry no longer determines behavior. At this point the altered state of consciousness is replaced by the normal state of consciousness. This occurs automatically in the case of the recovering alcoholic who doesn't drink and goes to the meetings.

Encounter group theory assumes that all participants are in a normal state of consciousness—one in which behavior determines chemistry. The same is true of the teaching, training, and counseling models—each assumes that both superior and subordinate are in a normal state of consciousness. As illustrated in Exhibit 9-1, MAD chemicals and/or MAD behavior change the brain biochemistry in such a way that the person operates at the level of the emotional or visceral brain rather than at the intellectual or new brain level.

When a person is in an altered state of consciousness—whenever chemistry is determining behavior—it is fruitless to accuse that individual of lacking will power or self-control. Such a person is controlled by the MAD chemical or the MAD behavior rather than controlling it. Internal control, or responsibility, can occur only when the addict takes the first step and abstains so that in time chemistry no longer determines behavior but instead behavior now determines chemistry.

Exhibit 9-1: **Old Brain Behavior/New Brain Behavior**

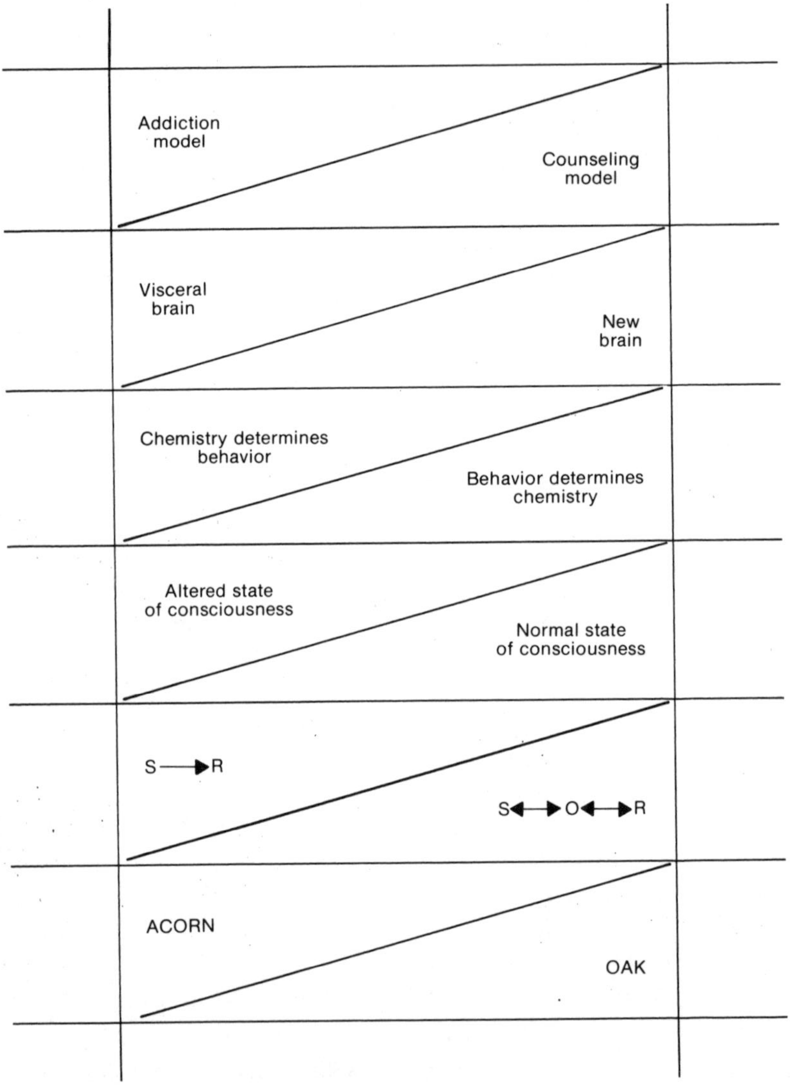

Addiction model — Counseling model

Visceral brain — New brain

Chemistry determines behavior — Behavior determines chemistry

Altered state of consciousness — Normal state of consciousness

S ➡ R — S ⬅➡ O ⬅➡ R

ACORN — OAK

The Genesis of ACORN Behavior

ACORN behavior is extremely widespread, both in organizations and among American managers. We use the acronym

ACORN to refer to both chemically dependent and MAD behaviors. In this context ACORN stands for *A*ddictive, *C*ompulsive *O*bsessive, *R*eally *N*utty behavior. The OAK is an *O*pen, *A*daptive, *K*nowledgeable human being. The OAK can be viewed as (a) the person who has never been addicted to a MAD chemical or a MAD behavior or (b) as an ACORN who has taken the first step and is now on the way to becoming an OAK again.[5]

The neurophysiological literature suggests that many people are stress-creators and stress-carriers because they get a high from the turmoil, turbulence, and agitation that they create either at work or in the home situation.[6]

Tepperman refers to the propensity of the ACORN to get turned on as a hereditary catecholamine metabolism pattern. According to this analysis, the hereditary catecholamine metabolism pattern of each individual is different—some people are quickly turned on by a crisis or a precipitating psychological disturbance, such as making the first bet on the part of the compulsive gambler. An OAK, on the other hand, has learned how to cope with precipitating psychological disturbances. Many American managers cannot wait for a precipitating psychological disturbance to occur; instead "they build fires just to put them out" or "they are so proud of their ability to stand up under a crisis that they are always manufacturing crises to stand up under." Management theorists frequently point out that "American managers actually enjoy crises; they often get their greatest personal satisfaction, the most recognition, and their biggest rewards from solving crises. Crises are part of what makes work fun."[7]

The attempt to change this kind of behavior by relaxation techniques or by attendance at sensitivity training programs seldom results in permanent change. The person may experience relief when relaxing or when participating in a sensitivity training program. The ACORN behavior almost always returns, however, when the person goes back to the environment that cues the precipitating psychological disturbance and the hereditary catecholamine metabolism pattern.

The addiction model asks that the ACORN "change playgrounds and playmates" in order to stay sober or to avoid compulsive gambling. The "winner" learns to cope with social situations that expose him or her to drinking or to gambling as time in the program increases. This is quite in contrast to the problems faced by the ACORN who returns to work (after stress therapy or T-group training) and to the same territory, the same colleagues, and the same situations that initiate the precipitating psychological disturbance. In the absence of a supportive group, "emotional sobriety" becomes difficult and perhaps even impossible of achievement.

There appears to be a common link among the early hyperactive behavior of children, the Type A Behavior Pattern, workaholic behavior, and the increased resort to substance abuse by successful people throughout our society. The following quotation describes these relationships well:

> I'm sure you've seen executives who are constantly moving. I see them in my office. They're worse than the kids, fidgety kinds of personalities, bundles of energy. It is acceptable because it is controlled. The person has somehow learned to adapt and control his behavior. He's not pushing the kid next to him or running around the classroom. He fidgets with feet or his hands constantly. I think this is what happens to some of these kids—they do eventually become fidgety adults. . . . The most effective method of working with hyperactive children is to channel the child's energy appropriately. Most successful people . . . are hyperactive; otherwise, how could they get so much done?[8]

As the hyperactive child grows up and becomes an adult, the arena of work replaces the classroom. The general manager, the line officer in the military, the professional, and the creative person tend to be tension-seekers in a stress-filled world. They are heterostats who glory in change. This tendency builds on the earlier hyperactive behavior of the individual and those work environments in which the Type A Behavior Pattern is viewed positively as an indicator of individual performance.[9] It is our contention that hyperactivity is a MAD behavior that causes the ACORN to become invisibly entrapped within a high-stress environment.

Much of the literature on workaholic behavior assumes that managerial ACORN behavior is necessary—that success requires this kind of adult hyperactivity. History confirms that many ACORNs have become successful people. It is significant that those factors that predispose to managerial success also tend to be associated with chemically dependent and MAD behaviors. They also are at the root of a lot of organizational and family stress.

The line manager, whether driven by the need for power or pushed by the need for achievement, or both, is a tension-seeking heterostat. The following describes the tension-seeking behavior pattern of such a person:

> Human beings need not be driven by outside pressures to explore, to think, to dream, to imagine, to seek out problems for a solution; their mental functions are constituted to do just that. They are not only *stimulus-reducing* and *problem-solving*, but also *stimulus-seeking* and *problem-finding* organisms.... The two explanatory paradigms—the tension-reducing and the tension-seeking accounts of behavior—are different ways of explaining motivation for creativity.[10]

The Two Faces of Power

In 1970, David C. McClelland published a paper with the title that appears at the head of this section.[11] As many readers are aware, McClelland devoted much of his early research to the study of the behavior patterns of people who are motivated by the need for achievement and how this need correlates with entrepreneurial behavior. McClelland frequently makes the point that such behavior is basic to industrialization.

Paradoxically, however, innovators and entrepreneurs with high needs for achievement seldom succeed as the professional managers of large organizations. To put it differently, entrepreneurship, or starting an organization, is a function in which need-for-achievement people excel. However, managing it after it has acquired a track record calls for professional managers with a very strong need for power.

McClelland argues that truly effective professional managers are motivated much more by the need for power than by the need for affiliation. He points out that there are two sides to the need for power—one malign, the other benign. The benign face he terms Authoritarian Institutional Power. The malign face is Authoritarian Personal Power (APP). It is the Authoritarian Personal

Power need that turns on the adrenalin afterburner of the ACORN who lusts for power and who is also turned on by thinking of drinking.

Many aspects of the behavior pattern of the Authoritarian Personal-Power individual remind us of the youthful bully who is cruel and mean to those who are younger and weaker. The Authoritarian-Personal-Power person is the impulsive, tough guy who continuously strives for a position of dominance over other people. He tends to be rude, often gets into fights, and uses women as pawns. Men with a strong Authoritarian-Personal-Power behavior pattern tend to drink heavily, are mean drunks, and have high rates of alcoholism. They use their cars as weapons and have a high incidence of automobile accidents. To the Authoritarian-Personal-Power type of person, personal loyalty is more important than individual responsibility or organizational commitment. Almost all the conquistadores and dictators of history have been motivated by a messianic, Authoritarian-Personal-Power drive to conquer the world.

Adolph Hitler provides the pristine example of a person driven by an overwhelming Authoritarian-Personal-Power need to conquer the world. The paranoia of power was not his only problem. The "adrenalin afterburner" to his hereditary catecholamine metabolism pattern and precipitatory psychological disturbance was addiction to amphetamines. This, according to medical authorities, "induced the recklessness that led him to run amok faster and faster until he attained his frightful goal."[12]

The Hestons point out, however, that it was not "speed" alone that fueled Hitler's drive for power. As they point out, "exercising unrestricted power in the long run is bound to have intolerable effects upon the ruler. *Power itself was the main drug underlying his activity.*"[13]

The Authoritarian-Personal-Power syndrome matches that of the Type A Behavior Pattern almost word for word. This face of power is turned on by drinking alcohol or by those situations in which the personal dominance of the (usually male) person is threatened. At that level of action, the two patterns may be described as a caricature of male chauvinism. McClelland argues that Authoritarian Personal Power is closely associated with heavy drinking, gambling, macho-type aggressive and competitive behavior, and the collection of "supplies" representing power such as convertible automobiles, male hunting trips, and Playboy Club keys.

The positive side of power is exemplified by Authoritarian Institutional Power. This type of manager behaves more like a coach than a drill instructor. In contrast to Authoritarian-Personal-Power person behavior, the Authoritarian-Institutional-Power person is more mature, less defensive, older and wiser, and less worried about his personal future. As McClelland and Burnham put it:

> The institutionalized-power manager is more successful at creating a good climate for regular work. His subordinates have both a sense of responsibility and a clear knowledge of the organization. They stick to the work rules, not because they are hit over the head, but because they become loyal to the institution.[14]

APP Behavior and Alcohol Use

McClelland suggests that Authoritarian Personal Power behavior correlates very closely with heavy drinking at the cultural, organizational, group, and individual levels. The essence of macho in many societies is to be able to drink a lot and to be able to hold one's liquor. The two go together—a high capacity for liquor is viewed as dysfunctional only if the drinker loses control of his behavior.

The first drink or two of an alcoholic beverage serves as a central nervous system stimulant although ethanol is actually a central nervous system depressant. Alcohol, particularly of the distilled kind, creates a burning sensation in the mouth and throat and this, according to McClelland, "stimulates the secretion of the adrenalin."[15]

Heavy drinking and low inhibition correlate very closely with a high need for power in virtually all parts of the world. McClelland points out that folktales from heavy drinking societies contain numerous references to hunting, to sharp weapons such as arrows, spears, and knives, and to violent vocabulary as manifested by such terms as smash, stab, cut, and chop. One would assume from this that an individual with high need for Authoritarian Personal Power would be very likely to choose drinking as a means by which to accentuate the feeling of power.

Authoritarian-Personal-Power drinking fantasies are focused on seeking to win over other active adversaries. To win, in the Authoritarian-Personal-Power context, is to exercise authority over the other members of the group. Thoughts about this face of power are strengthened by the drinking of alcohol—perhaps one reason why heavy drinking and manliness have been historically equated.

The Authoritarian-Personal-Power view of the world is "a 'zero-sum game' in which 'if I win, you lose' or 'I lose, if you win.' The imagery is that of the 'law of the jungle' in which the strongest survive by destroying their adversaries."[16]

The Jungle Fighter and the Gamesman

In 1976 Michael Maccoby reported on his study of 250 or so top managers in a dozen, highly successful, technologically advanced corporations. During the years since its publication, *The Gamesman* has become a management classic.

Maccoby classified the 250 managers he studied into four separate categories. These four categories were the jungle fighter, the gamesman, the company man, and the craftsman. The gamesman is virtually the same person as McClelland's Authoritarian-Institutional-Power-type, present-day, successful manager. In Maccoby's words:

> The modern gamesman is best defined as a person who loves change and wants to influence its course. He likes to take calculated risks and is fascinated by technique and new methods. He sees a developing project, human relations, and his own career in terms of options and possibilities, as if they were a game. His character is a collection of near paradoxes understood in terms of its adaptation to the organization requirements. He is cooperative but competitive; detached and playful but compulsively driven to succeed; a team player but a would-be superstar; a team leader but often a rebel against

bureaucratic hierarchy; fair and unprejudiced but contemptuous of weakness; tough and dominating but not destructive. Unlike other business types, he is energized to compete not because he wants to build an empire, not for riches, but rather for fame, glory, the exhilaration of running his team and of gaining victories. His main goal is to be a winner; his deepest fear is to be labeled a loser.[17]

Maccoby indicates that the jungle fighter resembles the gamesman very closely. The principal difference is that the jungle fighter uses power, not in the service of the organization, but to satisfy the jungle fighter's own ACORN needs. In doing this, the jungle fighter destroys himself in the process. The term jungle fighter is well chosen. Jungle fighters become "hooked" on power just as much as the addict becomes dependent on a substance. Because of this, jungle fighters who refuse to recognize their problems tend to succumb to this compulsion just as surely as practicing drunks are ruined by their addiction. The reader should note the resemblance to Hitler—both Maccoby's jungle fighter and McClelland's Authoritarian-Personal-Power-type manager are power-driven to the point that their behavior can actually ruin the organization.

Conclusion

Our research into the behavior of ACORN managers—those hooked to MAD chemicals or to MAD behavior or both—indicates that a serious flaw exists in both management theory and psychological theory about motivation and leadership behavior. We can illustrate this flaw by reference to Exhibit 9-2.

Cell number one of the four cell matrix in Exhibit 9-2 describes OAK-OAK interaction behavior in which both the superior and the subordinate behave in the normal state of consciousness. The other three cells illustrate situations in which the subordinate, the superior, or both are in altered states of consciousness. In these three cases either of the two or both may be hooked to a MAD chemical or a MAD behavior.

Study of Exhibit 9-2 suggests why T-groups and sensitivity training fell apart at the seams in recent years. It also explains why employer assistance plans work so well. T-groups and sensitivity

Exhibit 9-2: **ACORN—OAK Interaction Model**

	Superior	
	OAK	ACORN
OAK	1	2
ACORN	3	4

Subordinate

training assume that participants are in the normal state of consciousness—that change occurs as a result of rational discussion and intellectual persuasion.

By contrast the integrative theory as illustrated in Exhibit 9-1 is based on the fact that a large number of people are ACORNS who are hooked on MAD chemicals and MAD behavior. For those who would argue that we are making too big an issue of addictive behavior, it is worth noting that one leading authority on addiction recently discovered that about half the population is hooked to one form or another of MAD chemical or MAD behavior or both.[18] Given the prevalence of denial, we estimate that at least three out of five Americans are hooked on some form of MAD chemical or MAD behavior.

To the best of our knowledge, this chapter suggests for the first time in the management literature why change is so hard to initiate in organizations. This is particularly true of those cases in which the superior is the ACORN as indicated in Exhibit 9-2. Our discovery suggests that radical changes will have to occur in currently accepted theories of motivation and leadership behavior if American organizations are once more to become competitive on the world scene.

ENDNOTES

1. For a brief discussion of how catecholamines mediate behavior, see Chapter 8. Chapter 8 also develops much of the rationale for this chapter, including the literature survey.

2. A. T. W. Simeons, *Man's Presumptuous Brain: An Evolutionary Interpretation of Psychosomatic Disease* (New York: Dutton, 1961), 32.

3. John L. Weil, *A Neurophysiological Model of Emotions and Intentional Behavior* (Springfield, Illinois: Thomas, 1974).

4. Alcoholics Anonymous World Services, Inc., *Alcoholics Anonymous* (New York: 1955), 59.

5. For fuller discussion of ACORN and OAK behaviors, see Chapter 8.

6. Jay Tepperman, *Metabolic and Endocrine Physiology*, 3rd ed. (Chicago: Yearbook Medical Publishers, 1975), 162.

7. Robert H. Hayes, "Why Japanese Factories Work," *Harvard Business Review* (July-August 1981): 61.

8. Richard Hughes and Robert Brewer, *The Tranquilizing of America: Pill Popping and the American Way of Life* (New York: Harcourt Brace Jovanovich, 1979), 127-128.

9. M. Friedman, and R. H. Roseman, *Type A Behavior and Your Heart* (New York: Knopf, 1974).

10. Jacob W. Getzels and Mihaly Csikszentmihalyi, *The Creative Vision* (New York: Wiley, 1976), 240-241.

11. Dorothy N. Harlow and Jean J. Hanke, *Behavior in Organizations* (Boston: Little, Brown, 1975), 430-440. Republished from the *Journal of International Affairs*, 24, no. 1 (1970): 29-47.

12. Leonard F. Heston and Renate Heston, *The Medical Casebook of Adolf Hitler* (New York: Stein and Day, 1980), 20.

13. Ibid., 1. Italics supplied.

14. David C. McClelland and David H. Burnham, "Good Guys Make Bum Bosses," *Psychology Today*, December 1975, 70. A longer version of their study appears in the *Harvard Business Review* (March-April 1976): 100-110, under the title, "Power is the Great Motivator."

15. David C. McClelland, "The Power of Positive Drinking," *Psychology Today*, January 1971, 71.

16. Harlow and Hanke, *Behavior in Organizations*, 435.

17. Michael Maccoby, *The Gamesman* (New York: Simon and Schuster, 1976), 100.

18. Dava Fobel, "Almost Half of Sample in a Poll Reports Addiction," *New York Times*, 27 January 1981.

Part IV

Creativity, Education,
and Management for the Future

10

Creativity, Management, and the Minds of Man

Waino W. Suojanen

The creative process is undoubtedly one of the most personal and elusive through which human beings seek fulfillment and self-validation. Because of this, and because even the most articulate of people encounter blocks in attempting to analyze and describe something that is so personal and individual, very little has been done in the way of introducing an understanding of creativity and innovation into the mainstream of the management literature. Creativity is difficult to analyze and describe because it follows no fixed rules and appears to be based on no visible patterns of logic. In almost every respect, the creative process appears to be at variance with the frames of reference that are applicable to currently accepted theories of management and organizational behavior.

The management of creativity and the scheduling of invention were matters that drew a considerable amount of attention during the halcyon days of the aerospace age—roughly the time period from 1940 to 1970. The American government, and particularly the military-industrial complex, poured large sums of money not only into research, development, test, and evaluation, but also into projects that were focused on doing "research on research" itself. Particularly notable in the latter instance were the individual and institutional grants made by the National Aeronautic and Space

Reprinted with permission from *Human Resource Management* (Spring 1976).

Administration.

Numerous tools and techniques of management were developed within the military-industrial complex. Project management, matrix organization, and PERT (Program Evaluation Review Technique) have become so commonplace that they now hold an established position within the more traditional management literature. Courses on the management of research and development have been incorporated into the curricula of those schools of management that are located in geographical areas where numbers of scientists and engineers are employed in the technologically advanced industries.

During World War II, and subsequent years, many managers of research and development, along with management scientists, became convinced that linear, rational, and quantitative methods could be employed within the larger organization to improve problem-solving and decision-making processes. This despite the fact that the decision-making and problem-solving processes within the university and the laboratory, from which managers had come to work for the government, were much more oriented in the direction of autonomy and colleague authority than they were toward discipline and efficiency.

In recent years, this sort of logical, Cartesian philosophy has become ever more deeply embedded into the value systems of professional research and development managers whether in the public or private sector. More recently, a number of universities have embarked on crusades to improve efficiency and effectiveness. Many university administrators, who in the past preferred to rely on intuition, now feel impelled to pay at least a certain amount of lip service to a philosophy of management that focuses on Management by Direction and Management by Results as exemplified by the left end of the continuum in Exhibit 10-1.

There is little question that management science techniques have provided the professional manager with a far more rigorous and analytical kit of tools than were available prior to World War II.

Operational management prior to 1940 really consisted of nothing more than a potpourri of so-called "principles" that in some more or less mystical way were supposed to provide a frame of reference within which the manager could move toward efficiency and effectiveness. Whatever may be one's personal biases and

Exhibit 10-1: **Contingency Model of Leadership Behavior**

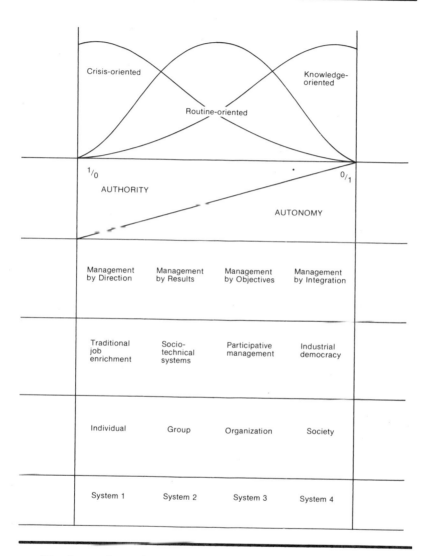

Management by Direction	Management by Results	Management by Objectives	Management by Integration
Traditional job enrichment	Socio- technical systems	Participative management	Industrial democracy
Individual	Group	Organization	Society
System 1	System 2	System 3	System 4

predilections, there is little question that operations research, systems analysis, and management science played a vital role in moving the industrialized world to undreamed heights of prosperity between 1940 and 1970.

Managers, whether they are operating within the orbit of the

Exhibit 10-2: Continuum of Leadership Behavior

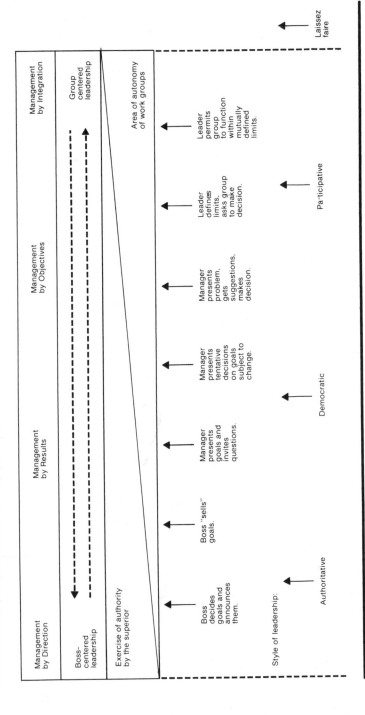

Management by Direction

Boss-centered leadership

Exercise of authority by the superior

Management by Results

Management by Objectives

Management by Integration

Group centered leadership

Area of autonomy of work groups

Boss decides goals and announces them.	Boss "sells" goals.	Manager presents goals and invites questions.	Manager presents tentative decisions on goals subject to change.	Manager presents problem, gets suggestions, makes decision.	Leader defines limits, asks group to make decision.	Leader permits group to function within mutually defined limits.

Style of leadership:

Authoritative

Democratic

Participative

Laissez faire

simpler, more naive theory of operational management, or whether they are being guided by the more complicated and sophisticated concepts of rational management, or by a combination of both, must constantly focus efforts on the *control* of the activities of other people. Any sort of control is based on explicit or implicit standards of production, the measurement of performance, the comparison of the actual work turned out against the standards, and correction of performance wherever that may be deemed neccessary. Management is almost totally an evaluative activity and, as such, requires that the person in charge continually *judge* the behavior of those working for him or her. In other words, without control and without judgment, the rationality of technology and the logic of organization structure lose their meaning. To put it differently, boss-centered leadership tends to be highly authoritarian—a point that is easily perceived by referring to the left side of Exhibit 10-2.[1]

In the years that have followed World War II, the advances in the cognitive aspects of management have been partially matched by advances in the behavioral aspects of the discipline. Some behavioral scientists, following the lead of the physical sciences, concentrated their efforts on the discovery and development of tools and techniques that would increase the efficiency and profitability of the organization. In one sense, it is plausible to argue that behavioral scholars of this persuasion have attempted to be as rational in their approach as their colleagues working in operations research or management science or systems analysis. At this stage in time, their successes have been no greater than their failures, yet they continue to try. Unfortunately, in the attempt to copy the physical and biological sciences, these behavioral scientists have either ignored or been unaware of recent advances in the neurophysiology and psychobiology of the human brain.

These advances suggest that human consciousness occupies a very important role in the creative process of discovering new knowledge and problem solving as well as in many aspects of decision making. Furthermore, our advancing knowledge of the mind of man provides evidence that suggests that behavioristic psychology provides an incomplete explanation of human motivation. By the same token, these research findings tend to confirm the position of humanistic psychology and the importance of autonomy in the affairs of men.

Determinism, Free Will, and the Old Brain

During the past ten years or so, significant progress has been made in the study of the human brain and its functioning. With every advance that occurs in our understanding of this most important and complex human organ, it becomes increasingly clear that many of our ideas about administration, and particularly the management of science and technology, will have to undergo drastic modification. As an example, scholars have discussed the issue of determinism versus free will for a number of centuries. Concerning this issue, Gevarter points out:

> The widespread existence of ardent supporters of both views suggests that each might possess some validity. Is there some way that one can resolve this dichotomy or fit the separate views into a more complete picture? A tantalizing approach is to try to utilize our evolving knowledge of the brain as an aid in seeking a solution.[2]

According to Gevarter, man has both an "old brain" and a "new brain" in the confines of his skull. The old, or visceral brain, consists of the hindbrain, the midbrain, and the limbic region of the forebrain. The visceral brain controls the animal drives of man as well as his motivational and emotional behavior. The visceral brain also appears to control memory, brain activation, program organization, and is concerned with selecting the behaviors that are appropriate to a given set of stimuli.[3] The medulla in the visceral brain serves as a switchboard that enables the reticular formation to alert the forebrain. The cerebellum, which is another part of the old brain, serves a "management by exception" function by deciding which situations and stimuli are worth noting and which can be ignored by being relegated outside the realm of awareness.

In crisis-oriented situations, according to Gevarter, the visceral brain automatically produces

> a response based upon a weighted integration of one's true values (old brain values), one's knowledge of the situation, and one's internal psychological stress. The decision is made so as to minimize the stress which would result from the failure to satisfy one's basic values and internal psychological pressures

in regard to the situation. It appears that this automatic reaction (gut decision) is usually heavily biased toward the present, with future needs given little weight. Particularly under emotional stress, there appears to be little choice as to the decision (i.e., short-range determinism). Free will is generally not associated with instantaneous action, but with awareness of what is taking place (see London, 1969, p. 269).[4]

The Gevarter-London thesis is consistent with the argument of the ethologists that a good deal of human behavior can, in a topological sense, be mapped by analogy from observations of the behavior of animals. Man, in terms of one perspective, is an animal who frequently behaves in emergency situations in ways that are prescribed by genetic endowment just as appears to be the case with primates and the higher animals.[5] In a more recent study, A.G. Kefalas and I discuss the repertoire of emergency behaviors of man which are ethologically consistent with the behavior of animals in critical situations.[6] From the viewpoint of management theory, this is highly significant. Man's earliest nonfamilial organization was probably the hunting group and even today this structure from the all-but-forgotten past still continues to determine much of our behavior in present-day institutions. In a very basic and almost blind sense, man as an animal still retains a penchant for the quick fix, the Band-Aid, the jury rig, because the visceral brain tends to overwhelm the new brain when man is confronted by a crisis situation or contingency.

A model of the "old brain" and the "new brain" or, alternatively, of the "three minds of man" is presented in Chapter 3, Exhibit 3-2. A detailed description of the new brains of man appears in the next section.

The Functioning and Unique Asymmetry of the New Brain

As the understanding of the neurophysiology and psychobiology of the cerebral cortex of man has advanced, it has become apparent that its structural symmetry is not matched by a similar pattern of functioning. Quite the opposite. The cerebral cortex consists, not of twin functional hemispheres, but of a left new brain and a right new brain.

In the normal, right-handed person, the left new brain is basically linear, time-oriented, rational, and analytic in nature. Mathematical and verbal capacities are located in the left new brain. By contrast the right new brain is nonlinear, intuitive, artistic, and creative in nature. It specializes in orienting us in space and is responsible for body images and the recognition of faces.[7] In connection with this, a comment by Levy is noteworthy:

> Considering these various results, I was led to the idea that perhaps there is an intrinsic antagonism between the modes of information processing of the two hemispheres. Perhaps a hemisphere which is capable of expressing itself in language does not merely have the capability of symbolic-analytic reasoning, but is, in fact, constrained to use such reasoning. Such a hemisphere thinks in terms of symbolic and not visual relationships. It tends to look at stimuli analytically, as if it intended to describe what it sees. If true, this idea provides a basis for understanding why in man, but in no other animal, there is such a profound functional differentiation of the two half brains. Once the ancestral hominids acquired the capacity for language, there would be an obvious adaptive advantage for that capacity to be confined to a single hemisphere, leaving the other free to carry on the perceptive Gestalt functions. Had both sides of the brain possessed language, there would have been a loss in visualization abilities. The old adage, "He can't see the forest for the trees" possibly expresses most succinctly the proposed antagonism. Perhaps a language-competent hemisphere is simply incapable of seeing forests.[8]

The ability of the right new brain to see the forest rather than the trees is overwhelming in its implications. Not only does the right new brain form patterns and structures and Gestalts of the world that exists—it can also do the same thing apparently insofar as future states and arrangements and even value systems are concerned. If there is a ghost in the machine, then it is located in the right new brain. Most significantly, the right new brain sometimes performs most optimally under states of consciousness other than the one of ordinary, everyday experience.[9] In this context, the right new brain thinks laterally and makes observations of the kind that ultimately result in new hypotheses.

The left new brain performs the judging-controlling-assessing functions that are necessary to observation, experiment, and induction in the scientific method. If research and development are functions of the right new brain, the left new brain performs the test and evaluation. Both, of course, are necessary to the process of conceptual (right new brain) variation and intellectual (left new brain) selection. The left new brain is rational and specializes in vertical thinking—that which is stepwise, correct, and relevant.[10]

It is clear that the truly creative individual is one in whom a balance exists between the cerebral hemispheres. The three princes of Serendip, according to Horace Walpole, were always making discoveries, by accident and sagacity, of things they were not seeking. Today serendipity is more often viewed in terms of the expression, "chance favors the prepared mind."

Chance, of course, is the perceiving right new brain which, in the creative person, can be likened to a radar which is continuously scanning the inner self and the outer environment for hypotheses which are ideally both simple and elegant. The prepared mind is the left new brain of the disciplined specialist. Serendipity then is a symbiosis of the Gestalt of the right new brain and the analytical functioning of the left new brain out of which new knowledge emerges. One way of summarizing some of the relations is presented in Exhibit 10-3.

Exhibit 10-3: **Scientific Method and Creativity**

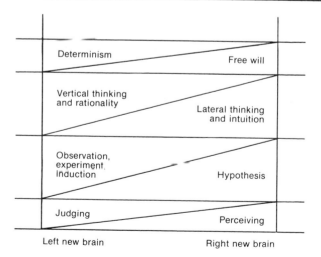

Left new brain	Right new brain
Determinism	Free will
Vertical thinking and rationality	Lateral thinking and intuition
Observation, experiment, Induction	Hypothesis
Judging	Perceiving

As we look to the future in this troubled world, in which policy has been formulated by crisis for six decades or more, it becomes clear that mankind must move from the quick fix, jury-rig, Band-Aid mentality of the visceral brain to something quite different. The following section outlines one approach toward identifying and cultivating creative potential early in life.

The Faces of Able Adolescents

In the fifties and early sixties, Elizabeth Drews was focusing her attention on the study of able adolescents and seeking a solution to the problem of identifying them while they were still relatively young.[11] The results of her research have been widely used by guidance counselors and admissions officers to determine which students constitute "college material" and which do not.

Drews developed a four-cell matrix and used the matrix as a means of classifying the students included in her samples. The matrix she used is shown in Exhibit 10-4.

According to Drews, about 20 percent of the members of her sample referred to themselves as social leaders, 60 percent felt they were high-achieving studious, and 20 percent thought of themselves as creative intellectuals. Only a small fraction, less than 1

Exhibit 10-4: **Types of Creative Adolescents**

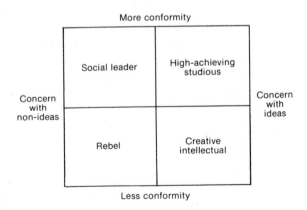

percent, were classified as fitting into the rebel cell of the matrix.

The basic values of the social leaders were described by Drews as being highly materialistic and hedonistic. They were competitive but tempered this by good-natured togetherness. In their day, the social leaders exemplified the vision that the outer-directed personality represented not only the soul of the present but also the savior of the future.

The high-achieving studious were followers of what is now called the Work Ethic but which a few years ago was known as the Protestant or Puritan Ethic. As indicated by the matrix, they were highly conforming in nature. This conformity was far more responsive to the demands of teachers than it was to the pressures exerted by their peer groups.

Drews discovered that male social leaders tended to become doctors, lawyers, and corporation executives when choosing their career patterns. Similarly, high-achieving studious males tended to become engineers and accountants (shades of Herzberg and the two-factor theory), whereas the females in many instances gravitated toward such traditional career patterns as teaching and nursing.

The creative intellectuals were far more interested in behavior and in process than they were in popularity and product. They tended to lend more weight to internal life than to external effect. Their efforts leaned toward the achievement of ultimate objectives rather than to the completion of immediate tasks. Teachers were apt to view them as prickly personalities who liked to ask below-the-belt questions and to make irreverent comments. Each tended to have his own system of values—to march in step with a different and individual drummer rather than to the peer group marching band or the symphony orchestra of their teachers. Drews pointed out that these were the adolescents who were to become the scientists, artists, writers, musicians, and scholars-at-large of a future generation.

The rebels, in the Drews sample, accounted for only a small percentage of the sample. The rebel, in the fifties and the early sixties could be viewed as an individualistic, creative nonintellectual. Rebels were clearly at odds with the school and the community but Drews felt that their alienation was largely a reaction to the kinds of rejection that they had experienced throughout their lives.

However, when attempts were made to relate to them in ways they understood and when they could "make sense" from their school work, Drews discovered that they could become highly motivated.

Some two decades later, the Drews matrix appears more explanatory of the past than predictive of the future. From an intuitive, right new brain point of view, there is little question but what the percentage of rebels has increased considerably and, given the matrix, the "new" rebels must have migrated into that cell from the "social leader" and the "creative intellectual" cells. The creative intellectuals and the rebels of the sixties are aware that there are creative solutions to the problems we face as a nation. This is well expressed in the following:

> We have exchanged old contradictions for new ones between our belief in social equality and our desire for self-validation and esteem. . . . The generation of the sixties, drawn to a vision of a society of equals more radical than our historical democratic ethic, represents only a new form in which this contradiction has been encountered.[12]

As one studies the Drews matrix from the viewpoint of the neurophysiology of the brain, it can be modified as indicated in the bottom part of Exhibit 10-5.

This brings us to the paradox of creativity. On the one hand, we profess to be highly concerned with the discovery and nurture of people who are right-new-brain dominant and can come up with solutions to the problems that beset mankind on every hand. In this approach, our "espoused theory" is supportive of creativity and innovation. On the other hand, or should I say on the "other brain," most managers have a "theory in use" that rejects creativity and innovation. This is true not only of the organization; family, the school, the religious association, all tend to act in a similar way. The objectives are there; they are determined by people in positions of higher authority, and woe unto the one who rocks the boat or rattles the cages or makes waves. Typically, the left new brain and the visceral brain function together to smother the questions and the hypotheses which are the natural output of the right new brain.

A number of years ago, one of the more innovative managers of research and development put together a set of guidelines for one who would change a right-new-brain, knowledge-oriented organ-

Exhibit 10-5: **Management and Creativity**

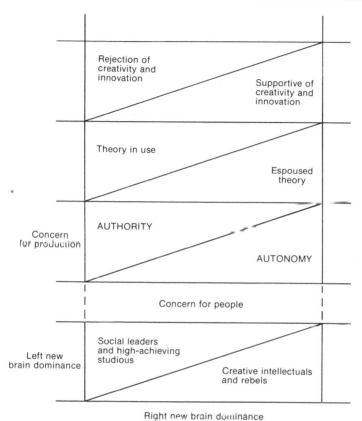

izacion into one doing routine, left-new-brain-type work. The reader should bear in mind that these guidelines are of the tongue-in-cheek variety and should interpret them from that point of view.

(1) Coordinate work carefully to avoid duplication. Everything new can be made to look like something we have done before or are now doing.

(2) Keep the reins tight; define tasks clearly; follow the rule book. If this is done, nothing very new will get a chance to be inserted.

(3) Concentrate on planning and scheduling and insist on meeting time schedules. New and interesting ideas may not work and always require extra time.

(4) Assure full output by insisting on rigorous adherence to the proper work day—in other words, don't be late. The creative man sometimes remembers his new ideas, but delay in working on them helps to dissipate them.

(5) Insist that all plans go through at least three review levels before starting work. Review weeds out and filters good ideas. More levels will do it faster but three are adequate, particularly if they are protected from exposure to the enthusiasm of the innovator. Further, insist that all proposals be put in writing.

(6) Suboptimize to assure that each component is as nearly perfect as possible. This leads to a wealth of "sacred" specifications that will be supported in the mind of the creative man by his earlier "believe teacher" training.

(7) Centralize as many functions as possible. This creates more review levels and cuts down on direct contact among people.

(8) Strive to avoid mistakes. This increases the filtering effect of review.

(9) Work for a stable, successful, routine-oriented organization. This decreases the need for change and justifies the opposition to it.[13]

Implications for the Manager

Since the end of World War II, we have lived in a world marked by continuing and accelerating "future shock" or, at least, that is what we have been told by the pundits and the publishers and the public opinion pollsters. Professors and politicians, by the peck, have climbed on this bandwagon.

I would like to suggest that this is wrong—that we have been fed a diet of change not knowing that the real staple has been stability.

Most management theorists, myself included, have acted under the *presupposition* that leadership styles were changing as a result of the new ideas that were being developed in our knowledge-oriented institutions, when actually we were operating under the old French heuristic rule of "plus ca change, plus c'est la meme chose"—"the more things change, the more they remain the same." If this observation is correct, and the current worldwide crisis in economic affairs as well as the almost universal concern with matters of survival tend to support this conclusion, then management theorists have a great deal of rethinking to do.

A first step toward such a reexamination has been taken by Frederick Herzberg in an article which bids fair to become a classic.[14] In this article, Herzberg recommends orthodox job enrichment as the organization improvement strategy that offers the most promise. If we take another look at Exhibit 10-1, we can see that this means going back to where we were before World War II to Management by Direction and to what Rensis Likert refers to as a System 1 philosophy of management.

It is my contention that Herzberg would have us turn back the clock at a time when it should really be turned ahead. With a wave of his hand, he has dismissed the results of a quarter century of creative and innovative behavioral science research. A much more useful perspective from which to view the future of management would be to ask, "What elements of behavioral science research are worth saving, given our current knowledge of the evolution of man, and the neurophysiology of the human brain?"

In contrast to the Herzberg thesis, our knowledge of the minds of man and their evolution are supportive of the behavioral science research findings of recent decades. The right new brain has a normative function—it seeks for the *ought to be* in human affairs just as humanistic psychology tells us to do. This means that work can be structured to satisfy human needs and to provide more meaning to the lives of people. Concern for production and concern for people do go together and can be jointly attained. There is no need, as Herzberg appears to imply, to move ahead by utilizing a retrograde strategy—that concept should have been well dispelled at the practical level by the Lordstown experience.

For those of you who are right-new-brain dominated, my parting words are hardly necessary. They are addressed to the great majority of American managers who are dominated by left-new-brain thinking. When your bucket is empty, twenty more people with empty buckets will not help put out the fire, but one long-haired radical with a full bucket can make all the difference. Next time an oddball idea crosses your desk, don't send it off to more left-new-brain reviewers. Your best filter is your own right new brain. The suggestion is hardly revolutionary, nor will it require anything extra in the way of time or money. All that is required is that you learn how always to give your right new brain and that oddball idea a fighting chance. And that decision could be the most important one you will ever make as a manager.

ENDNOTES

1. The original version of Figure 1 appeared in my book, *The Dynamics of Management* (New York, Holt, Rinehart and Winston, 1966), 104. Subsequent versions can be found in W.W. Suojanen, "Evolution, Ethology, and Organization," *Southern Journal of Business* (October 1970): 107-116; W.W. Suojanen and Stephen Brooke, "The Management of Creativity," *California Management Review* (Fall 1971): 17-23; W.W. Suojanen, "Motivation and Leadership," *Modern Office Management and Administrative Services,* Carl Heyel ed. (New York, McGraw-Hill), Section 8, 14-27; and W.W. Suojanen, "The Minds of Man and the Uses of Management Science," *Clemson University Review of Industrial Management and Textile Science* (Spring 1975): 51-66.

2. William B. Gevarter, "Man—His Brain and His Freedom," *The Journal of Humanistic Psychology,* 15, no. 4 (Fall 1975): 79-90

3. J.R. Smithies and W.R. Adey, *Brain Mechanism and Behavior* (Oxford, Blackwell, 1970), 154-155.

4. Gevarter, *Man—His Brain,* 5. The other reference is to P. London, *Behavior Control* (New York, Harper & Row, 1971).

5. See Chapter 1.

6. See Chapter 2.

7. For a more detailed, popular discussion of the functions of the left half brain and the right half brain, see Robert E. Ornstein, *The Psychology of Consciousness* (New York: Viking Press, 1972), 50-73, and Maya Pines, *The Brain Changers: Scientists and the New Mind Control* (New York, Harcourt, Brace, Jovanovich), 138-159. An excellent scientific discussion

can be found in Jerre Levy, "Lateral Specialization of the Human Brain: Behavioral Manifestations and Possible Evolutionary Bias" in *The Biology of Behavior*, J.A. Kiger ed. (Corvallis, Oregon: Oregon State University Press, 1972), 159-180.

8. Levy, "Lateral Specialization," 171-172.

9. See, for example, O.W. Markley, *Changing Images of Man* (Menlo Park, California: Stanford Research Institute, 1974), 199.

10. For a more detailed discussion of vertical and lateral thinking, see Edward de Bono, *New Think* (New York, Basic Books, 1967) or his article, "The Virtues of Zigzag Thinking," *Think*, May-June 1969, 8.

11. "The Four Faces of Able Adolescents," *Saturday Review*, 19 January 1963, 68-71.

12. Paul Starr, "Who Are They Now? Rebels after the Cause: Living with Contradictions," *New York Times Magazine*, 13 October 1974, 10.

13. A paraphrase of remarks by William B. McLean, Thirteenth National Conference on the Administration of Research, Rensselaer Polytechnic Institute, 29 September 1959.

14. "The Wise Old Turk," *Harvard Business Review* (September-October 1974): 70-80.

11

Creativity, Education, and Behavior: A Triune Brain Approach

Waino W. Suojanen

The numerous articles on the differing modes of functioning of the two halves of the human brain view the "left hemisphere" as a verbal-analytic brain and the "right hemisphere" as a spatial-intuitive brain. All of these articles appear to be based on the twin assumptions that (a) the two parts of the new brain have separate minds of their own and (b) that consciousness or awareness is located in the new brain.

Neither of these assumptions appears to be correct. A recent volume, to which all of the contributors are brain researchers, points out that "The split brain research, formerly so far-removed from data on normals, has recently done an about-turn, revealing that, at least after surgical recovery, the right hemisphere is not as different functionally from the left as originally thought."[1] In a more recent study, Niels A. Lassen et al. point out that "We have investigated speech processing in detail. Here we were impressed to find that both the right and the left hemispheres become active in much the same manner."[2]

The research literature indicates that cerebral asymmetry is much more pronounced in human males than it is in human females. Many popular articles understate the case for asymmetry because male data are combined with female data. At the present time it is almost impossible to bring to the surface the biological

181

paradigm that points out that the human brain is really a sex organ, because of a deeply rooted cultural paradigm based on the incorrect assumption that there is no difference between the male brain and the female brain. The following quotation covers this controversy in a very frank way:

> Though a great many topics in psychology are now politicized, nowhere is the ideological bias more entrenched, more unabashed and more arrogant than in the study of gender. The prevailing orthodoxy runs along these lines: that sex differences are trivial or superficial, in both degree and effect; that they exist only because of social conditioning; that this conditioning is designed to insure male hegemony; and that the ideal personality type is androgynous. Because there is very little evidence to support any of these beliefs, the case is often made not by argument but by intimidation. To question these ideas is to risk jeers and hissing when the issues are discussed in public and a torrent of abusive letters when they are debated in print. When a psychological topic becomes so completely hostage to ideology, we lose any capacity to think about it freshly or in depth. Contention absorbs all our intellectual energy. Granted that the adversarial posture is useful at certain moments in history of a scientific issue; more often it is not, and the more so when our knowledge is scant and the issue itself formidably complex. And what can be more complex than the question of sex differences? Both biological and social influences are at work in forming the differences; culture and class condition their expression; there are an extraordinary number of variables on which the sexes may—and generally do—differ; and the differences are unstable and change over the course of the life cycle.[3]

Although not all the facts are yet in, it is now clear that most of the early split-brain patients were males rather than females. In a well-known study in which male and female subjects were compared, Jeanette McGlone discovered that males indeed did appear to have virtually all their verbal abilities located in the left new brain but that women did not. The verbal abilities of the women whom McGlone studied were localized in the right hemisphere as much as they were in the left hemisphere. This led her to the conclusion that the "splitting of the brain into the rational, linguistic left and the feeling, spriritual, cosmic right was too elegant." Her findings suggest that language competence in men and women is organized quite differently. Females have speech control areas located in both the right and the left sides whereas in the North American male language tends to lateralize to the left.[4]

However, even in the case of the male of the species, language tends to lateralize to the left only in monolingual individuals. M. L. Albert and L. K. Obler make the following four points:

1. Language organization in the brain of the average bilingual may be more bilateral than in that of a monolingual.

2. Patterns of cerebral dominance may be different for each language in the brain of a bilingual.

3. Differential cerebral lateralization for each language is not random but is influenced by many different factors, including age, manner, and modality of second language acquisition.

4. Cerebral dominance for language in the bilingual is not a rigid, predetermined, easily predicted phenomenon; it is, rather, a dynamic process, subject to variation throughout life and sensitive to environmental, especially education, influences.[5]

Albert and Obler also emphasize that "it would no longer be correct to accept the traditional dogma that the left hemisphere is necessarily dominant for language in right-handers. This doctrine was obtained from many years of study in monolinguals and it probably remains correct for most monolinguals."[6]

They speculate further that the right hemisphere "may have as much capability to acquire language in adulthood as in childhood" and that "it may even be dominant for one of the languages of the bilingual."[7]

I can personally attest to the correctness of this speculation insofar as my own thinking is concerned. My first language was Finnish—a language rooted in the images and metaphors of a nomadic folk whose very nature has been shaped by the demands of a harsh and unyielding environment. When I think in terms of pictures or images or patterns or models of Gestalt, I use my right brain in a Finnish modality. Then, as I examine my plan or hypothesis, or daydream or fantasy, I revert to English and my left brain. In essence, my spatial-intuitive right-hemisphere mode of thought is Finnish and my verbal-analytic, left-hemisphere style is English.

This mode of switching from one language to another used to be a problem for me. Now, understanding the brain as well as I do, I am grateful for a gift that is quite rare and has proven of inestimable value to me in my professional work. Not many people are proficient in two languages, one of which fits into the spatial-intuitive right brain with the other processing data in the verbal-analytic style of the left brain. These two complementary languages represent the gift of creativity—the right side specializing in concept formulation and the left side in intellectual selection.

In contrast to some authors who write about the brain, I no longer use the terms "left hemisphere" and "right hemisphere" or "left half brain" and "right half brain." The reason for this is that human beings have a triune brain and consciousness appears to be located in the old, or visceral, brain as much as it is in the new brain or the cerebral cortex.

Since the publication of Ornstein's *The Psychology of Consciousness*, an unending stream of articles has appeared in the popular media explaining the separate ways in which the two hemispheres of the new brain process information. It is my contention that the principal reason for this popular preoccupation with the new brain is an anthropomorphic value system that assigns consciousness in man to the new brain level in order to prove that he is different from and, therefore, presumably superior to other social mammals, including the higher primates. Insofar as current research is concerned, there is virtually no evidence that the centers for consciousness or awareness are localized in the neocortex. Instead, recent advances in neurophysiology strongly indicate that the human brain is triune both in physiology and function, as suggested in Chapter 4, Exhibit 4-1. Following MacLean, who originally postulated the three-part brain, I assume that man's reptilian brain and his old mammalian brain together make up the "old," or visceral brain. The human "reptilian" brain includes the hindbrain and the midbrain—the paleomammalian brain consists of the limbic region of the forebrain. Man's neomammalian brain is composed of the left new brain (LNB) and the right new brain (RNB) as shown in Exhibit 4-1—these two parts of the cerebral cortex are connected to each other by the *corpus callosum*.[8]

In recent years, our understanding of the interplay between the left new brain and the old brain has advanced at a rapid rate. We can now view the brain, not as a device to do work, but as a communications machine to develop concepts and to select those that appear to be the most reasonable. At the heart of this process lies the right new brain and its activity. The right new brain continues to function both during sleep and during the normal state of consciousness, carrying on its functions at the preconscious level. The right new brain continuously develops concepts and hypotheses by scanning, ordering, selecting, and rejecting ideas. These ideas are then arranged in sequences by complementarity and separation on the basis of time, space, and causality. Operating cooperatively, the right new brain and the left new brain condense concepts into ideas on the basis of similarity and dissimilarity, nearness and distance, and finally by summarizing and coding.

The right new brain processes data at an extraordinarily rapid rate and with great freedom as it assembles and disassembles fantasies and daydreams into plans and hypotheses. The kind of processing performed by the right new brain is analogic. The left new brain, by contrast, takes the concepts and symbols of the right new brain and processes them digitally into words and numbers. A good many aspects of creative thought are unconscious—the right new brain operating in a preconscious mode in tandem with the subconscious operations of the visceral brain. Much of this processing takes place during REM (rapid eye movement) sleep.

Input into the brain originates from the surface of the body, from the internal organs, and from the environment. In common with the central processing functions that take place between the left new brain and the right new brain, the major part of this input is subliminal, that is, it is outside the conscious awareness of the neocortex.

At the neocortical level, input, internal processing, and output operate at the level of the right new brain. This highly developed symbolic processing system is continuously sampled by the left new brain. It is this conscious sampling of the stream of right-new-brain input, right-new-brain central processing, and right-new-brain output that is frequently referred to as "thinking" or "intellectual selection." The left new brain samples the "conceptual formulations" of the right new brain, tests and evaluates them, thinks about them at length, and communicates and relates these thoughts to other persons. All of this, in turn, is fed back into the right-new-brain stream where it undergoes modification on a delayed or a real-time basis, depending on the situation. In this sense learning, thinking, and creativity are all functions of the right new brain while the processes of sampling, thinking about, testing, and communication are functions of the left new brain.

How does the visceral brain enter into this picture? There is always distortion in the relationships of left-new-brain signs in their roots in the animal nature of man. The word or the number itself is never a visceral brain construct; rather it is the relationship between the sign and what it represents that becomes distorted and displaced and is incorporated into the visceral brain. This distortion, in turn, feeds back many visceral brain disturbances to the new brain, particularly in stressful situations and in addictive and habitual maladaptive behaviors. This sequence follows a new brain-old brain-new brain pattern.

There are many ways of formulating the relationships that exist among the minds of man. However, the most relevant is the one which we are faced with here, namely, the problems of learning and, most importantly, the problems of how to protect the freedom of right-new-brain processing in learning, in education in general, and in creativity. The freedom that must be preserved is the "conceptual" function of the right new brain in a world that is concerned almost totally with left-new-brain education and training. What is needed here is the freedom from an excessive concern with literal, pedestrian, left-new-brain realities along with its liberation from the addictive, compulsive, and obsessive distortions of the visceral brain. This is a challenge that education has not had to face in the past. We must come to grips with these issues now—the world of the "third wave" is one of crisis and continuous change. Crisis, emotion, and the fight-or-flight response are the province of the visceral brain, just as continuous change is mediated by the right new brain.

Both left-new-brain and visceral brain processes tend to be fixed and rigid because the former holds its intellectual values almost as strongly as the latter clings to its evolved instincts. In the normal state of consciousness, the symbolism of the right new brain is anchored to a literal reality. This symbolism is very much akin to the behavior of a patient who has gone to see a psychiatrist with secret orders never to tell the truth to any question that the therapist may ask. This stereotyping influence of the combined visceral brain/left new brain is found in the works of certain creative people in almost every field. The artist paints the same painting time and time again. The poet writes and rewrites the same poem. The social scientist continues to grind the same scientific axe throughout a lifetime. This kind of behaviorism leaves its personal signature on the painting or the poem or the theory. This mentality explains the behavior of the person who produces only one painting or only one first-rate piece of theoretical work during a career. This is the price that is paid when the sense-feel-do survival instincts of the visceral brain combine with the sense-feel-obey intellect of the left new brain so strongly that the sense-feel-create expression of the right new brain emerges only once in a lifetime.

The human brain, in a sense-feel-create mode, swiftly condenses and combines the intellectual inputs of the left new brain and the emotional inputs of the visceral brain. It readjusts experience on a real-time basis, while condensing reality, because it does not have to operate in the space-and time-bound constraints of the verbal-quantitative left new brain.

Many dissimilar ingredients can be rapidly reshuffled in creative thought, provided that the visceral brain is operating in a complementary mode with the right new brain. The visceral brain will compete with the right new brain when it feels that the survival of the organism is threatened. Such a threat need not be physical, that is, one originating in the environment. Much more destructive to creative thought is a high level of arousal—so high in fact that the visceral brain shifts into the fight-or-flight response. When this takes place, chemistry determines behavior, and all the resources of the human organism are deployed for self-preservation.

How, then, can creativity flourish if it has to operate between the strictures imposed by the visceral brain and the left new brain? The answer to this depends on the autonomy of the right new brain as it shifts into the creative, problem-finding, intuitive mode. The visceral brain and the left new brain complement the right new brain, as they complement each other, through "Janusian thinking" and "homospatial thinking." Janusian thinking includes "actively conceiving of two or more opposite, contradictory or antithetical concepts, images, or ideas simultaneously" whereas "homospatial thinking" consists of "actively conceiving two or more discrete entities occupying the same space, a conception leading to the articulation of new identities."[9]

Remember that the three minds of man operate concurrently as one total system. Anything that we do, anything that we say, anything that we think (whether we are sick or well) is the composite result of these three minds operating together. Because each mind also performs its own processing, it is permissible to use the terms *processing* and *mind* as synonyms. When we dream, when we are consciously creative, or when we are preoccupied with the routine affairs of life, the three minds tend to work and function together. The only important difference lies in the relative role played by each of these components in a given situation. When a manager is concerned with a crisis, the visceral brain does most of the processing. When a file clerk is routinely filing a folder, the left new brain is responsible for the greatest share of the processing. When a scientist is studying a biological process and developing hypotheses about its operation, the right new brain predominates in the total functioning.

Some years ago, A. Harry Klopf explored the hypothesis that each individual neuron in the brain seeks pleasure and avoids pain.[10] In common with current neurophysiological theory, Klopf localized consciousness in the midbrain and the thalamic reticular formation rather than in the new brain. Klopf argues "that intelligence in complex systems (such as the brain) is a concomitant of a striving for a maximal condition. We may term this heterostasis." According to this theory, the classroom would be a limited heterostat. Such a system is defined with respect to the controlling subsystem. In the case of the classroom situation, the limited heterostat also may be said to be the teacher, in that when the teacher seeks to maximize his or her own pleasure, the teacher also largely determines the course of the learning because other participants subsume their own need achievement to that of the teacher. They do so because they are subordinate to the teacher and obey the teacher's authority.

By contrast, the left-new-brain, problem-solving approach to education is based on the concept of left-new-brain homeostasis. Educators often equate their goals with personal survival. For this reason many of them get along by "going along." Klopf points out that homeostasis is a subgoal to the maintenance of heterostasis. To the extent, then, that we focus our attention on educating and training people to operate in a left-new-brain, routine-oriented environment, we are training children to be functionaries rather than heterostats who can deal with constant crisis and continuing change.

These ideas are especially relevant to the education and training of administrators. Organizations pursue both internal goals and external goals. Homeostatic left-new-brain behavior is directed at maintaining an equilibrium between the organization and its environment. Visceral brain behavior is heterostatic—each partici pant must adjust to change and this increases arousal. High arousal is present in creative behavior and even higher arousal is present in the fight-or-flight response. Educational administrators tend to have a strong, sense-feel-do, visceral brain approach to crisis-oriented situations in which decisions must be made rapidly and correctly. This is the behavior of Michael Maccoby's "gamesman" or David McClelland's "authoritarian institutional power" type manager exemplified in Exhibit 11-1.

As shown in the figure, administrative functions are more crisis-oriented and knowledge-oriented than they are routine-oriented. Line administrators avoid the homeostatic, sense-feel-obey functions of the technical staff functionary almost like the plague, seeking instead high arousal heterostatic situations. Decision making, visceral-brain situations and problem-finding, right-new-brain situations are pleasurable and are sought; problem-solving, left-new-brain situations are avoided by delegating them to technicians.

As our understanding of the functioning of the human brain increases, it is increasingly evident that many of the things we are doing, both as teachers and as administrators, will have to be changed if we are to meet the challenges of the crisis-oriented, continually changing world that now is looming on the horizon. As soon as possible, we must accept the fact that "the brain can change, and the teacher is responsible, in part, for providing the environment in which these changes can occur."[11]

Exhibit 11-1: **Balance in Leadership**

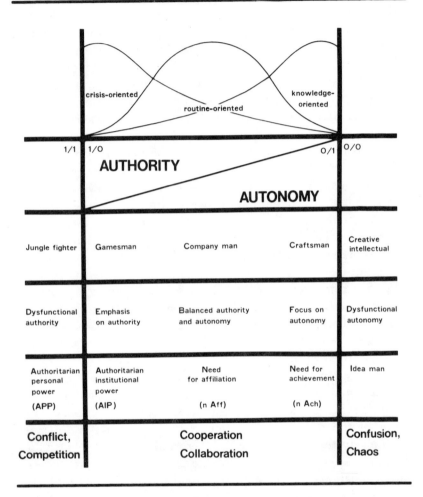

ENDNOTES

1. Stevan Harnad and Robert W. Doty, Sr., "Introductory Overview" in *Lateralization in the Nervous System*, Stevan Harnad, et al., eds. (New York: Academic Press, 1977), XLVIII.

2. "Brain Function and Blood Flow," *Scientific American*, October 1978, 69.

3. Joseph Adelson, "The Dream of Androgyny," *New York Times Book Review*, 9 March 1980, 3.

4. *Psychology Today*, October 1978, 29-31. See also Jeanette McGlone, "Sex Differences in Functional Brain Asymmetry," *Cortex*, 14 (1978): 122-128; Jeanette McGlone and Wilda Davidson, "The Relationship Between Cerebral Speech Laterality and Spatial Ability with Special Reference to the Sex and Hand Preference," *Neuropsychologia* 2 (1973): 105-113; and Diane McGuinness and Karl H. Pribram, "The Origins of Sensor Brains, Development of the Gender Differences in Perception and Cognition," reprinted from *Cognitive Growth and Development Essays in Memory of Herbert G. Birch*, Morton Bortner, ed. (New York: Brunner-Mazel, Inc., 1978).

5. *The Bilingual Brain: Neuropsychological and Neurolinguistic Aspects of Bilingualism* (New York: Academic Press, 1978), 253.

6. Ibid.

7. Ibid.

8. Paul D. MacLean, "The Brain's Generation Gap: Some Human Implications," *Zygon* (June 1973): 113-127. MacLean, Director of the Laboratory of Brain Evolution and Behavior, National Institute of Health, has written extensively on the triune brain. In common with Penfield, he locates the decisive mind in the old brain, the visceral or emotional brain.

9. Albert Rothenberg, "Homospatial Thinking in Creativity," *Archives of General Psychiatry*, 33 (January 1976): 18.

10. *Mental and Physical Phenomena: Toward a Unified Theory* (Air Force Avionics Laboratory, Wright-Patterson AFB, Ohio 45433), mimeographed draft, 1977.

11. Marcanie Frosting and Phyllis Maslow, "Neuropsychologic Contributions to Education," *Journal of Learning Disabilities*, 12, no. 8 (October 1979): 40.

12

Productivity, Creativity, and Managerial Behavior: A Triune Brain Approach

Waino W. Suojanen
R. Carlton Bessinger

Recently, much attention has been devoted to the twin problems of the apparent lack of pride in productivity and the decreasing concern for craftsmanship in the American organization. Much of this criticism has focused on such factors as the adverse effect on productivity of government regulations, the problems posed by inflation and increasing energy costs, and the stultifying effect of labor unions on output. Instead, may it not be the case that we are managing our way to economic decline?[1]

Robert Hayes and William Abernathy argue that lack of pride in productivity and concern for craftsmanship represent a failure of leadership on the part of American industry. This, in turn, is at least partly a function of the way management is taught in our leading business schools.

Current management theory evolved during the quarter century extending roughly from 1948 to 1973. In that routine-oriented world only a few members of top management had to behave in a "holistic" manner—only they, of all those in an organization, assumed the role of heterostat in crisis- and knowledge-oriented situations and as homeostat in routine-oriented situations. Hetero-

Reprinted with permission from the Southern Management Association *Proceedings*, Atlanta, Georgia, 1981.

stats can be described as those managers who are most effective in dealing with crises and continuing change, as those who actively seek high arousal, tension-generating situations. Homeostats, on the other hand, are more effective in intellectual problem solving and in the maintenance of a stable, routine environment.

Arousal and Management Behavior

The sense-feel-do, crisis-oriented situation, and the sense-feel-create, knowledge-oriented contingency, both call for and reward heterostatic, tension-seeking behavior. The basic problem, of course, is that a system functions best when there is minimal deviation from a prescribed course of action. A smooth course of action and a low level of tension go together—this is the practice of "management by exception" as that concept is discussed in management literature. A smooth course is best attained, however, by tension-seeking heterostats who are motivated by sense-feel-create and sense-feel-do challenges. These three types of managerial behaviors, and the relationship among them, are presented in Exhibit 12-1.

Many managers tend to overreact to *tension-seeking*, crisis-oriented and knowledge-oriented situations. In neurophysiological terms, these managers have a hereditary catecholamine metabolism pattern that is turned on by a "precipitating psychological disturbance."[2] The manager with the high hereditary catecholamine metabolism pattern often displays a Type A behavior pattern.[3] There is considerable evidence that the hereditary catecholamine metabolism pattern is turned on much more by crisis-oriented and knowledge-oriented precipitating psychological disturbances than it is by routine-oriented situations.

As our understanding of the functioning of the human brain increases, many of the concepts of the current paradigm that focuses on routine-oriented behavior will have to be changed if we are to meet the challenges of the crisis-oriented, continually changing world of today. We must accept the fact that "the brain can change, and the teacher is responsible, in part, for providing the environment in which these changes can occur."[4]

Recent advances in neurophysiology strongly indicate that the holistic, macro, human brain is triune in the micro in both physiology and in function. This three-part brain is composed of the old, or visceral, brain and the two halves of the new brain, or neocortex. In a recent monograph, A. Harry Klopf has explored the implications of the visceral brain concept along with the hypothesis that each individual neuron in the brain seeks pleasure and avoids pain.[5] In agreement with the most recent neurophysiological theory, Klopf localizes consciousness in the midbrain and the

Exhibit 12-1: **Situations and Managerial Behavior**

	Crisis oriented situation	Routine oriented situation	Knowledge oriented situation	
	Heterostasis	Homeostasis	Heterostasis	
	Sense- feel- do	Sense- feel- obey	Sense- feel- create	
	Decision making	Problem solving	Problem finding	
	Tension seeking	Tension reducing	Tension seeking	

thalamic-reticular formation of the visceral brain, rather than in the new brain.[6] He argues that intelligence in complex systems (such as the brain) is a concomitant of a striving for a maximal condition, and he defines this maximal condition as *heterostasis*. Following this line of thought, the organization can be viewed as a limited heterostat with the chief executive officer occupying the key position. When the chief executive officer seeks to maximize his own pleasure, he also determines the course of the organization and other participants subsume their own need achievement to his. That is, they are subordinate to him and obey his authority.

The present-day line manager has to cope with many more crisis-oriented situations and knowledge-oriented contingencies than was the case just a few years ago. The tension-reducing style of the sense-feel-obey manager of the past was relevant to the stable, routine-oriented, pre-OPEC world. The world today, by contrast, is characterized by crisis—one follows another almost in a routine fashion. The tragedy of American managers and American management theory today is that both continue to focus on the routine-oriented situations, which makes sense only if the situation requires behavior in which the manager can "repeatedly follow a given course of action."

Management Theory and the Brain

Articles discussing the differing modes of functioning of the "left hemisphere" and the "right hemisphere" of the human brain now appear with increasing frequency both in the management and the training and development literature. This literature views the "left hemisphere" as an analytical-verbal brain and the "right hemisphere" as an intuitive-synthesizing brain. In a widely quoted article, Henry Mintzberg argues that planning takes place in the left side and managing is a function of the right side of the human new brain.[7] Mintzberg bases much of his discussion on the volume by Robert Ornstein titled *The Psychology of Consciousness*.[8]

The publication of Ornstein's book ignited a spate of articles about the new brain in the media. Virtually all of these articles assume that (a) this new brain has a mind of its own and (b) that consciousness or awareness is located in the new brain.

Neither of these assumptions appear to be correct. In agreement with Klopf, we assign consciousness to the older visceral brain.

The Triune Brain

The current theory assumes that managers almost always behave rationally. Because of this, the Ornstein and Mintzberg approach ties in perfectly to an anthropomorphic value system that assigns consciousness in man to the new brain level. This approach assumes that man is different from, and therefore presumably superior to, other social mammals, including the higher primates. Insofar as neurophysiology and psychobiology are concerned, there is little evidence that there are centers for consciousness or awareness in the neocortex. Instead, and we repeat ourselves in order to underline what we are saying, recent empirical advances strongly indicate that the human brain is triune both in physiology and in function as suggested in Exhibit 5-1, Chapter 5. Following MacLean, we assume that man's reptilian brain and his old mammalian brain together make up the "old," or visceral, brain. The human "reptilian" brain includes the hindbrain and the midbrain—the paleomammalian brain consists of the limbic region of the forebrain. Man's neomammalian brain is composed of the left new brain and the right new brain. These two parts of the cerebral cortex are connected to each other by the *corpus callosum*.[9]

Why use the term "old brain" when referring to the visceral brain and the expression "new brain" when discussing the neocortex?[10] According to Simeons and many other theorists, the old brain dates back about two hundred million years.[11] The new brain evolved on top of the old brain and the new brain is about twenty million years old. Many animals have little or no neocortex; clearly, in these cases, the decisive mind is located in the old brain.

In 1961, a 48-year-old war veteran underwent a surgical procedure in which the *corpus callosum* was severed.[12] The important thing to bear in mind is that this surgical procedure, known as a commissurotomy, causes very little change in the temperament, personality, or general intelligence of the "split brain" patient. The sensory input system remains virtually comparable to that of a person who has not undergone the operation.

This suggests that the integrative mind is not in the new brain but in the old brain. Even though the left new brain and the right new brain cannot communicate with each other directly, they can do so indirectly through the decisive mind as illustrated in Exhibit 5-2, Chapter 5.

The Pain and Pleasure Areas of the Visceral Brain

The decisive mind receives input also from the pain areas of the visceral brain as well as from the pleasure areas. As MacLean puts it, in referring to this part of the brain, "many of the creative, emotional, and spiritual impulses ascribed to the right hemisphere are more properly attributable to the limbic system" i.e., the visceral brain.[13]

The pleasure areas are located on the right side of the brain along with the right new brain. Similarly, the pain areas are located on the left side of the left new brain. This makes for a symmetrical model and one that has support in the neurophysiological literature.[14]

The left new brain and the pain areas work together in sensing pain and mediating the emotional behavior of the individual. Similarly, the right brain, consisting of the right new brain and the pleasure areas, mediates pleasure-producing behaviors. In the normal state of consciousness, the pain and the pleasure inputs into the decisive mind are in balance and the organism is in a state of homeostasis. Movement either to the "right" or the "left" moves the animal to pleasure or to pain respectively and thus to a state of heterostasis.

Movements to the right characterize euphoria, eustress, experimental drug use, and positive addiction. Movements to the left are illustrated by dysphoria, distress, addictive substance use, and negative addiction. Homeostasis, or an equilibrium situation, is exemplified by equiphoria, stress, and the normal state of consciousness.

Summary

General management functions in the future will be much more crisis-oriented and knowledge-oriented than routine-oriented.

General managers and military line officers tend to avoid the homeostatic, sense-feel-obey, functions of the technical staff functionary as they seek instead to become involved in high arousal, heterostatic situations. Decision making satisfies the arousal needs of the visceral brain and problem/opportunity finding provides a similar outlet to the right new brain. The heterostatic, line manager avoids problem-solving, left-new-brain situations by delegating them to staff functionaries.

Some years ago, two articles commented on the proper role of operations research/systems analysis in the broader field of management theory and organizational behavior.[15] The authors felt that a number of proposals, suggesting that change was overdue in management theory, had died because of a general lack of interest. They felt that the Star Trek television series provided an analogy that could be used to explain to management theorists and to practitioners what the management scientists and operations researchers do and how their work relates to the broader goals of the organization.

Rick Hesse and Steve Altman viewed the decision-making process on board the USS Enterprise as a responsibility shared jointly by Captain Kirk, Mr. Spock, and Dr. McCoy. In their model, Captain Kirk was the decisive, line manager; Mr. Spock the analytical, management science specialist; and Dr. McCoy the intuitive, behavioral science expert. The essence of decision, according to this model, is triune—three minds combine to select an optimal course of action. We agree with their analysis and have embodied aspects of their analysis into this chapter.

Captain Kirk is the key figure in every crisis-oriented situation in which the USS Enterprise is involved. It is his responsibility to make decisions—to evaluate and select one from a number of alternative courses of action. Decisions of this kind are characterized by high stress, short time intervals, and value conflict. Captain Kirk, however, does not work in isolation. As shown in Exhibit 12-2, he is the decisive line officer; Mr. Spock represents the analytical (left new brain) management science specialist; and Dr. McCoy is the intuitive (right new brain) behavioral "scientist." The essence of *deciding what to do*, according to the model, is triune. Three minds combine to select an optimal course of action. Captain Kirk, however, always remains in charge of the *doing* and is responsible for his actions. (For a fuller discussion of the Star Trek model, see Chapter 4.)

Exhibit 12-2: **Star Trek, Management, and the Brain**

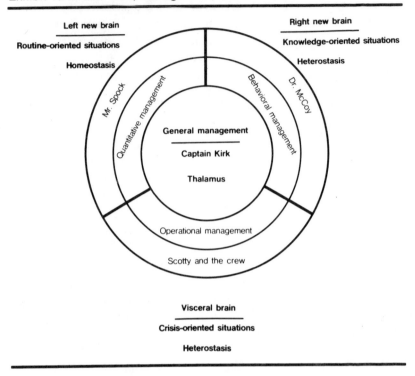

Knowledge-oriented situations, like their crisis-oriented coun- terparts, are also characterized by a high degree of arousal. People who are creative, who are motivated by a need for achievement, tend to be tension-seekers. They enjoy the "high" they experience when they find an opportunity or when they create something new. Knowledge-oriented situations appeal to the person with a strong, right-new-brain, sense-feel-create orientation. The point is that it is just as exciting to "formulate and develop new courses of action" as it is to make decisions, that is, "to select one from a number of possible, alternative courses of action."

Present-day management theory, as it has evolved since the end of World War II, has focused its attention almost totally on left- new-brain, routine-oriented situations. Traditional theory and the systems approach both emphasize problem solving and a world in which the solutions to these problems "repeatedly follow a prescribed course of action." Current management theory and practice assume that the environment is one of certainty, when it is basically one of risk and crisis-oriented situations on the one hand and uncertainty and knowledge-oriented contingencies on the other.

Exhibit 12-3: **Situations, Primary Ability Called For in that Situation, and Location in Organization**

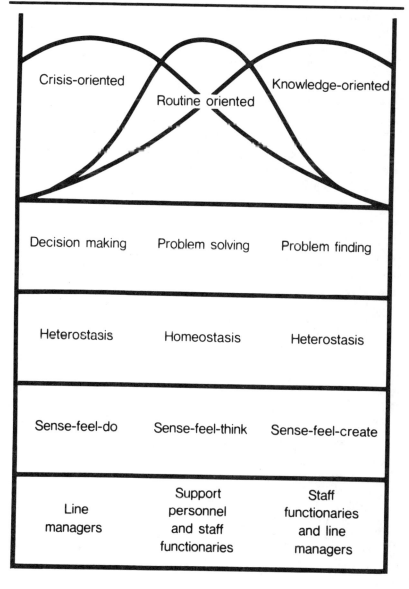

Crisis-oriented	Routine oriented	Knowledge-oriented
Decision making	Problem solving	Problem finding
Heterostasis	Homeostasis	Heterostasis
Sense-feel-do	Sense-feel-think	Sense-feel-create
Line managers	Support personnel and staff functionaries	Staff functionaries and line managers

Significantly, the newer generation of management theorists consists largely of "number crunchers" whose specialty is to teach us more and more about less and less as they foray ever deeper into the numerical abysses of the A QUIVER, left new brain. Incongruously enough, their generation was preceded by one that was as much concerned with developing the "sense-feel-obey" concepts of bureaucracy as the current generation is obsessed with sense-feel-think and sense-feel-obey rational behavior patterns. Both cases illustrate the old axiom—"give a child a hammer and he will find nails to pound."

We would like to point out that the integrative theory, as we have partially outlined it in this paper, indicates quite clearly that the management theory jungle exists only because the current paradigm makes assumptions about the world and about the functioning of the human brain that are incorrect.

We are not suggesting we throw out the routine-oriented, left-new-brain approach to management theory that says we "repeatedly follow a given course of action." We must retain that approach, but we must also pay greater attention in our theory to the crisis-oriented, visceral-brain situation in which the manager "evaluates and selects one from a number of possible alternative courses of action" and the knowledge-oriented, right-new-brain contingency in which Captain Kirk, along with Mr. Spock and Dr. McCoy, focuses on "formulating and developing new courses of action." Exhibit 12-3 summarizes what we have said in this Chapter and what is presented in the other Exhibits.

ENDNOTES

1. Robert H. Hayes and William J. Abernathy, "Managing Our Way to Economic Decline," *Harvard Business Review* (July-August 1980): 67-77. For the military counterpart to this, see Richard A. Gabriel and Paul L. Savage, *Crisis in Command: Mismanagement in the Army* (New York: Hill and Wang, 1978).

2. Jay Tepperman, *Metabolic and Endocrine Physiology*, 3rd ed. (Chicago: Yearbook Medical Publishers, Inc., 1975), 162.

3. Meyer Friedman and Ray H. Roseman, Type A Behavior and Your Heart (New York: Knopf, 1974).

4. Marcanie Frosting and Phyllis Maslow, "Neuropsychologic Contributions to Education," *Journal of Learning Disabilities*, 12, no. 8 (October 1979): 40.

5. *Mental and Physical Phenomena: Toward a Unified Theory* (Air Force Avionics Laboratory, Wright-Patterson AFB, Ohio, 1977), mimeographed draft.

6. Ibid., 67-118.

7. "Planning on the Left Side and Managing on the Right Side," *Harvard Business Review* (July-August 1976): 49-58. See also, Benjamin B. Young, Jr., "A Whole Brain Approach to Training and Development," *Training and Development Journal* (October 1979): 44-50.

8. San Francisco: Freeman, 1975.

9. Paul D. MacLean, "The Brain's Generation Gap: Some Human Implications," *Zygon* (June 1973): 113-127. MacLean, Director of the Laboratory of Brain Evolution and Behavior, National Institute of Health, has written extensively on the triune brain. In common with Penfield, he locates the decisive mind in the old or visceral or emotional brain.

10. A. T. W. Simeons, *Man's Presumptuous Brain* (New York: Dutton, 1961), 11-28.

11. Glynn U. Isaac and E. R. McCoron, eds., Human Origins: Louis Leakey and the East African Evidence (Menlo Park, Calif.: Staples Press, 1976), 1-54.

12. Michael S. Gazzaniga, "The Split Brain in the Man," *Scientific American*, August 1967, 24.

13. Constance Holder, "Paul MacLean and the Triune Brain," *Science* (8 June 1979): 1068. For a much more detailed description of the functioning of the pain areas and the pleasure areas, see John L. Weil, A Neurophysiological Model of Emotional and Intentional Behavior (Springfield, Ill.: Thomas, 1974). Weil, like MacLean, locates pain and pleasure behaviors in the old brain.

14. Frank H. Netter, *Nervous System*, vol. 1 (Summit, N.J.: CIBA Pharmeceutical Co., 1975), 76.

15. Dieter Klein and Paul Butkovich, "Can the Professions of Operations Research/Management Science Change and Survive?," *Interface*, (May 1976): 47-51; and Rick Hesse and Steve Altman, "Star Trek: An Optimum Decision Making Model," *Interface* (May 1976): 60-62.

13

Management Theory, Behavior, and the Biohavioral Sciences: A Focus on Gender

Gary B. Roberts
Waino W. Suojanen

Major advances in understanding and theory have occurred during the past decade in the "biohavioral" sciences: biology, ethology, sociobiology, and neurophysiology. It is our contention that, as soon as possible, teachers and practitioners of management must begin to incorporate these concepts into both theory and practice. Management theory, except for a few articles in the journal literature, and a few nods in this direction in the textbooks, has virtually ignored the fact that the biohavioral sciences are moving rapidly into the area staked out only recently by the behavioral sciences: psychology, sociology, and anthropology. The purpose of this chapter is to discuss the reasons why management literature ignores or resists the data of the biohavioral sciences. To this end, we focus on the topic of sex differences and management as illustrative of both the challenges and difficulties present in this integration.

Ignorance of the literature is one reason why management theory continues to ignore the results of research in the biohavioral sciences. This, however, need not be a major obstacle. Some thirty years ago, management theorists were ignorant of or ignored the

Reprinted with permission from the Southern Management Association *Proceedings*, Atlanta, Georgia, 1981.

findings of the behavioral science literature. During the decade of the fifties, behavioral science material was integrated into the body of management theory, serving both the theorist and the practitioner better than the older "principles" approach alone had done.

Two other assumptions that management theorists have adopted are also to blame. According to this concept, management theory evolved in an enlightened and truth-seeking discipline, open to opposing views and subject to change as necessary. At the present time, however, many theorists feel that the discipline is in good repair and that its basic content need not be changed. Although a few have expressed concern about this refusal to change, most theorists are content with the status quo. There is really no compelling need to subject the discipline to continuous, intellectual account-taking, they contend, because the foundations are so firmly established.

This first assumption allows a second to exist. Because of the behavioral orientation, theorists denigrate the practical application of the biohavioral sciences. This contentment with subject matter content is a function of the fact that the field has avoided much of the controversy that has plagued so many of the other behaviorally oriented disciplines during the past thirty years. Some go so far as to argue that the paradigm that guides management research enables the discipline to steer clear of political and ideological biases. This is dangerous, because as Robert Duban indicates, a discipline only does research into those areas recognized as viable by the prevailing paradigm and avoids investigation of those areas that do not fit into it.[1] It is our contention that the current management paradigm does not allow for empirical research that tests biohavioral hypotheses because of the single-minded focus on the testing of hypotheses based solely on environment and to the exclusion of those arising from nature. Stereotypes are an acceptable subject for research, because the paradigm knows how to deal with them; genotypes and phenotypes, however, fall outside the bounds of the paradigm, and are simply not the subject of "polite" investigation and discussion within the profession. To suggest that behavior may be biologically determined is to drop over the edge of the paradigm into an area that really states, "don't confuse me with the facts, my mind is already made up."

By failing to consider much of the relevant information about human action developed outside of the accepted behavioral science and management research channels, we water down our contribution to the practitioner. Is this really a serious issue? Are there areas where the biohavioral sciences could contribute?

We believe that the data of biohavioral sciences will make a far greater contribution to management theory in the future than will the behavioral sciences. The assumptions of the biohavioral sciences stem from empirical scientific studies, whereas the assumptions of the behavioral sciences are based on cultural values.

Nowhere is the research need greater, the ideological bias more entrenched, the positions more arrogant, than in the study of gender and management. The prevailing orthodoxy dogmatically holds the following to be fact:

(1) Sex differences are trivial or superficial in both their degree and their effect when it comes to managerial success.

(2) Sex differences exist only because of social conditioning.

(3) Social conditioning is designed to ensure male dominance in the managerial arena.

(4) The ideal managerial style is androgynous.

(5) The appropriate purpose of both law and management theory is to move as expeditiously as possible toward this ideal style.

Little empirical research exists to support this orthodoxy, and hence the case is often made not by argument but by intimidation and law. When one questions these ideas in public, one does so at the risk of jeers and hissing, and when one questions them in print, one risks a torrent of abusive letters.

> When a psychological topic becomes so completely hostage to ideology, we lose any capacity to think about it freshly or in depth. Contention absorbs all our intellectual energy. Granted that the adversarial posture is useful at certain moments in the history of a scientific issue; more often it is not, and the more so when our knowledge is scant and the issue itself formidably complex. And what can be more complex than the question of sex differences? Both biological and social influences are at work in forming the differences; culture and class condition their expression; there are an extraordinary number of variables on which the sexes may—and generally do—differ; and the differences are unstable and change over the course of the life cycle.[2]

The literature of the biohavioral sciences is replete with empirical research that will help us increase our understanding of those differences between male and female that have a biological basis and that result in differences in behavior. Almost none of this material has found its way into the management literature. How long can we safely continue to ignore biohavioral research data such as that which follows?

As illustrative of our case, Camilla Benbow and Julian Stanley recently published the results of a very sophisticated study of sex differences in mathematical ability.[3] Their research strongly suggests a substantial sex difference in mathematical reasoning ability (scores on the mathematics portion of the Scholastic Aptitude Test) in favor of boys in a study of 9,927 intellectually gifted junior-high-school students. Their data contradict the assumption that differential course taking accounts for observed sex differences in mathematical ability and supports instead the hypothesis that these differences are gender-related. Similar conclusions, in less rigorous form, have been reported by Eleanor Maccoby and Carol Jacklin.[4] In their review of over two thousand books and articles on sex differences, they found that males are better at mathematics. Although the two sexes are similar in their early acquisition of quantitative concepts, at the age of twelve or thirteen, boys improve in mathematical skills much faster than do girls.

We are concerned about the implications of the Benbow and Stanley study for practicing managers, management researchers, and for teachers of managers. We are also convinced that management theory will ignore these data because they fall outside of the bounds of the literature that are within the accepted paradigm and because they challenge the current cultural orthodoxy. Past experience with similar research intensifies our concern.

Management theory, as we know it today, is based on the assumption that all behavior is learned and that its shaping is totally a function of nurture—of the environment. Each of us, according to this approach is born a tabula rasa—a clean slate. As we grow and learn, our behavior is shaped by those individuals, objects, and processes in the environment that are unique to each human being. This assumption comes to management theory from the behavioral sciences of psychology and sociology—disciplines that have provided so much to the shaping of management theory since the end of World War II. The assumption that human behavior is totally a matter of nurture currently dominates every aspect of management theory. Recent findings in the disciplines of ethology, sociobiology, and neurophysiology indicate otherwise— that human behavior is as much a function of nature or heredity as it is of nurture or environment.

A recent publication in the *Academy of Management Review* discussed at length the study of the sex structuring in organizations and commented that "Major findings for studies relating to sex differences in leadership style suggest that there may be fewer differences in the leadership behavior or style of males and females than *commonly held stereotypes* might suggest."[5]

This article has an excellent review of the management and psychological literature pertaining to the topic. However, not one of the 83 items included in that bibliography makes any reference to any publication in the biohavioral literature. A reader not familiar with the biohavioral literature may, as a result, conclude that the only relevent factors that should be investigated are commonly held sexual stereotypes and that such stereotypes all arise from the culture; that is, they are totally a result of environmental factors. By contrast, reference to the biohavioral literature shows conclusively that there are sexual differences in the brain and that these result in sexual variations in behavior. The biohavioral approach then asks the question: what differences in behavior result from these imparities? Causality, from the biohavioral point of view arises not only from cultural stereotypes but is also a function of the genotype and the phenotype. Sociobiology, the biology of sociology, goes so far as to suggest that the environmental stereotype is virtually always rooted in a biological foundation. We cannot understand these environmental behaviors, these commonly held stereotypes about differences in sexual behavior, unless we explore the hypothesis that many culturally conditioned patterns of behavior do indeed rest on some very basic sort of a biological substrate.

Management theory and its offshoots have systematically ignored and indeed, actually rejected, the results of biological research since the beginning of the twentieth century. Now, along with the behavioral sciences of sociology, psychology, and anthropology, management theory faces a fundamental intellectual challenge from the biohavioral sciences that will not only not go away but that will instead come to change our discipline completely by the end of the century. This challenge is so sweeping that our initial inclination may be to dismiss it or to ignore it. To accept it will require a complete reorientation of management theory. The findings of Edward Wilson,[6] and of many other ethologists and sociobiologists, are so encompassing in their scope that we dismiss them and ignore them only at the peril of maintaining an obsolete theory.

The recent lawsuits by Sears, Roebuck and Company against the federal government attest to the fact that national policy, by incorporating the assumptions of the behavioral and social sciences into application, now operates in such a way that obeying one law often forces one to be a lawbreaker in some other area. For this, the theory of management is as much to blame as is the law. The tragic aspect of all this is that both management theory and the law fail us at the very moment that American society is facing the worst crisis in its history—the decline in productivity, the loss of pride in craftsmanship, and the challenges posed by reindustrialization.

The inclusion of the biohavioral sciences into the management paradigm will force us to address the concepts of genotype and phenotype on a par with the issue of stereotype. This will change management theory in many respects. As long as we focus on the relatively straightforward concept of stereotype, the solutions are easy. Get rid of the stereotype and things will go well. Thus, Executive Order 11246 specified that any contractor with the federal government was required to develop a detailed plan to eliminate any sexual discrimination within the organization. Just as management theory focuses on discrimination based on stereo-types, national policy solves the problem by passing laws.

Both management theory and the law assume that a combination of sanction and training will break the cycle of stereotyping and discrimination. Some of the literature even hints of an unidentified male conspiracy that seeks to reinforce the prevailing stereotypes. The current response to conspiracy and discrimination based on stereotype is training and legal action. From a biohavioral point of view these responses to genotype and phenotype are poor biology and hence will prove to be poor policy. Law and theory raise the level of expectations of women, without addressing the basic biohavioral factor that it is the female who bears the baby and it is the mother who nurtures the child in all mammalian species. Only the human female pursues both motherhood and career—the current cultural stereotype states she can do both well if only her mate will share in the nurturance functions. Recently, in a front page article the *New York Times*, however, proclaimed that "Many Young Women Now Say They'd Pick Family Over Career."[7]

How will addressing the issues of genotype and phenotype help management theory? On the assumption that much of the research on stereotype is still valid, what we are suggesting is that biohavioral research is complementary with such an orientation. The integrative management theory should prove more useful because it recognizes innate differences between the sexes and among individuals. These differences are not deficits, but they do set biases and limits on behavior. From this realization, the course is clear. Diane McGuinness puts it as follows: "In a highly evolved species like *Homo sapiens*, culture can effectively alter biases, but unless the predispositions are recognized, intervention can proceed only by trial and error."[8] Many observers, for example, have described affirmative action and equal opportunity as being based on trial and error. The failure of these two programs has come about largely because the current paradigm—both in management theory and the law—is based on poor biology or better yet, on no biology at all.

One implication derived from biological data that requires immediate action on the part of the academic management community relates to the Benbow and Stanley study about sex differences and mathematical ability. These research results have a direct and immediate impact on one of the controversies raging within the profession. This debate is addressed to the issue of how much of the management curriculum should be devoted to quantitatively oriented subject matter. Accredited business schools must follow the recommendations of the American Assembly of Collegiate Schools of Business (AACSB) and now require a considerable number of quantitative courses within the management curriculum. Decision making and problem solving, in this context, are viewed as largely quantitative endeavors. The content of many required courses is determined by this viewpoint. The AACSB has adhered to this policy in spite of the fact that recent research by such authorities as Henry Mintzberg, John B. Miner, David McClelland, Michael Maccoby, and Charles H. Ford, suggests that there is virtually no correlation between quantitative skills and managerial success.[9]

When we combine these observations with those of Benbow and

Stanley, it becomes apparent that it is actually the AACSB and its member schools, in their curriculum policies, that are actually perpetuating discrimination against women! One-half of the Graduate Management Admissions Test (GMAT) measures mathematical ability and approximately one third of the required courses in the typical management program are quantitatively oriented. This, despite the fact that the evidence suggests that successful managers need be neither mathematicians nor statisticians. If equal opportunity is one of the bedrocks of our democracy, then we can hypothesize that our schools of business are sabotaging this policy if, as Benbow and Stanley point out, there are basic sexual differences in quantitative competence.

Do we argue that mathematics should be eliminated from the curriculum? For everyone? Only for women? By no means! The biohavioral perspective does not argue that there is a genetic determination of what men can do compared to women; rather, it suggests that the biological contributions shape what is learned and that there are differences in the ease with which the sexes learn certain things. What is clearly called for is a rethinking of the quantitative content of much of the curriculum of the American business school. What is predictive of success must be identified and retained. If it calls for a certain level of mathematical aptitude, then compensatory training must become an accepted, mandated part of the management curriculum.

By concentrating on problems purportedly caused by sex stereotyping, current management theory has increasingly come to ignore information that suggests that many of our most pressing management problems have their roots as much in genetics and "biohavior" as they do in environment and behavior. Until we include research data from the biohavioral sciences in our discipline, management theory will remain an inadequate guide to the practitioner. This is particularly true as far as sex differences are concerned. Biology tells us that:

> Women in all cultures are likely to care for the newborn and to prepare food for household consumption. Men can learn such skills, but as a group, they are less apt to show ease in infant handling and food preparation than women are. We know from the Soviet experience in training women cosmonauts and the Israeli experience in training women soldiers that

specialized training of women is necessary to compensate for the male advantage in large musculature. A similar compensatory training may become necessary if more men are to care for young infants. This is an important point to realize in an era when egalitarian ideology argues against innate sex differences and assumes that a unisex education will suffice to remove whatever sex differences currently exist. It is unrealistic to expect that we will achieve within a few generations a 50-50 distribution by sex in most human activities and occupation. It is doubtful that a unisex socialization alone can have that effect; it will require compensatory training of girls in some areas, boys in others. Since evolutionary changes take place at an infinitely slow pace through long stretches of time, each generation of males and females would require compensatory training. For many generations to come, any slackening of institutional effort directed to compensatory training of the sexes will quickly be followed by a return to sex differentiation as a consequence of the ease with which certain skills are learned by one sex and not by the other.[10]

As soon as possible, management theorists must become familiar with the research data of the biohavioral sciences and begin to incorporate these findings into the mainstream of the discipline. The issue of sex differences, as we have discussed it here, will not be resolved until the biohavioral aspects are thoroughly understood and judiciously applied. This is true for every area of concentration and special interest in the field. Just as management theory incorporated the data of behavioral sciences into the discipline in the early decades after World War II, so it is now time in the 1980s to begin to integrate what the biohavioral sciences have added to what we know about human behavior. We look forward to a time when management theory is enriched by these new concepts and ideas, and when we have a biohavioral special interest section in the Academy of Management.

ENDNOTES

1. Robert Duban, "Theory Building in Applied Areas" in *Handbook of Industrial and Organizational Psychology*, Marvin Dunnette, ed. (Chicago: Rand-McNally Co., 1976).

2. Joseph Adelson, "Dream of Androgeny," *New York Times Book Review*, 9 March 1980, 3.

3. Camilla Persson Benbow and Julian C. Stanley, "Sex Differences in Mathematical Ability: Fact or Artifact?" *Science*, 210 (12 December 1980): 1262.

4. Eleanor E. Maccoby and Carol N. Jacklin, *The Psychology of Sex Differences* (Stanford: The Stanford University Press, 1974).

5. Kathryn M. Bartol, "The Sex Structuring of Organizations: A Search for Possible Causes," *The Academy of Management Review*, 3, no. 4 (October 1978): 805.

6. Edward O. Wilson, *Sociobiology: The New Synthesis* (Cambridge, Mass.: Belknap Press of Harvard University Press, 1975), 242-335.

7. Dena Kleiman, "Many Young Women Now Say They'd Pick Family Over Career," *New York Times*, 28 December 1980, 1.

8. Diane McGuinness, "How Schools Discriminate Against Boys," *Human Nature* (February 1979): 82.

9. Henry Mintzberg, *The Nature of Managerial Work* (New York: Harper & Row, 1974); John B. Miner, *The Challenge of Managing* (Philadelphia: Saunders, 1975); David McClelland, *Power, The Inner Experience* (New York: Free Press, 1973); Michael Maccoby, *The Gamesman* (New York: Simon and Schuster, 1976); Charles H. Ford, "The 'Elite' Decision-Makers: What Makes Them Tick?" *Human Resource Management* (Winter 1977): 14.

10. Alice S. Rossi, "A Biosocial Perspective on Parenting," *Daedalus* (Spring 1977): 4.

14

Situational Management: Today's Theory, Tomorrow's Practice

Waino W. Suojanen

Every manager, in the course of a day or a month or a decade, is called upon to manage in three basic types of situations or circumstances or contingencies. Each of these situations is as old as mankind itself and, as a matter of fact, there is an increasing amount of evidence to suggest that the development of the minds of man is a response to the requirements of coping with these three fundamental circumstances of life.[1] In this chapter, I shall look at each of these circumstances in turn and suggest how the reader should behave in situations that call on him to be a boss, a manager, or a leader as the case may be.

Depending on the issue at hand, each manager is called upon to operate in three basic problem-solving or decision-making environments. These three contingencies focus on (a) adaptability to a crisis, (b) productivity or efficiency in the performance of established procedures, and (c) planning for changes initiated within the organization. The three types of situations are identified in Exhibit 14-1 as (a) crisis-oriented (b) routine-oriented, and (c) knowledge-oriented in nature.

Each of these contingencies can be related to a fundamental form of human organization. The tactical combat unit in the military provides the model for the crisis-oriented organization although

Reprinted with permission from *Business and Public Affairs*, Volume 3, Number 1 (Fall 1976).

many paramilitary associations resemble it very closely. For example, public safety functions such as firefighting and police work are performed by highly structured, authoritarian organizations.

The factory, or the mass data processing operation, provides an example of a routine-oriented organization. The "ideal type"

Exhibit 14-1: **Contingency Model of Leadership Behavior**

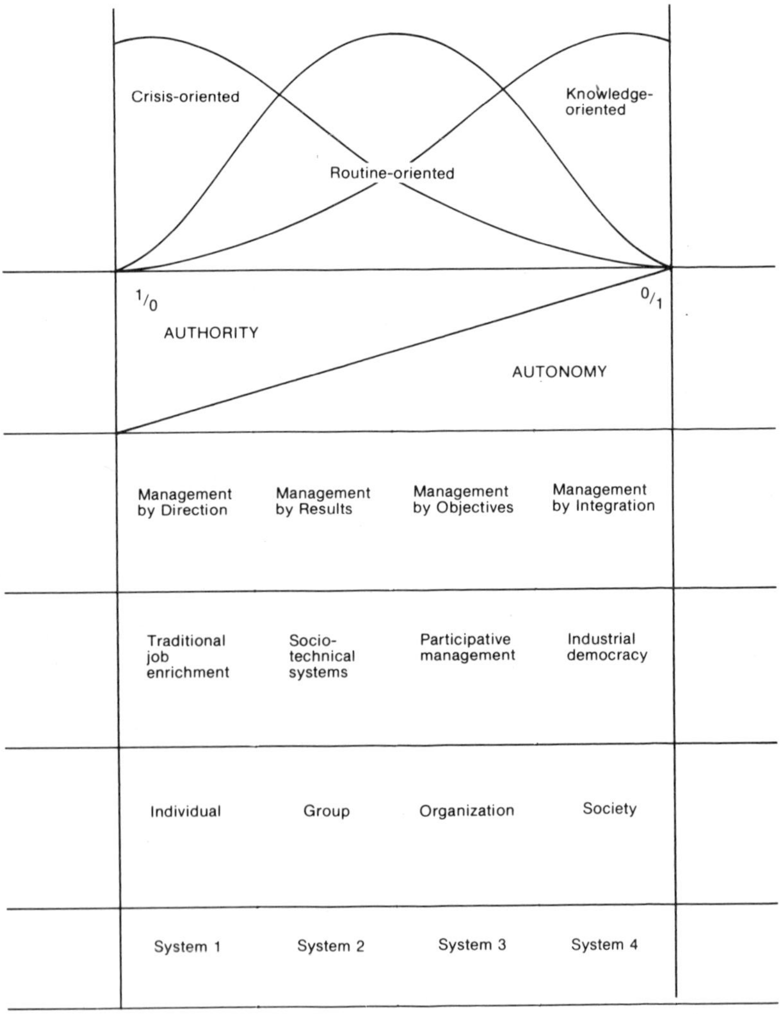
Crisis-oriented
Knowledge-oriented
Routine-oriented
1/0
0/1
AUTHORITY
AUTONOMY
Management by Direction
Management by Results
Management by Objectives
Management by Integration
Traditional job enrichment
Socio-technical systems
Participative management
Industrial democracy
Individual
Group
Organization
Society
System 1
System 2
System 3
System 4

bureaucracy, discussed by Max Weber, focuses its attention on routine activities in which relations and activities are regularized and simplified. In organizations of this kind, routine operations are governed by rules that prescribe exactly how the work is to be performed.

A good example of a knowledge-oriented organization is a long-range planning group in a large corporation. The probability that an organization will survive is much greater if it *initiates* or *generates* change rather than if it is so managed that it is almost always *reacting* or *adapting* to change. The expression "a good offense is the best defense," with which all of us are familiar, is the reason for being of all knowledge-oriented functions in the organization.

Leadership Styles

The continuum of motivational styles ranges from Management by Direction through Management by Results and Management by Objectives to Management by Integration. These various approaches are listed in Exhibit 14-2.

Management by Direction is boss-centered as indicated in the second panel of Exhibit 14-2. By contrast, Management by Results and Management by Objectives fall in-between the two extremes of the continuum and tend to be manager-centered. Management by Integration, in turn, is leader-oriented.

A few decades ago, one often heard the phrase "the manager gets things done" as a nutshell description of the process of motivation. It is evident, from a scrutiny of Exhibit 14-2, that this definition is boss-centered and highly authoritative. If the boss does not delegate authority—if he tries to do everything himself—he will move his organization from one crisis to another. A motivational style that is totally boss-centered, no matter what the situation, will tend to be ineffective because the essence of management is coordinating the efforts of other people rather than making all the decisions and solving all the problems. Nonetheless, many people continue to rely on a boss-centered leadership style because they find it hard to adjust their approach to the requirements of the given situation.

The boss who gets things done may be suffering from a Type A behavior pattern. As the discoverers of this kind of behavior put it:

> The great difficulty the Type A subject experiences in delegating work to others is only in part due to his "hurry sickness." It is also due to his belief that *all* his activities require his right hand and only *his* right hand. Nothing can be delegated to anyone else. This chronic refusal grows out of the basic insecurity of the Type A subject. He fears that even the slightest error in performing a task may topple his total structure of past achievements. Each task to be done appears to be too important to risk failure—and trusting an associate or subordinate simply increases the risk to an unacceptable point.[2]

Under the traditional concept of *management by exception*, most of the time of the person in charge should be devoted to work that is either problem-solving and knowledge-oriented in nature or to decision making of the crisis-oriented kind. The Type A finds it impossible to plan for and initiate change or to handle emergencies calmly. Being obsessed by time, he tries to do everything himself. He treats almost every issue that occurs as a flap or a fire fight. The typical Type A boss cannot operate except in terms of *reactive*, crisis management. By contrast, the Type B person is *proactive*—one of his basic responsibilities is constant improvement utilizing the genius in the organization as a resource to this end.

More recently, the phrase "the manager gets things done through people" was in vogue for a number of years. The human relations movement made a lot of managers realize that people are different from buildings and equipment—that they often react in predictable yet different ways to dissimilar leadership styles. There were, however, two basic flaws in this approach to motivation. First, the phrase smacked of master-slave type manipulation rather than of motivation. "Working through" people sounds quite condescending. Second, this concept tended to become confused with the issue of managerial prerogatives. This was particularly true in the United States. Admit it or not, motivational styles in this country are still mainly boss-centered and give every indication of remaining so for a number of years to come.

Management by Integration is based on the fundamental assumption that "the leader gets things done with people." The difference between this idea, and the one in the previous paragraph, is the distinction between *through* and *with*. Management by

Exhibit 14-2: Continuum of Leadership Behavior

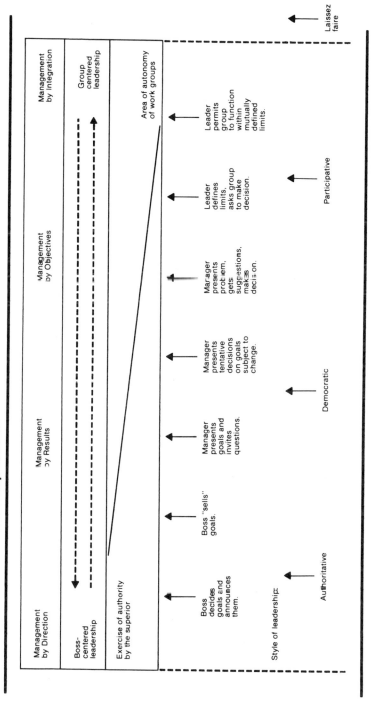

Results and Management by Objectives, are *through* and, as suggested in Exhibit 14-2, they tend to be democratic rather than participative in nature. By contrast, Management by Integration views the person in charge as a teacher-leader-counselor who relies on a highly participative style of the kind discussed in the following parts of this chapter.

Management by Direction and to a lesser extent both Management by Results and Management by Objectives are based on assumptions about human behavior and motivation that were in vogue until roughly the middle of the twentieth century. In all of these older management theories, decision making about important issues is viewed as the prerogative of the top management of the organization. The structure is a pyramid of superior-subordinate channels of command like those which characterize the armed forces. Obedience to formal authority is the highest value held by the members of the organization. External punishment, direction, and control are fundamental. The task is of central importance: people are replaceable. The boss, as the agent of higher authority, sees to it that people stick to their jobs and to the work in the way that has been prescribed by top management.

Management by Integration, which lies toward the right end of the continuum in Exhibits 14-1 and 14-2, makes completely different assumptions about human behavior. We know that people tend to resist objectives, tasks, and changes which are imposed upon them by management. Knowing this, we substitute for centralized decision making and employ human creativity (the genius in the organization) to help attain the objectives of the organization rather than permitting it to be focused on subverting them. Under Management by Integration, the leader recognizes both that he is an integral member of the work group and that he must also serve as its agent in representing it to top management. Because he is both a member of management and the spokesman and the motivator of his group, the leader relies more on acceptance authority than on formal authority. One of his principal responsibilities is to help the members of his group to grow and become self-actualizing human beings rather than serving merely as a policeman for higher authority.

Analysis of Leadership Styles

The alert reader will already have noticed that Exhibits 14-1 and 14-2 share many features in common. Every model in Management by Integration always reads from the left to the right—from the old to the new, from the less desirable to the more desirable, from authority to autonomy. This means that the best combination of efficiency of output and equity for people is on the right-hand side of these exhibits.

Both Exhibits 14-1 and 14-2 have a panel that contains a diagonal line. This diagonal line announces that the manager encounters a number of situations every day that are neither black nor white but consist rather of varying shades of gray. The diagonal tells the reader that the model is a spectrum or a continuum or a scale and that an infinite number of situations or contingencies or circumstances are covered by it. This is in contrast to a dichotomy, which is limited by its very nature to only two opposites such as black and white.

Think of the continuum between the two vertical lines in Exhibits 14-1 and 14-2 as a society, an organization, a group, an individual. Between the lines we have a system of cooperation or collaboration. Given the association, the boss can retain all the authority indicated by a 1/0 at the left end of the continuum, and delegate none to his subordinates. Conversely, the leader can delegate all of his authority to the members of the group, illustrated by the 0/1 at the right end of the spectrum, and retain none for himself. The most common situation is one of shared authority. It includes those contingencies such as .7/.3 or .2/.8, lying between the ends of the 1/0-0/1 scale.

Management by Direction, Management by Results, and Management by Objectives tend to focus on the principles of management as the source of guidance to the leader. Management by Integration is quite different. Rather than trying to apply universal principles across the board to any given contingency, Management by Integration instead defines leadership as follows:

1. The leader understands the situation.

2. The leader understands the requirements of the situation.

3. The leader decides or acts in accordance with the needs of the situation.

Over the course of time, the style of leadership under Management by Integration will move toward the group-centered approach and away from the boss-centered arrangement. However, this does not mean that there is no authority under Management by Integration. Without authority, leadership becomes meaningless and the organization perishes. Even in the most group-centered situation someone has to have the final say. President Harry S. Truman said it both elegantly and simply with a sign he had on his desk—"the buck stops here."

The important point to bear in mind about Management by Integration is that we never eliminate authority, but that it must always be exercised in accordance with the

1. Values of the society;
2. Policies of the organization;
3. Norms of the group;
4. Needs of the individual.

If there is a lack of congruence among these four areas, problems will arise.

The Venerable Vintage Vikings

The move from traditional job enrichment to industrial democracy in the United States will be extremely slow and will probably not come to pass in this century. It is indeed sad that the country that has been the world leader in political democracy has at the same time become the most autocratic of nations as far as the industrial and economic spheres are concerned. The overwhelming tragedy is that the United States may possibly become a political dictatorship in the next quarter century if we continue our present heedless course of treating each problem that we face as a crisis instead of relying much more than we do on policy and planning.

The Scandinavian countries—Denmark, Iceland, Norway, Sweden—are much farther along the road to participative management and industrial democracy than we are in the United States.[3] According to news stories, workers in the Scandinavian countries are more intelligent and management is more enlightened than is the usual case in the United States. The following indicates how prerogatives are divided in the work place.

The patterns for change have been to form an action committee of management and shop stewards at the plant. They then involve workers in meetings to see what changes can be made.

The general thrust has been to give workers more control and autonomy. They get more training, learn about the whole operation of their area. They then meet in groups and decide if they want to rotate in jobs, if they need a foreman and what other areas they can handle themselves, such as quality control and ordering their own supplies.

They also begin to set their vacation schedules and days off and to hire new workers. Eventually they may supervise their whole department, seeking advice only when they need it.[4]

The Scandinavian example does not serve in isolation. In an article titled "Made in America (under Japanese management)," Richard T. Johnson and William G. Ouchi discuss the philosophy of the Japanese multinational corporations operating in the United States.[5] The Japanese style of leadership, according to them, is marked by:

1. 'Bottom-up' process
2. Senior manager, the facilitator
3. Middle manager, the molder
4. Decision by consensus
5. Concern for the employee

The philosophy that Johnson and Ouchi discuss is totally integrative in nature and fits the right hand of the continuum as illustrated in both Exhibits 14-1 and 14-2.

According to another recent report, the Scandinavians are moving ahead much more rapidly than we are in the United States as far as improving the quality of work life is concerned. As Northrup points out:

> Swedish industrialists see the same symptoms of employee disaffection—high personnel turnover, absenteeism and malingering—as their American counterparts. What distinguishes the most ambitious Swedish efforts to cure the problem are the dual themes of decentralization and dialogue.[6]

Conclusion

Exhibit 14-1 shows that System 1 and Management by Direction apply to crisis-oriented situations; that Systems 2 and 3 and Management by Results and Management by Objectives work best in routine-oriented circumstances; and that System 4 and Management by Integration are most appropriate to knowledge-oriented contingencies. To put it differently, as illustrated by Exhibit 14-2, various situations call for boss-centered, management-centered, or leader-centered behavior, *depending on the requirements of the situation.* As you develop skill in the analysis of situations, you will find that it will pay off in your area of delegated authority.

NOTE

Since the original publication of this material, Time *magazine featured Japan in a cover story (30 March 1981). The philosophy of management recognized by Dr. Suojanen as being totally integrative in nature is discussed in* Time, *along with other factors, as reasons for Japan becoming "the world's toughest competitor." The moral of the story: America's student has become the teacher.*

ENDNOTES

1. See Chapter 3 and also my paper, "The Minds of Man and the Uses of Management Science," *Clemson University Review of Industrial Management and Textile Science* (Spring 1975): 51-66.

2. Meyer Friedman and Ray H. Rosenman, *Type A Behavior and Your Heart* (New York: Knopf, 1974).

3. For example, see Chapter XIII, "Scandinavian Model (As Usual) for the World?" in David Jenkins, *Job Power: Blue and White Collar Democracy* (Garden City, New York: Doubleday, 1973), 246-281.

4. Agis Salpykas, "Improving the Workers Role," *New York Times* (20 October 1974).

5. Richard T. Johnson and William G. Ouchi, "Made in America (under Japanese management)," *Harvard Business Review* (September-October 1974): 61-69.

6. Bowen Northrup, "Working Happier: More Swedish Firms Attempt to Enrich Production-Line Jobs," *Wall Street Journal* (25 October 1974).

7. For an explanation of Systems 1, 2, 3, and 4 see Rensis Likert, *The Human Organization* (New York: McGraw-Hill, 1967).

15

Management Theory, Managerial Work, and Graduate Education for Management

Waino W. Suojanen
Wayne W. Suojanen

Does management education prepare students for management? Does management training improve the performance of practicing managers? Can college professors with a sense-feel-think approach to problems contribute much to the sense-fcel-do and sense-feel-create skills of the manager? Surely, many a manager has questioned the relationship of his present responsibilities to the expensive education he received as an eager, young MBA student. An increasing number of executives are coming to the conclusions that both education and training for management have been drifting toward a course that appears to be 180 degrees removed from what managers actually do in the real world.

Much of the literature concerned with improving the formal background of the manager has recognized the importance of finding answers to these questions. A number of articles addressed to this issue have appeared in the *Harvard Business Review* and elsewhere during the past five years or so. Significant among these contributions have been articles by J. Sterling Livingston, John Hammond, James T. McKenny and Peter Keen, Henry Mintzberg, and Theodore Levitt.[1]

Reprinted with permission from *The Finnish Journal of Business Economics*, Special Edition, Volume 3, 1980.

In his paper, Sterling Livingston argues that the analysis and action functions of the manager are quite distinct. Most American business schools have not yet incorporated this distinction into programs which are supposed to prepare students to become managers. Livingston makes the point that one kind of knowledge is required to recognize and think through a case problem which someone has organized in such a way that only a quantitative solution will fill the bill. It is quite something else to acquire the ability to discover problems and opportunities in the real world and to actively follow them through to a successful resolution.[2]

A similar distinction between action and deliberation also appears in the Hammond article. Hammond suggests that there are enormous differences between the functions of the manager and those of the management scientist.[3] According to Hammond, a number of the leading business schools and schools of management almost totally ignore the disctinction between doing and planning in their programs.

McKenny and Keen underline the point that schools of business administration and management tend to devote far too much attention to rational tools and techniques. In such cognitive aspects of business as resource allocation, financial forecasting, and logistical planning, there is no question whatsoever that quantitative techniques are extremely valuable. However, as they also point out, this approach has not proven very useful in those management problems which "do not lend themselves to explicit formulation... where the manager operates through intuition."[4] By implication, their paper raises the question as to whether the skills of intuition can be taught in an academic environment.

Henry Mintzberg has focused his research effort on what it is that managers really do in their day-to-day work. He feels that meaningful management information systems or planning techniques must wait until we have a much more thorough understanding of the nature of managerial work. Until this is done, it will be difficult—perhaps even impossible—to do a full-fledged job of teaching the discipline to prospective managers. Can we truly improve the performance of practicing managers until we have the answer to this and many related questions? Until this is done, our bureaucracies will become larger and larger at the same time that they are becoming more ineffective and inefficient. According to

Mintzberg, we must find answers to these and other specific questions before we can expect management training and management science to have a significant and meaningful impact on management practice.[5]

Levitt comments that "there is no such thing as the right way for a manager to operate or behave."[6] From this viewpoint, management skills are transferable only when the leadership skills and personability style of the executive are congruent with the requirements of the situation. As he puts it, "... if personality and style are out of phase with the new situation, nothing can prevent disaster."[7]

A number of years ago, Bowen argued that management development programs can return to fundamentals by posing and answering two questions:

"1. How can we identify the best people?
2. How can we test these people under fire?"[8]

Bowen answered the first question by suggesting that management potential should be judged on the basis of demonstrated performance and that this appraisal should be done by people who are skilled in this kind of assessment. Some managers, according to Bowen, have an almost intuitive knack for selecting the right people for the right jobs. Bowen would test managers under fire once they have been chosen by giving them the opportunity to make real decisions and he would judge their performance on how well they carried out their jobs.

Education for Management at CalSloan

In our research in this area, we came to the conclusion that top-ranking schools of management and business administration in the United States fall into a continuum. One end of this continuum consists of those schools which view education for management as an analytical-verbal, sense-feel-think activity. This "CalSloan" approach, as we have termed it, is a composite of the names of the University of California-Berkeley where the first author studied for his terminal degree and the Sloan School of Management at Massachusetts Institute of Technology where the second author

Exhibit 15-1: **Continuum of Schools and Educational View of Management**

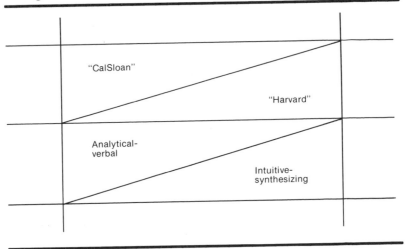

earned his MS and PhD. CalSloan schools, as we define them, focus on the development of the analytical, quantitative, intellectual, verbal, and rational skills of the prospective manager.

In Exhibit 15-1, we show the CalSloan approach to management education and training as analytical-verbal (A—V) in orientation as opposed to the "Harvard" model, which focuses its efforts on developing the intuitive-synthesizing (I—S) competence of the student. The I—S philosophy emphasizes case studies and other vicarious, experiential teaching methods. By contrast the CalSloan model relies on the more traditional, scholarly lecture method coupled with library research on the part of the student.

Prior to World War II, very little scholarly literature about management had been published in the United States. Because of this, no A—V model of management education existed. Instead, writers in the management area focused almost all their effort on the development and use of "principles" of management. These principles were designed more to teach the manager how to plan, organize, and staff the enterprise than they were to assist him in the direction and control of its affairs. Most of the pre-World War II management writers were practitioners who had been moved, by one reason or another, to place their thoughts into article or book form. Until after World War II, this literature remained mainly descriptive and institutional in nature. Followers of the Harvard school, then and now, have tended to view this approach as being of little value in the teaching of management skills. As indicated in Exhibit 15-2, in recent years this outlook has often been called the *operational management* school.

During World War II and in subsequent years, many military leaders, government executives, and top management people in industry were exposed to the A—V, problem-solving processes that characterize the CalSloan model. These people, along with the operations researchers and management scientists who had come into their own during the war years, became convinced that the use of analytical, rational, and quantitative methods could be widely extended within large organizations to improve both the problem-solving and the decision-making processes. In the literature, this sense-feel-think view to the discipline has become known as the *quantitative management* school. Many of the leading graduate schools in the United States now concentrate the bulk of their

Exhibit 15-2: **Schools of Management Thought**

research and teaching effort on analytical-verbal aspects of management education to the neglect of the intuitive-strategic approach.

A third philosophy of management education, identified as *behavioral management* in Exhibit 15-2, came into prominence during the years following World War II. Until five or ten years ago, behavioral management was highly influential in determining the mix of courses offered in the curriculum of graduate business schools. Under the influence of a number of prominent behavioral scientists, this approach flowed over into and merged with the broader human potential movement, which is called human growth or humanistic psychology. Even today, many professors who belong to this school take the view that managers who are motivated by a need to manage and appear to enjoy the exercise of authority are, in some sense, immature. They feel that the problems of an industrial civilization could be solved with relative ease if only these managers would learn how to behave as mature, democratic people. Becoming mature is, under this approach, equated with the sharing of authority and the broader concepts of participative management. Many of these academicians continue to be perplexed by the fact that the theory in use of most managers is Theory X despite the fact that they have had long classroom exposure to the espoused theory of Theory Y. Partly because of this conflict between theory and practice, behavioral management presently exists in somewhat of a state of somnolence. It is taught in many classrooms but it is applied in very few boardrooms.

Management Training at Harvard

The Harvard Graduate School of Business Administration, where the first author received his MBA, has developed an approach to management education that is quite different from that of the CalSloan schools. The first year of the MBA program at Harvard Business School immerses the student in the sense-feel-do, stressful, crisis-oriented environment of the line manager. By contrast, the second year concentrates much more leisurely and almost completely on the sense-feel-create, largely intuitive, knowledge-oriented atmosphere of strategy formation. The student may choose instead to focus the efforts of his second year on learning how to sharpen those skills that are of value to the entrepreneur. In either event, the abilities that make for success as a policymaker in a large organization are much the same as those that prove useful to the entrepreneur. At Harvard, as at CalSloan, most students opt for careers as staff functionaries rather than as line managers. In these cases, many of the second-year course offerings provide a grounding in the functional areas of business.

Wherever the Harvard prototype exists, the orientation teaches the student how to become a manager by almost total reliance on the case method. This remains true whether the focus is on the sense-feel-do, crisis-oriented environment of the first year of the MBA program or on its analog in shorter development programs or whether the focus is on the second-year, sense-feel create atmosphere of the strategy formation process. The way to learn how to get things done is to study and analyze what happens in the experiences of both successful and unsuccessful organizations and managers. Whether the situation is knowledge-oriented or crisis-oriented, the cornerstone of the Harvard approach continues to be the case method.

The lesson to be learned from the Harvard experience is that it is uniquely different—and has remained so for much of this century—from its "competition." Unlike many other elite schools that concentrate on the A—V aspects of management education, the Harvard curriculum directs its emphasis on turning out potential chief executive officers, skilled in the arts of intuition and strategy. The CalSloan model concentrates on the routine-oriented skills of the problem-solving, staff functionary, whereas the Harvard approach centers on developing the sense-feel-do, intuitive abilities and sense-feel-create, synthesizing competence of the general manager.

At Harvard, the atmosphere during the first year is one in which each student performs an enormous amount of work under conditions of high stress against the pressure of one deadline after another. As a result, there is very little time left over to pursue the leisurely niceties of scholarship that are more highly esteemed in the CalSloan schools. No graduate of the Harvard Business School will ever forget the frantic treks to Baker Library to drop a report through a slot before it slammed shut.

The question arises whether an atmosphere of near panic is of significant value to the education and training of the manager. Fortunately, a recent study by a former student covers this issue in considerable detail.[9] Cohen compares the first year of the Harvard MBA program with "boot camp" in the Marine Corps or basic training in the Army. According to Cohen, the Harvard Business School can be viewed as the "West Point" of American capitalism. Basic to the philosophy of the first-year program at Harvard is the deep and extensive, crisis-oriented indoctrination that old Marines and old soldiers know so well. Essential aspects of this indoctrination are the continuing pressure, the never-ending deadlines, and the stress that are the earmarks of the crisis-oriented situation.

Cohen does not discuss the second year of the MBA program as vividly and incisively as he does the first. In any event, the second year at Harvard, just like the first, is a unique experience. The crisis-oriented sense of impending doom disappears. The student now has more time to delve into strategy formulation, long-range planning, and the wider aspects of social and environmental issues.

In the first year there is so much to be done—so many cases to be analyzed each day and each week and each month—that no task is ever more than half-done, or so it appears to the student as he or she moves from one crisis to another. In the second year the emphasis shifts and the neophyte manager now has time to taste the vicarious pleasures of serving as the chief executive officer (CEO) of the corporation. Just as the first year emphasizes the sense-feel-do aspects of decision making, so the second-year program stresses the sense-feel-create, intuitive-synthesizing (I—S) approach of the CEO. One reason for the success of the Harvard approach, in contrast to its competition, lies in the way in which these two aspects of the educational experience in the classroom actually replicate the actual behaviors of the general manager. Before turning to that issue, let's take a closer look at the record, as Al Smith used to say, and see how well Harvard graduates do in the real world as contrasted to the graduates of the other leading schools of business administration and management.

In the *Gospel*, Cohen compared the track records of Harvard MBAs with the graduates of competitive schools. When he looked at who became the captains of industry—board chairmen, presidents of major corporations, senior partners, and vice-presidents— not to mention major policymakers in the public sector, it is clear that the Harvard graduate far outpaces the pack. According to his data:

—Forty-five out of Fortune's 500 corporations are run by graduates of the Harvard Business School

—About one in seven of the top 500 chairmen or presidents are either Harvard graduates, nondegree Harvard attendees, or participants of the school's management training programs

—Even though Harvard has the largest graduating classes, and has been in existence the longest, Chicago, Wharton, Columbia, and Stanford have collectively produced as many MBAs as Harvard; but only nine of them (as compared to Harvard's forty-five) have made it to the top of one of Fortune's 500.

There are those who argue that the Fortune 500 companies are selected on the basis of asset size rather than profitability and that a better measure of the Harvard factor than the one used by Cohen would be data that showed that Harvard graduates managed the most profitable rather than the largest corporations. That argument does not wash. Harvard graduates develop the will to manage in the course of their graduate training. Corporations seek executives who have that will—especially when their profits are down or are threatened—so that current profitability performance often does not measure the ingredients of the Harvard factor. In any event, if success is a matter of personal performance in corporate infighting, and the evidence indicates that indeed it is, then Harvard must be doing a lot of things correctly.

The Harvard factor may still remain unidentified but it is easy, given the above data, to understand why the approach is being emulated in major management training centers around the world. This is often done with the cooperation of the Harvard Business School and its faculty members. These institutions are interested, not in the study of management as a scholarly, research exercise, but as a sense-feel-do activity that is practiced daily on a real-time basis by millions of individuals in the factory and the marketplace. Although they have not identified the Harvard factor, they know that it exists. If this factor can be partially identified, then we will possess some clues to a theory that relates closely to the real world of the bottom line. Even more important, this theory should provide us with an understanding of the roles that education and training can play in developing people who can meet the challenges of the management world of the future.

What Do Managers Actually Do?

In his study of the real-world behavior of managers, Henry Mintzberg came to the conclusion that current theories—whether operational, quantitative, or behavioral—fall far short of explaining what it is that managers actually do.

Mintzberg makes a number of real-world observations about the work of the practicing manager. As he separates fact from folklore, a completely new picture of what top managers actually do comes to the surface. Some of the most important of his observations are the following:

1. *Managers are not scientists, nor does management appear to be turning into a science.* Managers are very little concerned with developing scientifically analytical procedures or sophisticated management information systems. Their work is so varied and crisis-oriented in nature that they have neither the time nor the patience to follow the step-by-step thinking pattern of observation, hypothesis, experiment, and induction that characterizes the scientific method.

2. *The manager is not a systematic, reflective planner.* Lacking the luxury of time, the manager can seldom afford to prepare a daily work program to plan his work and work his plan because he must continuously turn aside for interruptions, emergencies, and unexpected contingencies. Nearly every issue he faces is characterized by brevity, variety, and discontinuity. Almost as a matter of routine he works at an unrelenting pace on propositions that require that he make many on-the-spot decisions. His work is much more of the action-oriented, sense-feel-do type than it is reflective or deliberative. Competent managers accept the torrid pace, realizing that all these disruptions are essential to their major task—that of communication.[10]

3. *Managers rely much more heavily on brief, to the point, verbal communication than they do on written presentations or reports.* Mintzberg discovered that chief executives pay little attention to the bulk of their mail, ignore much of the computer-spun garbage that crosses their desks, and dislike reading long reports and lengthy intellectual studies. They much prefer to do their business by telephone or in face-to-face meetings. From these meetings and telephone calls, along with tidbits they receive from informers or from subordinates, they put together models in their minds, which

they retain and which they can retrieve as necessary.

4. *Manager's jobs are integrated.* The three major roles of the manager—the *informational,* the *interpersonal,* and the *decisional*—cannot be separated into independent subunits because they are integrated to form a gestalt. None of the ten responsibilities that are included in these three major roles (figurehead, leader, liaison, monitor, disseminator, spokesman, entrepreneur, disturbance handler, resource allocator, negotiator) can be detached from the manager's total job without limiting his or her overall effectiveness.

5. *Pressures on the managers are getting worse.* The overall result of an ever-increasing buildup of knowledge and organizational complexity is to force more and more reliance on the efforts of fewer and fewer individuals. Managers end up working harder because nobody else in the organization can possibly know as much as they do, and it takes far too much time to brief someone else to do their tasks rapidly and correctly. Management stress spirals as work loads become heavier. The medical journals attest to the high price the manager pays for a Type A Behavior Pattern.

Mintzberg underlines this by saying: "If there is a single theme that runs through this article, it is that the pressures of his job drive the manager to be superficial in his actions—to overload himself with work, encourage interruption, respond quickly to every stimulus, seek the tangible and avoid the abstract, make decisions in small increments, and do everything abruptly."[11] And in spite of all this the manager has to remain effective, and he or she does this by making the right decisions and getting things done.

Mintzberg implicitly suggests that education for the kinds of managers he has studied is best done by using the Harvard approach rather than the CalSloan model. He feels that powerful, skill-development techniques that are experiential and creative should be more widely used. Among these are role playing of the kind that is basic to the case method, behavior laboratories, and greater use of videotape. In his own words: "Educators need to put students into situations, whether in the field or in the simulated experience of the laboratory, where they can practice managerial skills, not only interpersonal but also informational and decisional."[12]

There is little question in our minds that the Harvard approach fits Mintzberg's model far better than does the CalSloan philosophy. Another leading institution, the Stanford Graduate School of Business has, in the past at least, followed a course somewhat more like that of the Harvard approach than of the pure CalSloan model. Let's turn in that direction and see what their experience can tell us about graduate education for management, and how what is done there may relate to the minds of the manager.

Stanford MBA Graduates

For a number of years, Thomas W. and Margaret S. Harrell have been studying the career patterns of MBA graduates of the Stanford Graduate School of Business. Their research is highly significant in determining the directions in which graduate education for management should proceed in the years to come, because the Stanford School of Business, in the past at least, adhered to a philosophy of management training that bore a closer resemblance to the Harvard model than it did to the approach of the CalSloan schools. As a second factor of importance, the Harrells' research reinforces the findings of Mintzberg discussed in the preceding section.

The Harrells break down their data on MBA graduates into two categories. One group includes graduates who choose general management as a career field—the other part of the sample consists of Stanford graduates who enter functional areas such as marketing and finance. As we have indicated earlier, graduate education for management too often focuses on educating students in rigorous intellectual and analytical skills despite almost general agreement that the training needed for general management is something else again. Other than those oriented to the Harvard model, this "something else" tends to be largely ignored by many graduate schools of business and management.

In one study, the Harrells examined the career patterns of 205 MBA graduates of Stanford University who had been out of school for ten years. They related the Verbal (V) and Quantitative (Q) scores of these alumni on the Admissions Test for Graduate Study in Business (ATGSB) to several criteria of business manager success.[13] The Harrells discovered that there was a negative relation between the (V) scores of their sample managers on the ATGSB and their later success in their executive careers. Ten years after graduation, those Stanford MBA students who had placed in the lowest decile in (V) in the ATGSB were earning more and had reached higher general manager positions than their cohorts who had ranked in the highest decile in this examination.[14] Because Stanford, in common with other leading business schools, prefers to admit students who do well on the GMAT, a number of applicants are denied admission each year because their test scores fall below the minimum acceptable level.

The Stanford data suggest that business schools sometimes refuse admission to the less intellectual, sense-feel-do applicant who seeks the action associated with line management and instead choose candidates who feel more at home in deliberative, sense-feel-think activities such as reading books and articles. Many of these potential staff functionaries have little aptitude for, nor desire to participate in, the rough and tumble aspects of general management. If we were to extrapolate into the baccalaureate classes—those who compose the MBA candidate pool—the paradox might be even more disconcerting. It is clear that many baccalaureate graduates—some of whom would develop into excellent general managers—never apply for graduate work because of their low grade point averages or because they feel that they might not do well on the GMAT. Others, with similar line management career potential, will not be admitted because their scores fall below minimums set by the individual schools in adherence to the policies of the American Assembly of Collegiate Schools of Business.

In the course of their research, the Harrells have also discovered that successful managers have personality profiles that differ significantly from those that the behavioral management school has been promoting for the past quarter century. The lowest decile graduates, in the study discussed above, were superior in ascendance, had higher scores on a decisiveness scale, and tended to be more authoritarian than classmates with higher admission test scores. The more successful managers had a strong need to manage despite the fact that behavioral management theorists had been proving for the previous quarter of a century that successful managers should be more concerned with affiliation and achievement. Significantly, this Harrell study also discovered that the successful managers were superior in social extroversion and in preference as friends than were their less successful, more intellectual classmates. Apparently, the "gamesman" has been on the management scene for most of the post-World War II years.

The Harrells define the general manager as working in a multifunctional mode rather than concentrating on a single, functional specialty. As such, he or she operates at a high level of authority in a line capacity rather than in a staff position. The general manager always has some responsibility for some supervision of employees.[15]

A general manager may be in charge of an entire organization, a division, or an important subunit, such as a profit center. The Harrells have been very careful to place in this category only those managers whose job descriptions fit the rigorous requirements the Harrells have developed.

In another report, the Harrells showed that Stanford Business School graduates occupying general management positions had personality profiles very similar to those of the managers whom Mintzberg studied.[16]

The Stanford Business School graduate who commits to a career in general management has a personality profile that fits a sense-do-feel behavior pattern. By contrast, Stanford Business School graduates who decide to become staff functionaries prefer a career pattern in which sense-feel-think or sense-feel-create activities predominate.

The behavior pattern of the successful general manager shows him or her to be:
• Decisive
• Authoritarian
• Superior in ascendance, particularly in speaking, speed, and health
• Socially extroverted

The Harrells point out that the qualities listed above apply as much to the military service as they do to the private sector.[17] Top ranking military officers come from the line rather than from the staff elements of their services. They are frequently rotated into staff positions but the sine qua non for promotion is progressively more responsible line billets.

Intelligence and academic achievement are important but not central to the achievement of high rank:

> In both the military service and in business it is likely that the pure staff types are smarter on the average than their line bosses—but it would be dysfunctional to promote on IQ alone, and the line managers have more leadership needs and skills. They are more effective in oral communication, which is primary to effective organizational leadership. This effectiveness in oral communication includes a complex pattern of social extroversion and ascendance.[18]

The Motivation to Manage—Cultural and Biological

John B. Miner, in an article in the *Harvard Business Review*, presented a profile that describes the behavior of successful, professional managers.[19] This profile not only describes the behavior of successful line managers, it also predicts whether a management student has the personality attributes that appear to underlie performance as a successful general manager.

Miner lists these attributes and motivations as follows:
- A favorable attitude toward authority
- The desire to compete
- The desire to exercise power
- Assertive motivation
- The desire to capture the attention of others through distinctive kinds of behavior
- A sense of responsibility

This list of factors virtually coincides with the description of the general manager position developed by the Harrells. The Stanford MBA graduate who becomes a successful general manager is motivated by a high need to manage, as Miner defines that concept. This individual is more authoritarian, more ascendant, and more decisive than are his or her more intellectual but less successful colleagues. Equally important, this person is superior to them in social extroversion and is more friendly—this despite the fact that the need for affiliation is not much of a factor in his or her motivations.

In the past, Miner used to refer to "the need to manage" factors as paralleling "the traditional assertive requirements of the masculine role as defined in our society." Recently, he has changed his mind somewhat on this point after discovering that female education majors and female public school administrators appear to have as high a need to manage as do their male counterparts.[20] The more recent, sociobiological literature tends to provide stronger support for Miner's earlier macho model of the need to manage than it does for his later finding that female executives exhibit this personality pattern. However, that is an issue that need not concern us in this discussion.[21]

The Harvard Factor, Decision Making, and Problem Solving

Exhibit 15-3 presents, in outline form, much of the previous discussion in this chapter. As the reader studies this Exhibit, many of the reasons why the Harvard approach produces proportionately more CEOs and chairmen of the board than its CalSloan competition become clearer.

The intuitive-synthesizing approach to management education is almost totally problem-focused. It teaches the student to understand a case in terms of *problem impact*—not "what is the apparent problem?" but the effect of the problem on the organization. Out of this grows a *profit awareness*—that the general manager has a bottom line responsibility for making money for the company. Although there may be much discussion of issues in class, the real-world I—S graduate learns to value *time* as an "important element in the psyche of decision makers."[22]

In both crisis-oriented and knowledge-oriented situations, the I—S student, through almost total immersion in the case method, develops both an *opportunity-orientation* and an ability to view high *risk-taking* as essential to the development of a healthy managerial style. The I—S manager tends to become a positive-thinker as he or she learns time and time again to gain an advantage from something new. This is in contrast to a routine-oriented staff mentality that turns away from the unproven and that which was "not invented here." Opportunity-orientation and high risk-taking thrive in a heterostatic, tension-seeking environment.[23]

Exhibit 15-3: **Situations, Abilities, Duties, and Educational Approach**

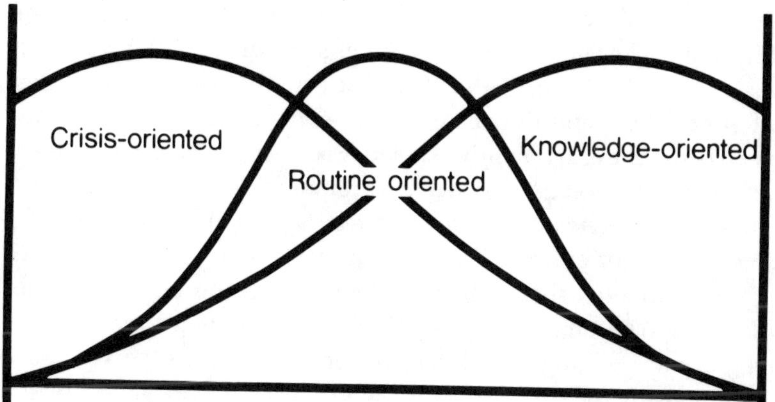

Crisis-oriented	Routine oriented	Knowledge-oriented
Decision making	Problem solving	Problem finding
Heterostasis	Homeostasis	Heterostasis
Sense-feel-do	Sense-feel-think	Sense-feel-create
Line managers	Support personnel and staff functionaries	Staff functionaries and line managers
Harvard	CalSloan	Harvard

The personality traits that survive and thrive in the I—S environment are those discussed by Mintzberg and Miner and the Harrells. The I—S graduate with a strong need to manage tends to picture himself as confident and impatient, whereas those from different backgrounds, often his or her subordinates, may view the manager as being arrogant. The distinction between the two is often not clear, and the perceptive I—S manager will consciously try to behave less arrogantly. This may be difficult, because the I—S manager tends to respect assertive argument on substantive issues just as much as he or she tries to discourage the nitpicking that is characteristic of much of what is called participative management.

The confidence that is nurtured by the I—S approach helps the graduates to become secure in their own faith in their own abilities. They become willing to rock the boat or to rattle the cage when the situation calls for this kind of behavior. They move over easily to the next issue because they do not wish to waste time with the possibility that they might later have to defend their decision. They become a cosmopolitan rather than a "local" secure in their assurance that if they move on they will have no problem picking up the threads elsewhere with little break in continuity or scope of income.

As contrasted to the A—V philosophy, the I—S approach develops a greater proportion of "tough-minded" managers, impatient as often with the worries of their quantitatively oriented colleagues as they are with the concerns of their more behaviorally oriented associates. The successful general manager will invariably "narrow the field of vision" on the closest path between problem-impact and problem-solution. If this means closing a plant or firing a subordinate, so be it. Whatever else may be said of I—S managers, "they tend to be the doers and the movers" of the corporate world.[24]

Summary and Conclusions

In a recent monograph, A. Harry Klopf argues that intelligence in complex systems is a concomitant of a striving for a maximal condition. He defines this maximal condition as *heterostasis*. According to Klopf, the organization is a limited heterostat. Such a system is defined with respect to the controlling subsystem. In the case of the organization, the limited heterostat may be said to be the

CEO. When the CEO seeks to maximize his or her own pleasure, he or she also largely determines the course of the organization as other participants subsume their own need for achievement to that of the CEO's. That is, they are subordinate to the CEO and obey his authority.

Organizations pursue both *external goals* and *internal goals.* When external goals are pursued, the efforts of the system are directed to altering the environment in some way. Living systems, by contrast, are better understood if they are viewed as pursuing internal goals through adaptive and variable endogenous procedures that operate on a relatively fixed external environment. The emphasis on coping with crisis-oriented situations and knowledge-oriented situations, as emphasized by the Harvard factor, suggests an identity between heterostasis and general management behavior. The organization attempts to make the largest possible profit by altering the environment in some way, say by increasing its share of the market. The "profit-aware" decision maker maximizes his or her pleasure by making decisions that make the largest possible contribution at the bottom-line level. The decision maker enjoys this because it gives him or her pleasure, or conversely, the pleasure makes the decision maker seek the sense-feel-do and sense-feel-create activities of heterostasis and causes him or her to avoid sense-feel-obey, homeostatic situations.

By contrast, the A—V approach to management education emphasizes the primary of *homeostasis.* The present-day bureaucrat, whether in the private or the public sector, must survive, and survival becomes both a necessary and sufficient condition. Klopf points out that homeostasis is a subgoal to the maintenance of heterostasis. To the extent, then, that the CalSloan approach focuses its attention on the education of people who, it is assumed, will operate in a problem-solving, routine-oriented environment, staff functionaries rather than line managers will be produced. Obviously, there is nothing wrong in training staff functionaries if this is recognized as the basic mission of the particular educational or training institution. Modern organizations need many people with such skills.

Exhibit 15-3 integrates Klopf's work into the integrative model and suggests that the opposition of heterostasis and homeostasis can provide us with additional insights about the future course of management education. As Exhibit 15-3 indicates, the Harvard approach produces I—S, tension-seeking managers who are at home in stressful, sense-feel-do and sense-feel-create situations in contrast to the CalSloan philosophy, which focuses more on the homeostatic, tension-reducing, sense-feel-think behavior that characterizes the role of the staff functionary.

The reader will note that Exhibit 15-3 summarizes many of the ideas we have presented in this article. This Exhibit suggests that the successful line manager excels at the heterostatic activities of decision making and problem finding. If heterostatic managers can be shaped from almost any sort of fairly bright and ambitious university graduate, there is little doubt that exposure to the I—S, Harvard experience will sharpen their sense-feel-do and sense-feel-create skills. These two kinds of skills comprise the essence of general management. The I—S experience appears to provide the kind of vicarious experience that develops the abilities of the manager as a heterostat.

All this is not to downgrade the relevance of the CalSloan philosophy. Modern bureaucracies, whether private or public, devote most of their resources to routine-oriented, problem-solving activities. As indicated in the center area of Exhibit 15-3, this calls for large numbers of support personnel and staff functionaries. Such people do not appear to be in short supply. What is needed, particularly in the future, are managers who can work well in the stressful areas of decision making and problem solving. The world now functions in a state of continuing crisis. It needs managers who can cope easily with crises, "who can keep their heads while those around them are losing theirs." Equally necessary are intuitive-synthesists who can find problems and convert them into opportunities before they deteriorate into crises. The Harvard model should prove as useful in the education of the general manager of the future as it has been in the past. The CalSloan model, on the other hand, will function better if it relaxes its basic assumption that the general manager of the future will remain a sense-feel-obey, routine-oriented, quantitatively focused individual.

During the past decade, the United States economy has shown a decline both in productivity and in the quality of this diminishing output. Pride in productivity and concern for craftsmanship appear to be virtues that relate to the "good old days" of the past. The debate as to the future directions the United States should take is now beginning to take shape. As one example, the president of

Harvard University suggests that the CalSloan model provides advantages that escape the case method of the Harvard approach.[25] On the other hand, two professors of the Harvard Business School indicate that we may well be managing our way into economic decline and that

> more disturbing still, true believers keep the faith on a day-to-day basis by insisting that as issues rise up the managerial hierarchy for decision they may be progressively distilled in easily quantifiable terms.[26]

In closing, we are dubious whether the American academic community can produce a realistic management theory out of the wreckage of the past decade, given the current paradigm that incessantly quantifies the unquantifiable, spinning out inductions that have little if any roots to the realities of the work place. An entirely new paradigm is needed—one that is grounded in sociobiology and neurophysiology and that is already proving its value in disciplines other than management.

ENDNOTES

1. J. Sterling Livingston, "Myth of the Well-Educated Manager," *Harvard Business Review* (January-February 1971): 79-89: John S. Hammond, "The Roles of the Manager and Management Scientist in Successful Implementation," *Sloan Management Review* (Winter 1974). 1-22; James T. McKenney and Peter G. W. Keen, "How Managers' Minds Work," *Harvard Business Review* (May-June 1974): 79-90; Henry Mintzberg, "The Manager's Job: Folklore and Facts" *Harvard Business Review* (July-August 1975): 49-61; Theodore Levitt, "The Managerial Merry-Go-Round," *Harvard Business Review* (July-August 1974): 120-128.

2. Livingston, "Myth," 82.

3. Hammond, "Successful Implementation," 1.

4. McKenney and Keen, "Minds Work," 79-90.

5. Henry Mintzberg, *The Nature of Managerial Work* (New York: Harper & Row, 1973), 3.

6. Levitt, "Merry-Go-Round," 121.

7. Ibid.,128.

8. Charles P. Bowen, Jr., "Let's Put Realism into Management Development," *Harvard Business Review* (July-August 1973): 86.

9. Peter Cohen, *The Gospel According to Harvard Business School* (New York: Doubleday, 1973).

10. Mintzberg, *Managerial Work*, 52.

11. Ibid., 60.

12. Henry Mintzberg, "Planning on The Left Side and Managing on The Right," *Harvard Business Review* (July-August 1976): 58.

13. The Graduate Management Admission Test (GMAT) has recently replaced the ATGSB.

14. The Relation of the Verbal and Quantitative Scores to Manager Success (U.S. Office of Naval Research, Technical Report No. 5, Arlington, Virginia, 9 August 1974.)

15. Thomas W. Harrell and Margaret S. Harrell, "Background, Personality and Vocational Interests of General Managers" (U.S. Office of Naval Research, Technical Report No. 2, 8 October 1973).

16. Thomas W. Harrell and Margaret S. Harrell, "The Personality of MBAs Who Reach General Management Early," *Personnel Psychology* (1973): 127-134.

17. Thomas W. Harrell and Margaret S. Harrell, "Career Path to General Management" (U.S. Office of Naval Research, Technical Report No. 2, 29 August 1975), 10.

18. Thomas W. Harrell and Margaret S. Harrell, "Career Path," 10.

19. John B. Miner, "The Real Crunch in Managerial Manpower," *Harvard Business Review* (November-December 1973): 146-158.

20. John B. Miner, "The Miner Sentence Completion Scale: A Reappraisal," *Academy of Management Journal* (June 1978): 288.

21. On this point, see for example, Edward D. Wilson, *Sociology: The New Synthesis* (Cambridge: Harvard University Press, 1975), 250-255, and *On Human Nature* (Cambridge: Harvard University Press, 1978); D. D. Thiessen, *The Evolution and Chemistry of Aggression* (Springfield,

Illinois: Thomas, 1976); and Steven Goldberg, *The Inevitability of Patriarchy* (New York: Morrow, 1973).

22. We have borrowed many of the expressions and phrases in the early part of this section from Charles H. Ford, "The 'Elite' Decision-Maker: What Makes Them Tick," *Human Resources Management* (Winter 1977): 14-20. Ford's analysis of the personalities of top line managers and the ways in which they behave is virtually identical with those of Mintzberg and the Harrells.

23. Ibid.

24. *Mental and Physical Phenomena: Toward a Unified Theory* (Air Force Avionics Laboratory, Wright-Patterson AFB, Ohio, 1977), mimeographed draft, 1977.

25. Derek Bok, *Harvard University: The President's Report, 1977-1978*, 1-29.

26. Robert H. Hayes and William J. Abernathy, "Managing Our Way to Economic Decline," *Harvard Business Review* (July-August 1980): 75.

Glossary

ACORN. An acronym that stands for *A*ddictive, *C*ompulsive, *O*bsessive, *R*eally *N*utty (behavior or the person with the behavior).

altered states of consciousness achieved through meditation. A state of consciousness not commonly experienced—it does not occur spontaneously but must be consciously and purposefully evoked. During this state, certain physiologic changes occur, such as decreased oxygen consumption, decreased respiratory rate, decreased heart rate, an increase in alpha waves (usually associated with feelings of well-being), and decreased blood pressure (usually in those with elevated blood pressure).

anthropomorphic. Interpretation of what is not human or personal in terms of human or personal characteristics.

antinomic. Contradictory or inconsistent.

A QUIVER. An acronym used to describe the functions of the left new brain—*A*nalytical, *QU*antitative, *I*ntellectual, *VE*rbal, *R*ational.

biobehavioral or biohavioral. Refers to behavior that is biologically determined as opposed to the environment-only school of learning; sciences that are drawn from include biology, ethology, sociobiology, neurophysiology, biochemistry, psychobiology, and linguistics.

biochemistry. Biological or physiological chemistry dealing with substances or chemicals found in the brain.

biogenetic structuralist. One who combines the insights of the neurological sciences, cognitive psychology, linguistics, human paleontology, and social-cultural insights with those obtained from ethology and sociobiology to learn more about organizational behavior.

250

catecholamines. Generic term for chemicals containing a catechol nucleus (a benzene ring with two adjacent hydroxyl groups) and a side chain ending with an amine (nitrogen-containing) group; act as neurotransmitters.

code of amity. Mutual acceptance and toleration among group members which acts to prevent aggression among group members, thus allowing the group to obtain objectives by cooperation and collaboration.

code of enmity. Ill will or dislike for an enemy; this applies to members of a different group. Discrimination among groups.

compleat. Stands for holistic as holistic is used today; complete. Taken from Izaak Walton, *The Compleat Angler* (1653).

corpus callosum (CC). A band of fibers, or commissure, connecting the left new brain and the right new brain.

decisive mind (DM). That part of the visceral brain responsible for decision making.

demophora. From *demos*, population; *phora*, production. Combined reference to human population and technological production consumption, using the latter term to encompass not only products of manufacture and cultivation, but also resources consumed and wastes generated in their production and use; stresses the unity and interdependence of biological and technological phenomena inherent in the "man-machine" concept; expresses the interplay of cause and effect relationships between human population phenomena and technological growth.

determinism. The doctrine that all acts of the will result from causes that determine them, in such a manner that either man has no alternative modes of action or that the will is still free in the sense of being uncompelled.

diencephalon. The posterior subdivision of the forebrain.

DNA. Deoxyribonucleic acid: any of various nucleic acids that yield deoxyribose as one product of hydrolysis, are found in cell nuclei (especially genes), and are associated with the transmission of genetic information.

epinephrine. Adrenalin; the principal blood-pressure-raising hormone of the medulla of the adrenal glands.

ergotropic. Nutritionally working.

ethology. A scientific study of animal behavior; also, a study of the relationship between animal behavior and human behavior.

euphoric state of consciousness (ESOC). The state of consciousness in which a person through the use of a chemical or an activity (such as gambling, overeating, work, etc.) moves from a normal state to a euphoric state—one that is characterized by feelings of warmth and exhilaration. That is, the person is on a "high."

evoked responses or evoked potentials. The brain's response to a stimulus; tiny electrical messages the brain emits in response to sensory stimulation.

Executive Stress Syndrome (ESS). The term used to describe a manager's reaction to psychological distress. The body may undergo changes just as in a physiological stress or a threat to life and limb (fight-or-flight response) situation.

fight-or-flight response (FFR). Reaction of the body to a perceived threat—that is, there is a chemical mobilization, or response that prepares the body to flee or defend itself. In the past it generally referred to a physical threat but now is used also to describe a perceived psychological threat. Fright-Flight-Fight Response (FFFR) is probably more descriptive of this psychological threat, also referred to as Executive Stress Syndrome—(ESS).

free will. The power asserted by moral beings of willing or choosing within certain limitations or with respect to certain matters without the restraints of physical or divinely imposed necessity or outside causal law.

General Adjustment Syndrome (GAS). Broader term for FFR. Used to describe the situation in which employees in an organization adjust to the workaholic, Type A, or addictive manager or management. This type of adjustment, or coping, on the part of employees to "get along" is highly dysfunctional as far as organizational effectiveness is concerned.

genome. One haploid set of chromosomes with the genes they contain.

genotype. The genetic constitution of an individual or group; comparable to potential in management terms.

glucocorticoids. Corticoids (as cortisone) that affect chiefly carbohydrate metabolism.

heterostat. A manager who is most effective in dealing with crises and continuing change; those who actively seek high arousal, tension-generating situations.

heterostasis. Maximal condition that is sought in crises by making optimal decisions; in knowledge-oriented situations a maximal condition is sought by formulating and developing new courses of action.

homeostasis. A constant or fixed environment.

homeostat. A manager who is most effective in intellectual problem solving and in the maintenance of a stable, routine environment.

hominid. Manlike creature; man.

male bonding. The uniting of males for a common cause or interest—to gain power, defend groups, acquire animal protein, etc.

negative addiction (NA). A chemical or an activity that causes a person to move from a normal state of consciousness to the euphoric state of consciousness, and finally to the painful state of consciousness.

negative normal state of consciousness (NNSC). The state of consciousness in which there are negative elements or unpleasant stimuli coming from the environment or from the new brain; this applies where life is nasty, brutish, demeaning, or when someone thinks in a negative or self-defeating manner. Along with the positive normal state of consciousness comprises the normal state of consciousness.

neurophysiology. Physiology of the nervous system; in text, refers mainly to the functions and vital processes of the brain.

neurotransmitter. A chemical substance that allows communication (synapse) between neurons (nerve cells); this is accomplished by the substance "bridging" the tiny gap (about 1/50,000,000 of a meter) between neurons.

norepinephrine. A catecholamine that acts as a neurotransmitter in the central and peripheral nervous systems.

normal state of consciousness (NSOC). The combination of the negative normal state of consciousness with the positive normal state of consciousness. The normal state is achieved when the negative and positive elements or stimuli cancel each other and a person exists on an even keel. The highs and lows of life are in balance.

OAK. Acronym standing for *O*pen, *A*daptive, *K*nowledgeable. Can be used to describe person or behavior.

pain areas (PAV). Area of the visceral brain that senses pain (along with the left new brain) and tells the animal (man) that it must change behavior to avoid this pain.

painful state of consciousness (PSOC). The state of consciousness a person who has a chemical or activity addiction finds that he or she has progressed to over a period of time. It is characterized by a deterioration of self-image, feelings of hopelessness, and possible suicidal tendencies.

phenotype. The detectable expression of the interaction of genotype and environment; actual performance in management terms.

phylogenetic. Based on natural evolutionary relationships.

pleasure areas (PLV). Area of visceral brain that mediates pleasure (along with the right new brain) and encourages the animal (man) to continue what it is doing.

positive addiction (PA). An activity that is noncompetitive, undertaken from 40 or 60 minutes daily, requires little or no conscious mental effort; the person undertaking the activity should feel that it is beneficial physically, mentally, or spiritually. To reach the state of positive addiction, one must continue the activity for a period ranging from six months to a year.

positive normal state of consciousness (PNSC). The state of consciousness in which there are positive elements or pleasant stimuli coming from the environment or from the new brain; this applies when someone is living "the good life" or when someone has a positive mental outlook on his or her situation. Along with the negative normal state of consciousness comprises the normal state of consciousness.

positive peer culture (PPC). Positive peer pressure and support within an institutional context. Based on the assumption that problem or addictive behavior can be contained and changed by giving the individual a positive role in a group process and subculture in which one can learn to know oneself and relate to other people. One very important aspect is the emphasis on the theme of "every member a counselor."

positive peer pressure and support (PPPS). A group process where individuals come to know themselves and relate to others by helping others as they help themselves. A supportive environment in which the group members aid each other in changing negative behaviors into positive behaviors. These groups are sometimes referred to as self-help groups.

proteinoid microspheres. Protein-like structures of organic material about the size of bacteria; formed by heating polypeptides, which can absorb various organic molecules from aqueous solution; may have once played a part in making cells.

proto-organisms. Primitive living things.

psychobiology. The study of mental life and behavior in relation to other biological processes.

relaxation response (RER). An innate physiologic response that is directly opposite that of the fight-or-flight response.

SCANS. An acronym used to describe the functions of the right new brain—Synthesizing, Creative, Artistic, Normative, Spatial.

sexual dimorphism. 1: a condition of having one of the sexes existing in two forms or varieties; 2: a condition of having the two sexes markedly dissimilar in appearance.

sociobiology, The study of society in terms of the methods and concepts of biological science.

split-brain. Refers to the two hemispheres of the brain after their surgical separation (commissurotomy).

steroids. Any of a group of compounds, including the sterols, bile acids, and sex hormones, that characteristically have the carbon ring structure of the sterols.

tabula rasa. Refers to the mind as a blank slate.

testosterone. A male sex hormone.

transcendental meditation (TM). A process whereby the mind experiences subtler and subtler levels of the thinking process with the goal of contacting the source of creativity and intelligence. Physiological responses like those occurring during the Relaxation Response are experienced during this process.

trophotropic. Relating to the orientation of cells or organisms in relation to chemical stimuli in which food or a nutritive substance constitutes the orienting factor.

visceral. The old brain, consisting of the hindbrain, the midbrain, and that part of the forebrain known as the limbic system. It regulates our subconscious behavior—fight or flight, freeze, feed, feel, flirt.

Bibliography

I. Biology and Organization

A. General

Asimov, Isaac. *The Genetic Code.* New York: New American Library, 1962.

Cole, Sonia. *Leakey's Luck.* New York: Harcourt Brace Jovanovich, 1975.

Dobzhansky, Theodosius. *Genetic Diversity and Human Equality—The Factors and Fallacies in the Explosive Genetics and Education Controversy.* New York: Basic Books, 1973.

Dubos, Rene *So Human an Animal.* New York: Scribner, 1968.

Eisner, Thomas, and Edward O. Wilson (eds.). *Animal Behavior.* San Francisco: Freeman, 1975.

Gould, Stephen Jay. *Ever Since Darwin: Reflections in Natural History.* New York: Norton, 1977.

Gribbin, John R. and Jeremy Cherfas. *The Monkey Puzzle: Reshaping the Evolutionary Tree.* New York: Pantheon Books, 1982.

Jacobs, David W. *Cliffs Rapid Reviews: Psychology.* Lincoln, Neb.: Cliff Notes, 1975.

Janis, Irving (ed.). *Current Trends in Psychology.* Los Altos, Calif.: Kaufman, 1977.

Jolly, Alison. *The Evolution of Primate Behavior.* New York: Macmillan, 1972.

King, James C. *The Biology of Race.* Berkeley, Calif.: University of California Press, 1981.

Leakey, Richard E., and Roger Lewin. *Origins*. New York: Dutton, 1977.

Luria, S. E. *Life: The Unfinished Experiment*. New York: Scribner, 1973.

Thomas, Lewis. *The Lives of a Cell: Notes of a Biology Watcher*. New York: Viking Press, 1974.

Wilbur, Ken. *Up From Eden*. Garden City, N.Y.: Anchor Press/Doubleday, 1981.

B. Ethology

Alland, Alexander, Jr. *The Human Imperative*. New York: Columbia University Press, 1972.

Ardrey, Robert. *The Hunting Hypothesis*. New York: Atheneum, 1976.

Claiborne, Robert. *God or Beast: Evolution and Human Nature*. New York: Norton, 1974.

Coon, Carleton S. *The Hunting Peoples*. Boston: Little, Brown, 1971.

Fisher, Helen E. *The Sex Contract: The Evolution of Human Behavior*. New York: Morrow, 1982.

Fromm, Eric. *The Anatomy of Human Destructiveness*. New York: Holt Rinehart & Winston, 1973.

Goldberg, Steven. *The Inevitability of Patriarchy*. New York: Morrow, 1973.

Gorney, Roderic. *The Human Agenda*. New York: Bantam Books, 1972.

Hall, Roberta L., and Henry S. Sharp (eds.). *Wolf and Man: Evolution in Parallel*. New York: Academic Press, 1973.

Jay, Antony. *Corporation Man*. New York: Random House, 1971.

Midgley, Mary. *Beast and Man: The Roots of Human Nature*. Ithaca, N.Y.: Cornell University Press, 1978.

Montagu, Ashley (ed.). *Man and Aggression*, 2nd ed. New York: Oxford University Press, 1973.

Thiessen, D. D. *The Evolution and Chemistry of Aggression*. Springfield, Ill.: Thomas, 1976.

Tiger, Lionel. *Men in Groups*. New York: Random House, 1969.

Tiger, Lionel and Robin Fox. *The Imperial Animal*. New York: Holt, Rinehart & Winston, 1971.

Worthy, Morgan. *Eye Color, Sex and Race*. Anderson, S.C.: Drake House/Hallux, 1974.

C. Sociobiology

Barash, David. *The Whisperings Within*. New York: Harper & Row, 1979.

Dawkins, Richard. *The Selfish Gene*. New York: Oxford University Press, 1976.

Freedman, Daniel G. *Human Sociobiology*. New York: Free Press, 1979.

Griffin, Donald R. *The Question of Animal Awareness: Evolutionary Continuity of Mental Experience*. New York: Rockefeller University Press, 1976.

Keith, Sir Arthur. *A New Theory of Human Evolution*. Gloucester, Mass.: Peter Smith, 1968.

Konner, Melvin. *The Tangled Wing: Biological Constraints on the Human Spirit*. New York: Holt, Rinehart & Winston, 1982.

Reynolds, Vernon. *The Biology of Human Action*. San Francisco: Freeman, 1976.

Rumbaugh, Duane M. (ed.). *Language Learning by a Chimpanzee: The Lana Project*. New York: Academic Press, 1977.

Wilson, Edward O. *On Human Nature*. Cambridge, Mass.: Harvard University Press, 1978.

II. The Brain and Behavior

Albert, Martin L., and Loraine K. Obler. *The Bilingual Brain: Neurophysiological and Neurolinguistic Aspects of Bilingualism*. New York: Academic Press, 1978.

Blakemore, Colin. *Mechanism of the Mind*. New York: Cambridge University Press, 1977.

Buzan, Tony. *Use Both Sides of Your Brain*. New York: Dutton, 1976.

Dimond, Stuart J., and J. Graham Beaumont (eds.). *Hemisphere Function in the Human Brain*. New York: Wiley, 1974.

Fair, Charles M. *The Dying Self*. Middletown, Conn.: Wesleyan University Press, 1969.

Furst, Charles. *Origins of the Mind: Mind-Brain Connections*. Englewood Cliffs, N.J.: Prentice-Hall, 1979.

Gardner, Howard. *The Shattered Brain: The Person after Brain Damage*. New York: Knopf, 1975.

Harnad, Stevan, et al. (eds.). *Lateralization in the Nervous System*. New York: Academic Press, 1977.

Jones, J. K. Chadwick, et al. *Environment and Social Psychology*. Baltimore: University Park Press, 1979.

Mayer, Andre, and Michael Wheeler. *The Crocodile Man: A Case of Brain Chemistry and Criminal Violence*. Boston: Houghton Mifflin, 1982.

Oatley, Keith. *Perceptions and Representations: The Theoretical Basis of Brain Research and Psychology*. New York: Free Press, 1978.

Penfield, Wilder. *The Mystery of the Mind*. Princeton, N.J.: Princeton University Press, 1975.

Pines, Maya. *The Brain Changers: Scientists and the New Mind Control*. New York: Harcourt Brace Jovanovich, 1973.

Restak, Richard M. *The Brain: The Last Frontier.* New York: Doubleday, 1979.

Sagan, Carl. *The Dragons of Eden: Speculations on the Evolution of Human Intelligence.* New York: Random House, 1977.

Simeons, A. T. W. *Man's Presumptuous Brain: An Evolutionary Interpretation of Psychosomatic Disease.* New York: Dutton, 1961.

Smith, C. U. M., *The Brain: Toward an Understanding.* New York: Capricorn Books, 1972.

Sommerhoff, Gerd. *Logic of the Living Brain.* New York: Wiley, 1974.

Sperry, Roger. *Science and Moral Priority: Merging Mind, Brain, and Human Values.* New York: Columbia University Press, 1983.

Taylor, David A. *Mind.* New York: Simon & Schuster, 1982.

Tyler, Timothy J. *A Primer of Psychobiology: Brain and Behavior.* San Francisco: Freeman, 1925.

Walter, W. Grey. *The Living Brain.* New York: Norton, 1963.

Wittrock, M. C., et al. *The Human Brain.* Englewood Cliffs, N.J.: Prentice-Hall, 1977.

Wooldridge, Dean E. *The Machinery of the Brain.* New York: McGraw-Hill, 1963.

Young, J. Z. *Programs of the Brain.* Oxford: Oxford University Press, 1978.

III. Addiction, Stress, and Individual Responsibility

Albrecht, Karl. *Stress and the Manager.* Englewood Cliffs, N.J.: Prentice-Hall, 1979.

Benson, Herbert, and Miriam Z. Klipper. *The Relaxation Response.* New York: Avon, 1976.

Blue Cross Association. *Blue Print for Health.* Chicago: Blue Cross Association, 1974.

Borman, Leonard D. (ed.). *Explorations in Self-Help and Mutual Aid.* Evanston, Ill.: Center for Urban Affairs, Northwestern University, 1975.

Brown, Barbara. *Stress and the Art of Biofeedback.* New York: Bantam Books, 1977.

Bry, Adelaide, with Marjorie Bair. *Visualization: Directing the Movies of Your Mind to Improve Health, Expand Your Mind, and Achieve Your Life Goals.* New York: Barnes and Noble, 1978.

Campbell, H. J. *The Pleasure Areas: A New Theory of Behavior.* New York: Delacorte Press, 1973.

Capra, Fritjof. *The Tao of Physics.* Berkeley: Shambhala, 1975.

Cheraskin, E., and W. M. Ringsdorf, Jr. *Psychodietetics.* New York: Bantam Books, 1974.

Cousins, Norman. *Anatomy of an Illness as Perceived by the Patient: Reflections on Healing and Regeneration.* New York: Norton, 1979.

Friedman, Meyer, and Ray H. Rosenman. *Type A Behavior and Your Heart.* New York: Knopf, 1974.

Gaylin, Willard. *Feelings: Our Vital Signs.* New York: Harper & Row, 1979.

Gendlin, Eugene T. *Focusing.* New York: Everest House, 1978.

Gibb, Jack R. *Trust.* Los Angeles: Guild of Tutors Press, 1978.

Glass, David G. *Behavior Patterns, Stress, and Coronary Disease.* Hillsdale, N.J.: Lawrence Erlbaum Associates, 1977.

Glasser, William. *Reality Therapy.* New York: Harper & Row, 1965.

Gordon, Barbara. *I'm Dancing as Fast as I Can.* New York: Harper & Row, 1979.

Hilgard, Ernest R. *Divided Consciousness: Multiple Controls in Human Thought and Action.* New York: Wiley, 1977.

Julian, Robert M. *A Primer of Drug Action.* San Francisco: Freeman, 1975.

Keyes, Ken, Jr., and B. T. Durkan. *How to Make Your Life Work or Why Aren't You Happy?* St. Mary, Kentucky: Living Love Institute, 1974.

Klopf, A. Harry. *Mental and Physical Phenomena: Toward a Unified Theory.* Air Force Avionics Laboratory, Wright-Patterson AFB.

Kovel, Joel. *A Complete Guide to Therapy: From Psychoanalysis to Behavior Modification.* New York: Pantheon Books, 1976.

Lair, Jess. *Ain't I A Wonder and Ain't You a Wonder Too.* New York: Doubleday, 1977.

Luks, Allan, (ed.). *Having Been There.* New York: Scribner, 1979.

McClelland, David C., et al. *The Drinking Man.* New York: Free Press, 1972.

McKenna, Marylou. *The Serenity Book: Sensory Awareness Training and How It Can Change Your Life.* New York: Rawson Associates, 1977.

McLean, Alan A. *Work Stress.* Reading, Mass.: Addison-Wesley, 1979.

McQuade, Walter, and Ann Aikman. *The Longevity Factor: A Revolutionary New System for Prolonging Your Life.* New York: Simon and Schuster, 1979.

Milam, James R. *The Emergent Comprehensive Concept of Alcoholism.* Alcoholism Center Associates, Ind., P.O. Box 286, Kirkland, Washington 98033.

Mowrer, O. Hobart. *The New Group Therapy.* New York: Van Nostrand Reinhold, 1964.

National Research Council. *Common Processes in Habitual Substance Use: A Research Agenda.* Washington, D.C.: National Academy of Sciences, 1977.

Oates, Wayne. *Confessions of a Workaholic: The Facts about Work Addiction.* New York: Abingdon Press, 1971.

Pelletier, Kenneth R. *Mind as Healer, Mind as Slayer: A Holistic Approach to Preventing Stress Disorders.* New York: Delacorte, 1977.

Selye, Hans. *Stress Without Distress.* New York: New American Library, 1975.

Shostak, Arthur B. *Blue Collar Stress.* Reading, Mass.: Addison-Wesley, 1980.

Vaillant, George E. *Adaptation to Life.* Boston: Little, Brown, 1977.

Vorrath, Harry H. *Positive Peer Culture.* Lansing, Mich.: Michigan Center for Group Studies, 1972.

Warshaw, Leon J. *Managing Stress.* Reading, Mass.: Addison-Wesley, 1979.

Watts, George O. *Dynamic Neuroscience: Its Application to Brain Disorders.* New York: Harper & Row, 1975.

Weil, John L. *A Neurophysiological Model of Emotional and Intentional Behavior.* Springfield, Ill.: Thomas, 1974.

Wright, H. Beric. *Executive Ease and Dis-Ease.* New York: Wiley, 1975.

Yablonsky, Lewis. *Psychodrama.* New York: Basic Books, 1976.

IV. The Integrative Theory of Management

Ackoff, Russell L. "Towards A System of Systems Concepts." *Management Science* 17, no. 11 (July 1971): 661-671.

Blake, Robert R., and Jane Mouton. *The Managerial Grid.* Houston, Tex.: Gulf Publishing Company, 1964.

Bronner, Rolf. *Decision Making under Time Pressure.* Lexington, Mass.: Heath, 1982.

Fiedler, Fred, Martin Chemers, and Linda Mahar. *Improving Leadership Effectiveness.* New York: Wiley, 1976.

Harragan, Betty Lehan. *Games Your Mother Never Taught You.* New York: Rawson Associates, 1977.

Hogarth, Robin. *Judgment and Choice.* New York: Wiley, 1980.

Hutschnecker, Arnold A. *The Drive for Power.* New York: Bantam, 1974.

Jones, Landon Y. *Great Expectations.* New York: Coward, McCann & Geoghegan, 1980.

Kepner, Charles H., and B. B. Tregoe. *The Rational Manager.* New York: McGraw-Hill, 1965.

Koberg, Don, and Jim Bagnall. *The Universal Traveler.* Los Altos, Calif.: Kaufman, 1976.

Lefrancois, Guy R. *Psychological Theories and Human Learning: Kongor's Report.* Monterey, Calif.: Brooks-Cole, 1972.

Maccoby, Michael. *The Gamesman.* New York: Bantam Books, 1978.

Maslow, Abraham H. *Motivation and Personality.* New York: Harper & Row, 1954.

McGregor, Douglas. *The Human Side of Enterprise.* New York: McGraw-Hill, 1960.

Mintzberg, Henry. *The Nature of Managerial Work.* New York: Harper & Row, 1973.

———. "Organizational Power and Goals: A Skeletal Theory," in Schendel and Hofer's *Strategic Management.* Boston: Little, Brown, 1979.

———. "Planning on the Left Side and Managing on the Right." *Harvard Business Review* 54 (July-August 1976): 49-58.

———. *The Structuring of Organizations, A Synthesis of the Research.* Englewood Cliffs, N.J.: Prentice-Hall, 1979.

Mintzberg, Henry, Duro Raisinghani and Andre Theoret. "The Structure of 'Unstructured' Decision Processes." *Administrative Science Quarterly* 21, no. 2 (June 1976): 246-275.

Muller, Ronald. *Revitalizing America.* New York: Simon & Schuster, 1980.

Perrow, Charles. *Complex Organizations: A Critical Essay.* Glenville, Ill.: Scott, Foresman, 1979.

Rychlar, John F. *Personality and Life-Style of Young Male Managers.* New York: Academic Press, 1982.

Schutz, William. *FIRO: A Three-Dimensional Theory of Interpersonal Behavior.* New York: Rinehart & Co., 1958.

Suojanen, Waino, and Stephen Brooke. "The Management of Creativity." *California Management Review* 14 (Fall 1971).

Suojanen, Waino, and Asterios G. Kefalas. "Organizational Behavior and the New Biology." *Academy of Management Journal* 17 (September 1974).

Suojanen, Waino, and Robert J. Massey. "Molding Organization Climate." *Advanced Management* 26 (October 1961): 5-7.

Tannenbaum, R., and W. H. Schmidt. "How to Choose a Leadership Pattern." *Harvard Business Review* 36 (March-April 1958): 95-101.

Vroom, V., and P. Yetton. *Leadership and Decision Making.* Pittsburgh: University of Pittsburgh Press, 1973.

Wright, J. Patrick. *On a Clear Day You Can See General Motors.* New York: Avon, 1979.

V. Creativity, Education, and Training for Management

Abramsson, Bengt. *Bureaucracy or Participation: The Logic of Organization.* Beverly Hills, Calif.: Sage Publications, 1977.

Austin, James H. *Chase, Chance, and Creativity: The Lucky Art of Novelty.* New York: Columbia University Press, 1978.

Buzan, Tony. *Use Both Sides of Your Brain.* New York: Dutton, 1974.

Cohen, Peter. *The Gospel According to the Harvard Business School*. New York: Doubleday, 1973.

Dahl, Robert A., and Charles E. Lindblom. *Politics, Economics, and Welfare*. New York: Harper & Row, 1953.

Davis, Gary A., and Joseph A. Scott. *Training Creative Thinking*. New York: Holt, Rinehart & Winston, 1971.

DeBono, Edward. *New Think*. New York: Basic Books, 1967.

Edwards, Betty. *Drawing on the Right Side of the Brain*. Los Angeles: Tarcher, 1979.

Getzels, Jacob W., and Mihaly Csikszentmihalyi. *The Creative Vision*. New York: Wiley, 1976.

Hayes, John R. *The Complete Problem Solver*. Philadelphia: Franklin Institute Press, 1981.

Hosti, Ole R. *Crisis Escalation War*. Montreal: McGill-Queens University Press, 1972.

Kotter, John P. *Power in Management: How to Understand, Acquire, and Use It*. New York: Amacom, 1979.

Lefcourt, Herbert M. *Locus of Control: Current Trends in Theory and Research*. New York: Wiley, 1976.

Lindblom, Charles E. *Politics and Markets: The World's Political-Economic Systems*. New York: Basic Books, 1977.

Margolis, Diane Rothbard. *The Managers: Corporate Life in America, Work, Family, and Community*. New York: Morrow, 1979.

McCall, Morgan W., Jr., Ann M. Morrison, and Robert L. Hannan. *Studies of Managerial Work: Results and Methods, Technical Report Number 9, May 1978*. Center for Creative Leadership, 5000 Laurinda Dr., Greensboro, N.C. 27402.

McClelland, David C. *Power: The Inner Experience*. New York: Irvington Publishers, 1975.

Miner, John B. *The Challenge of Managing*. Philadelphia: Saunders, 1975.

Motl, Paul E. *The Characteristics of Effective Organizations*. New York: Harper & Row, 1972.

Prentky, Robert A. *Creativity and Psychopathology: A Neurocognitive Perspective*. New York: Praeger, 1980.

Prince, George M. *The Practice of Creativity*. New York: Harper & Row, 1970.

Rothenberg, Albert. *The Emerging Goddess: The Creative Process in Art, Science, and Other Fields*. Chicago: University of Chicago Press, 1979.

Wolfe, Tom. *The Right Stuff*. New York: Farrar, Strauss, Giroux, 1979.

VI. Sex Differences

Arnold, A. P., and A. Saltiel. "Sexual Difference in Pattern of Hormone Accumulation in the Brain of a Songbird." *Science* 205 (17 August 1979): 702-704.

Bradshaw, J. L., A. Gates, and N. C. Nettleton. "Bihemispheric Involvement in Lexical Decisions: Handedness and a Possible Sex Difference." *Neuropsychologica* 15 (1977): 277-286.

Gorski, R. A. "Sexual Differentiation of the Brain." *Hospital Practice* (October, 1978): 55-62.

Jenni, D. A., and M. A. Jenni. "Carrying Behavior in Humans: Analysis of Sex Differences." *Science* 194 (19 November 1976): 859-860.

Lake, D. A., and M. P. Bryden. "Handedness and Sex Differences in Hemispheric Asymmetry." *Brain and Language* 3 (1976): 266-282.

Levy, J., and J. M. Levy. "Human Lateralization from Head to Foot: Sex-related Factors." *Science* 200 (16 June 1978): 1291-1292.

Lips, Hilary M., and Nina Lee Colwill, *The Psychology of Sex Differences*. Englewood Cliffs, N.J.: Prentice-Hall, 1978.

McGlone, J. "The Relationship Between Cerebral Speech Laterality and Spatial Ability with Special Reference to Sex and Hand Preference." *Neurophysiologia* 11 (1973): 105-113.

———. "Sex Differences in Functional Brain Asymmetry." *Cortex* 14 (1978): 122-128.

———. "Sex Differences in the Cerebral Organization of Verbal Functions in Patients with Unilateral Brain Lesions." *Brain* 100, Part 4 (December 1977): 775-793.

McGuinness, D., and K. H. Pribram. "The Origins of Sensory Bias in the Development of Gender Differences in Perception and Cognition," in *Cognitive Growth and Development Essays in Memory of Herbert G. Birch*, edited by Morton Bartner. New York: Brunner/Mazel, Inc., 1978.

Maccoby, E., and C. Jacklin. *The Psychology of Sex Differences*. Stanford Calif.: Stanford University Press, 1974.

Munroe, R. L., and R. H. Munroe. *Cross-Cultural Human Development*. Monterey, Calif.: Brooks-Cole, 1975.

Nash, John. *Developmental Psychology: A Psychobiological Approach*, 2nd ed. Englewood Cliffs, N.J.: Prentice-Hall, 1978.

Taylor, D. C. "Differential Rates of Cerebral Maturation Between Sexes and Between Hemispheres." *The Lancet* 297 (19 July 1969): 140-142.

Wachtel, S. S. "H-Y Antigen and the Genetics of Sex Determination." *Science* 198 (25 November, 1977): 797-799.

Witelson, S. F. "Sex and the Single Hemisphere: Specialization of the Right Hemisphere for Spatial Processing." *Science* 193 (30 July, 1976): 425-427.

VII. Ecology and the New Order

The books listed in this section cover the period from about 1963 to
1973—the decade of Woodstock and the first energy crisis. Almost every
volume focuses on the fact—not yet realized by American society—that we
live in a world of limited resources and infinite demands. Unless the
current paradigm of management changes, we are doomed to many years
of inflation. Far worse, however, is the discontinuity in basic values that
suggests the crisis as the basic model for management in the future.

Bell, Daniel. *The Coming of Post-Industrial Society.* New York: Basic
Books, 1973.
Boulding, Kenneth E., *The Organization Revolution.* Chicago: Quad-
rangle, 1968.
Brown, Lester R. *World Without Borders.* New York: Random House,
1972.
Carson, Rachel. *Silent Spring.* Boston: Houghton Mifflin, 1962.
Commoner, Barry. *The Closing Circle.* New York: Knopf, 1971.
Dubos, Rene. *A God Within.* New York: Scribner, 1972.
Editors of *The Ecologist. Blueprint for Survival.* Boston: Houghton
Mifflin, 1972.
Editors of the *Wall Street Journal. Getting Involved.* Princeton, N.J.: Dow
Jones, 1971.
Ehrlich, Paul R. *The Population Bomb.* New York: Ballantine, 1968.
Ellul, Jacques. *The Technological Society.* New York: Knopf, 1964.
Environmental Protection Agency. *Alternative Futures and Environ-
mental Quality.* Washington, D.C.: Government Printing Office, 1973.
Ferkiss, Victor C. *Technological Man.* New York: Braziller, 1969.
Gabor, Dennis. *The Mature Society.* New York: Praeger, 1972.
Galbraith, John Kenneth. *Economics and the Public Purpose.* Boston:
Houghton Mifflin, 1973.
_____. *The New Industrial State.* New York: New American Library,
1967.
Goodwin, Richard N. *The American Condition.* New York: Doubleday,
1974.
Gorney, Roderick. *The Human Agenda.* New York: Bantam, 1973.
Hailey, Arthur. *Wheels.* New York: Bantam, 1973.
Johnson, H. D. (ed.). *No Deposit—No Return.* Reading, Mass.: Addison-
Wesley, 1970.
Linowes, David F. *Strategies for Survival.* New York: Amacom, 1973.
Mead, Margaret. *Culture and Commitment: A Study of the Generation
Gap.* New York: Doubleday, 1970.

Meadows, D., et al. *The Limits of Growth: A Report for the Club of Rome's Project on the Predicament of Mankind.* New York: Universe Books, 1972.

Mumford, Lewis. *Interpretations and Forecasts: 1922-1972.* New York: Harcourt Brace Jovanovich, 1972.

Odum, Eugene P. *Ecology.* New York: Holt, Rinehart & Winston, 1963.

Odum, Howard T. *Environment, Power, and Society.* New York: Wiley, 1971.

Ramo, Simon. *Century of Mismatch.* New York: McKay, 1970.

Reich, Charles A. *The Greening of America.* New York: Random House, 1970.

Revel, Jean-Francois. *Without Marx or Jesus.* New York: Doubleday, 1971.

Rockefeller, John D., III. *The Second American Revolution.* New York: Harper & Row, 1973.

Roszak, Theodore. *Where the Wasteland Ends.* New York: Doubleday, 1972.

Schumacker, E. F. *Small is Beautiful.* New York: Harper & Row, 1973.

Servan-Schreiber, J. J. *The American Challenge.* New York: Atheneum, 1968,

Thayer, Frederick C. *An End to Hierarchy! An End to Competition!* New York: New Viewpoints, 1973.

Toffler, Alvin. *Future Shock.* New York: Random House, 1970.

Ward, Barbara, and Rene Dubos. *Only One Earth.* New York: Norton, 1972.

Weisskopf, Walter A. *Alienation and Economics.* New York: Dutton, 1971.

Wrigley, E. A. *Population and History.* New York: McGraw-Hill, 1969.

Index

Company man, 156
Competition, 6-8
Compulsive gamblers, 146
Compulsive gambling, 148
Compulsive overeating, 148
Conceptual variation, 61
  function of right new brain, 147
Consciousness, 57, 59-60, 80, 90
  altered state of, 61-62, 85, 107,
    122, 125, 146, 148-149
  dreaming state of, 67
  euphoric state of, 85, 95, 100,
    114, 122
  need for "high" and, 95
  negative normal state of, 121
  normal state of, 62, 78, 83-84,
    93, 95, 100, 107, 114, 145,
    147, 148-149
  painful state of, 100
  positive normal state of, 121
  seat of, 60, 189, 195-196
  stream of, 65-66
Cooperation, 6, 8, 10
  in hunting groups, 11
Corporate Man, 21
Corpus callosum (CC), 82-84,
  185, 197
Cortex, 43. See also
  Cerebral cortex
Craftsman, 156
Creative intellectuals, 174
  description of, 173
Creative people
  motivated by, 200
Creativity, 14, 163
  autonomy and, 167
  blocks to, 188
  "high" and, 200
  human consciousness and, 167
de Bono, Edward, 45
Decision-making, 246
  according to Star Trek model, 55
  arousal needs and, 199
Decision science, 56
Decisive mind, 56, 67, 73, 78,
  80-81, 83-84, 148
  seat of consciousness, 81

substitute for corpus callosum,
  83-84
Denial
  definition of, 146
Determinism, 168-169
Diencepalon, 57. See also
  Visceral brain
Dimethyltryptamine (DMT), 103-104
"Dis-ease", 129
Distance runners
  addiction and, 104
Distress, 130
Divorces Anonymous, 123
DNA, 10
Dobzhansky, Theodosious, 27-28
Dominance
  relation to male bonding, 11-12
  leadership and, 13
Drews, Elizabeth, 172-174
Duban, Robert, 206
Durkheim, Emile, 48
Dynamics of Management, 40
Economic man, 28, 47
  rationality of, 60
Economic rational man, 18
Educability
  assumptions made, 32-33
Education
  ability to deal with the
    nonroutine and, 189-190
Efficiency
  obsessive concern for, 49
Emotions Anonymous, 123
Employee assistance programs, 149,
  157
Encounter group, 149
  assumptions of, 149
Endorphins, 146
  altered states of consciousness
    and, 103-105
Enkephalin, 103
Epinephrine, 80, 128, 130, 146
Equiphoria. See Homeostasis
Ergotropic phenomena, 85
Ethological approach
  assumptions of, 27
Ethology, 18, 21, 28, 30, 68, 113,
  205. See also New biology